A MATTER
OF INCHES

A MATTER OF INCHES

HOW I SURVIVED IN THE CREASE AND BEYOND

CLINT MALARCHUK
WITH DAN ROBSON

TRIUMPH
BOOKS

TRIUMPHBOOKS.COM

To my mother, Jean Ilene Jones—for always being there for me. And to Joanie, my saint.

Contents

Prologue ix

1   The Crazy Game 1

2   Slaughterhouse 4

3   Shattered Glass 8

4   Wobblebottom 14

5   Stomach Pains 21

6   Empty Bottles 24

7   Butterfly 32

8   A Strong Defense 41

9   Training Camp 45

10   Hitched 52

11   A Fighting Chance 57

12   Traded 67

13   Capital Crimes 77

14   Jugular 84

15   Night Terrors 92

16   Whiskey and Pills 102

17   Can't Do This 114

18   Sin City 120

19   Dad 129

20   Retired 132

21   East 140

22   South 150

23   Open Wounds 157

24   Open Bottles 161

25   I'd Never 165

26   I Might 173

27   I Did 185

28   The Damage Done 189

29 Alcatraz 196
30 Warriors 203
31 Family Day 208
32 Post-Traumatic 218
33 On the Outside 225
34 Relapse 231
35 Lucky One 235
    Afterword *by Joanie Malarchuk* 245
    Acknowledgements 251
    Index 255

Prologue

I DIDN'T WRITE A NOTE. IT WASN'T THAT KIND OF THING. I STOOD in the dust, firing at old tin cans teetering on the edges of fence posts. It was target practice all morning, aiming through the sagebrush around our desert ranch in Nevada. I chased away rabbits, shooting at whatever moved. *Pop, pop, pop*—bullets to the mountains. I was sweating—booze mostly. Our horses circled in the corral; the dogs wrestled and snapped at each other. I kept sweating. Sweating and drinking. Can after can. Bullet after bullet. *Pop, pop, pop.*

The house was empty. She had stayed in a motel the night before; she'd been doing that a lot lately. The questions twisted and turned. *How does a man go through four marriages? How does he pick them wrong each time? It's her fault, all of this. The bitch.*

She wanted to hurt me; I was certain of it. She wanted to torture and humiliate me. *They're all the same. Can't trust them.* She'd drive for hours at a time just to get away from me. She'd go to a friend's house. Fly to her parents'. "Anywhere, just away," she'd say. "I can't be here." Her damn excuses were always the same. "You won't let me help you. You won't help yourself. There's nothing I can do anymore."

Screw it.

Part of me knew she was right. I could admit that much. Part of me could see the trap I was in. But that part was buried deep inside me now, and I couldn't hear it screaming. The surface was loud, swirling and swirling, and

I couldn't make it stop. The pills didn't work. The more I took, the worse it got. The booze settled me down, drowning it all out until the buzz turned and the rage took over. I was a human cyclone. All I could hear was the rising hum in my mind, my own head betraying me.

God, turn it off. Turn my goddamn mind off.

It was October 7, 2008—two-thirty on a grey, cloudy afternoon. I didn't hear the car pull up, and I didn't hear her call my name. She walked through the house and found my cell phone on a shelf next to the back door. She'd called all morning, but I had ignored her. She was tearing my life apart. *It has to be her. It's all her. She wants better things. Wants to embarrass me.* So the phone rang and rang and rang, and I didn't give a shit.

She opened the back door of our bungalow and called for me. I sat on the bench, eyes to the mountains. Sipped my beer. The .22 was on the table in front of me. Everything was a blurry rage, a crazy haze. Impossible to turn off. Impossible.

She found me beside the tack shed.

"What are you doing out here?" she asked.

"I'm looking for rabbits." I spat out my chew.

"What are we going to do about this?" she asked. My mind roared and my body shook. My face was wet with sweat and tears. There'd been moments like this before. Moments when I swore I'd do it. "I'll tie a string around the doorknob and attach it to the trigger. You'll come in and blow me away." A clear day later, and the words would haunt and sting. "You know I'd never do that kind of thing. I love you." And I did. I loved Joanie so much.

She didn't think anything of the gun sitting beside me. There were plenty around the ranch. We used them to get rid of the things that needed to be gone. I grabbed it, stood up and faced her.

"Is this what you want?" I yelled.

"What?" She didn't understand.

"I can't do it anymore," I said. "I can't turn my head off. This is all I can think about. I can't live inside my head anymore."

Joanie didn't have time to scream. I pushed the barrel under my chin and pulled the trigger.

1

The Crazy Game

THE PUCK DROPS AND YOU'RE TRANSFIXED. YOU DON'T HEAR THE crowd, just a buzz that rises and falls. You hunt for a black disc. The black disc cannot pass. *It shall not pass.* It moves like a laser. *Here . . . there. Up . . . where? Down . . . there . . . there! Where? Shit! Where? Shit— there!* This is the point of the game. The game is the point of life. Now the puck is on the point—or *was* on the point—and if you don't find it fast, find it now, it will cross a line from which you cannot bring things back. And your ass is on that thin red line, backed deep in the crease behind a wall of players who can't clear a path to the puck.

Then you hear the snap. Airborne. Incoming. Your synapses fire. Einstein couldn't calculate the shit flashing through your brain right now. Screw physics—you're giving sight to the blind. You reach out with faith in me-almighty and feel the weight of the world in your hand.

Whistle.

The buzz becomes a cheer. The referee lifts the puck from your glove. Your teammates tap your pads. You nod. You twitch. Check your straps. Clank the posts with your stick—centre yourself—and push out towards the circle. You crouch. You blink. The puck drops and you're transfixed.

Crazy—that's the word they always use to describe us. "You have to be crazy to be a goalie." Of course it's true. Standing in front of a hundred-mile-an-hour slapshot? Crazy. Having the outcome of every game rest on your shoulders? Crazy. Defending the net against Wayne Gretzky or Mario Lemieux or Sidney Crosby or Alex Ovechkin? *Crazy.*

Yes, you have to be crazy to be a goalie. It's the first rule. Watch closely during a game. Each has their own idiosyncrasies. No two are the same. Consider every perfectly adjusted strap, every twitch, every tantrum—they are all trying to cope. Goaltending is the most complicated, pressure-packed position in sport. A quarterback or a pitcher may be the closest to understanding the stress a goalie is under, but even they can't grasp the madness of the position. Why are goalies such unique personalities? It's the pressure. The physical, mental and emotional stress goalies face is incomparable. Does a person become unique under the pressure, or is a unique person drawn to the pressure? It has to be a little of both.

Look at modern keepers like Ilya Bryzgalov and his musings about the universe, or a legend like Patrick Roy, who used to talk to his posts. Or go back further to the infamously surly Terry Sawchuk, or Glenn Hall, who tossed his cookies before each game. They even played without masks until Jacques Plante's face exploded and he had the sense to protect it.

When I was a kid, Plante's book *On Goaltending* was my bible. I practically memorized every word. It was filled with exercises and drills that I did religiously. I trained like a madman. I remember running up and down the basement stairs—up and down, up and down, up and down, endlessly.

For me, from the start, it was an obsession. I had to be the best, and being the best meant perfection. I had to train, train, train or someone else would live my dream. I think every goalie understands obsession to a certain degree. But Plante didn't mention that in his book. I guess I learned about it on my own.

Crazy—I hate the word. It's haunted me since I was a kid. The truth is that I've been so many different kinds of crazy that its limitations insult me. Crazy is too simple a word to describe me. Throughout my career, I teetered on the edge of normal, even though my teammates would say I was the most ordinary goalie in the world. In public, things were fine. I was a clown in the locker room, always the centre of attention. But I was kidding myself the whole time. People like me are natural actors. And all shows end eventually.

Mental illness isn't something people like to discuss. Especially not in professional sports, where the only wounds that matter are physical. The rest is just weakness. But I've suffered from mental illness my entire life. I've battled debilitating bouts with anxiety, obsessive-compulsive disorder and depression. It was like I had jugs of gasoline poured all over me, waiting for the spark to ignite. I did my best to hide it, until it all came blazing out.

My kind of crazy let me live a dream—then took it away and put a bullet in my head. For most of you, my story begins on the evening of March 22, 1989, a regular-season hockey game between the St. Louis Blues and Buffalo Sabres. It was a routine play, just a minor collision. Then I grabbed my throat and felt the red warmth spray through my fingers.

Millions watched me bleed out that night. This is about the rest of me.

Slaughterhouse

THE RIFLE FIRED—A VIOLENT CRACK, AND THEN RINGING. I didn't expect the sudden deafness. It was dark and I could see only a silhouette outlined by the afternoon sun outside the silo doorway. The bear grunted and slumped.

I was a good four miles from help. There was nothing around, just green fields and pine trees and emptiness. If I could get to the pickup truck, I'd be fine. But the bear's big black body slouched in the small frame, blocking the door. I was only fourteen, but I'd worked at the ranch long enough to know that a motionless bear doesn't necessarily mean a dead one.

I lowered the .30-30 rifle to reload. *Thank God I have this gun.* But the bullet jammed when I cranked the lever, and I fumbled around until it fell into place. I'd handled a gun before, but this was the first time a bear had me cornered in a silo.

Crack. I shot him again.

Crack. Reloaded. I shot him four or five more times. Filled him full of holes; filled him good and dead. I shuffled forward and jabbed him with the gun. He didn't move. Blood pooled around his head. I climbed over his hot, bloody bulk to get outside. I got in the truck and drove like hell.

• • •

I've always thought of Grande Prairie, Alberta, as home. My family lived in the small town, about six hours northwest of Edmonton, for the first six years of my life. And I spent every summer of my youth there after we left for Edmonton when Dad got a sales job in the city. All of my uncles and aunts lived there. I stayed with my grandmother, who was sweet and grey and spoiled me. It's where I learned to skate and play hockey. It's also where I first learned to kill. Aside from the hockey rink, it was the only place where I really found peace as a kid.

When I was ten, I started working on the ranch with my cousin and her husband. His name was Bill Finch, and he owned the ranch with his father and two brothers. They were typical cowboys—all scruff and grit and chew—probably in their late twenties. I wanted desperately to be like them. We stayed in a single-wide trailer on an enormous property that stretched for miles of hills and pine trees and rivers. We did all kinds of things at the ranch. They had cattle and horses and sheep and pigs. They also had beef cattle, and sometimes we'd ride through the fields corralling them. They had about five hundred head. I loved riding the horses. I could go as fast as I wanted and never run out of land.

Wolves and coyotes were a real problem. When a cow was calving, you had to be up all night to make sure nothing got to the calf before you did. I saw a lot of dead ones after the coyotes were done with them. We'd milk the dairy cows twice a day. Some of them we'd do by hand because they didn't give to the machines. Each time, we'd dump the white pails of milk into a machine to separate the cream, which we sold. It was my job to carry the excess milk in big buckets across the barnyard to feed the pigs. I'd do shoulder shrugs as I went, packing some muscle onto my skinny frame.

The guys on the ranch knew I was tough. They liked to put me to the test. We'd work crazy hours, in the barn by four-thirty in the morning and sometimes still out baling hay well after midnight. We worked by the light of our tractors.

Of all the animals there, the bulls were the most dangerous. I watched the ranch hands try to offload the biggest bull I'd ever seen in my life. He must have been two and a half tonnes. They had two-by-six planks along the ramp, trying to guide him down into a pen. He didn't want to go. Next thing you know, he freaked out and started thrashing around, and the planks snapped into pieces and exploded in the air.

One time in the pasture, the Finch brothers tried to load a two-thousand-pound Black Angus bull onto a cattle liner. They had it roped up and they tried to pull it up a ramp onto the truck. Bill told me to get off my horse and give the bull a good smack on the ass to move him along.

"We've got him tight. He can't get away."

So I smacked him hard, as I was told, but they all let go of the ropes. The bull charged at me. I barely made it to the trees before the damn thing ran me over.

The Finch brothers were big rodeo guys, so they taught me how to ride. I loved the sport of it: hanging on and falling off and getting on and falling off and hanging on. I got bucked off the first time I tried it, and I was hooked. It didn't really hurt that much. I just had a few bruises—a sprained wrist here, a twisted ankle there. Rodeo is about competition—man versus beast. It's a rush. It's about still hanging on when you have no business being able to.

I had an uncle and cousin who had a farm up there, too. Tim, my cousin, was my age. He was my best friend back then. My uncle Ed, his dad, was a rugged woodsman. He killed a lot of bears. One time, he was building a house on land about an hour outside of Grande Prairie—I mean, we're talking the middle of nowhere. He lived in this old gutted-out school bus. He piled up bales of hay for heat. The motor was gone and there was plywood where the engine should have been. I loved living in that old rotting bus. It was just the wild and us.

This one night, a bear came sniffing around, looking for food. We heard him clawing at the bus. My uncle sat up in his cot and saw the bear standing on the plywood by the windshield. Without even getting up, he reached under the bed, pulled out a rifle and shot him through the glass.

"You kids don't go out there in the morning," he said. "We have to make sure he's dead." For me, it was a huge deal. For Uncle Ed, it was routine—he went right back to sleep. The next day, we cut off the bear's hide and cooked the meat. I could smell the bear on me for days.

I was twelve when I killed for the first time. We slaughtered cattle once a week and did all the cutting and wrapping ourselves. The father of the Finch brothers was the butcher. He'd lost a finger in the slaughterhouse. He was tough—a real cowboy. I wanted to be like him, and I was eager to impress.

They had the steer in this rigged-up pen. One of the guys shot him in the head with a .22. Another pulled a lever that dropped the bottom of the pen down on a slant. The cow slid out onto the floor, flailing his legs like he was trying to run away. I stood next to the trap door holding a large knife, because that's what they'd told me to do. The steer fell onto me and took out my legs. I landed half on top of him and half mixed up in his fighting hooves. They thought it was hilarious. I thought it was funny, too. I was just lucky I didn't land on that goddamn knife.

I fell off and took a few more kicks from the steer as I got up. Then I bent over, gripped the knife and opened his throat. He kept kicking as he bled out. One of the Finch men sliced both of his hind legs between the bone and the Achilles tendon. They put these big hooks in there and hoisted him up. He hung, stretched out, as the blood drained. We skinned him and used electric chainsaws to cut out his ribs. His guts flew, and we tied them up in his hide like it was a garbage bag.

I took the whole thing well, so the guys liked me. It was considered a rite of passage.

After that, my job was to shoot the steer or cut its throat. Done right, the process from bullet to blade to hook took about eight seconds. The guts went to this remote part of the ranch we called the "gut dump," where black bears always hid, waiting for food. After my first, I probably killed a dozen. I used to shoot bears like gophers.

3

Shattered Glass

DOCTORS ALWAYS WANT TO KNOW ABOUT THE PAST, BUT I'VE always tried to avoid mine. From the start, I was taught to cowboy up and move on. I thought that rehashing old things was senseless. Everyone has messed-up stories about their upbringing. Why would anyone care about mine? It's always the same, it seems. The first person doctors want to know about is my dad—the daddy issues—so let's start with him.

Mike Malarchuk was a good man. He was a salesman for Nabob coffee. He moved our family from Grande Prairie to Edmonton to work out of the office there. We lived in a white bungalow at 8112 163 Street in Elmwood, the west end of the city. It had a carport where he parked our family's Buick and a backyard roughly the size of two boxing rings. There was a big field behind our house that belonged to Elmwood Elementary School. It had a couple baseball diamonds. He coached my older brother Garth's Little League team. I used to watch from the bleachers.

Dad was an athlete. He wasn't big. I'm taller than he was. But he was strong and muscular. He was a hard worker. Everyone who knew him, all my uncles, said he was one of the best athletes in the Peace Country region of Alberta where he grew up. He was a star baseball player. He was a goalie too, and a damn good one. He played in the senior leagues, which were kind of like semi-pro way back then. He had a big, bent nose because he wore no mask. He was a really tough guy who boxed a bit as well. He taught me how to fight in our backyard. He taught me how to be strong. "If you get hurt, don't lie on the ice," he'd say. "Skate to the bench. Work hard."

Most memories of my dad involve sports. Mike Malarchuk was the kind of father who lived at the rink with his sons. Hockey was the most important part of our life. He was a timekeeper at my games when I was young. He'd come watch me play for hours on the outdoor rink near our house in the freezing Edmonton winters. Back then, we mostly played outdoors, even in organized league games. Playing indoors was a big-time reward. When I was a mite—probably nine years old—Dad was the manager of my team. On Saturday mornings, we had indoor ice out at the Enoch Cree reserve. We'd get up at four in the morning and climb into our old Gran Torino and drive through the freezing dark. We'd be on the ice at five-thirty, but often we'd have to go and wake up the rink manager, who lived next door, so he could let us in.

The Enoch arena was so cold it might as well have been outside, but those practices always felt special. It was the highlight of the week. After practice, I'd go home and watch a half-hour or so of Saturday morning cartoons—always Bugs Bunny and the Road Runner—on our black-and-white television in the basement. Dad had finished the basement himself—he was handy. There was a bedroom for my brother, Garth, a bathroom and the TV area, which was all carpeted. One of my earliest memories, when I was really young and small, is of falling asleep on my dad's chest while he lay on the couch and watched that old black-and-white TV. He had a toothpick in his mouth. I curled up into him and dreamed.

On those Saturday mornings, after practice and cartoons, I'd pull on my jeans and a heavy sweater and bundle up in my winter jacket. I had this huge old pair of gloves that were so ripped that my fingers came through. I'd put a smaller pair of gloves beneath them so I could grip my stick and still be warm. I thought that was great. The fingers would flop around because the gloves were so worn out. Then I'd tie up my skates and head to the rink out past the schoolyard behind our house. The ice had painted lines. It was smaller than a regular rink but had boards and was big enough for five-on-five shinny. There was no refrigeration system. The quality of the ice depended on the weather and the work of the attendant assigned to scrape it down each day. It had a chain-link fence on top of the boards—nothing fancy, but to us, it was Maple Leaf Gardens or the Montreal Forum. I'd be there by nine in the morning and play shinny with the neighbourhood kids all day. We didn't have goalies, so I played out. Sometimes Dad would come and stand out in the cold, just because hockey was what we did. It was us.

At dinner, around five, I'd walk across the snow-covered field in my skates, and when I got to our back door my mom would lay down towels on the kitchen floor and I'd shuffle on my hands and knees to the table. Then I'd shuffle back and be off across the field. I'd stay out there so long that they would turn the lights out on me. It'd be about ten at night. There was a man who took care of the ice—he'd drag out a hose to flood it down and I'd help him. "Don't you have to be home?" he'd ask me.

"No, Mom knows where I'm at," I'd say.

My parents could see the lights from our back window. They knew that once those lights went out, I'd be home as soon as the ice was ready for a new day.

When I wasn't playing hockey outside, my family practically lived between Jasper Place Arena and Coronation Arena in Edmonton. Garth was seven years older than I was and was one of the best goalies in the city, if not the province. Garth was my idol. He got to play indoors because he was older and on the best teams. I remember going to those games before he left home at seventeen to play junior in Calgary. I'd either run around and get into trouble while my mom and older sister, Terry, watched from the stands, or I'd be in the timekeeper's box with Dad, running the clock. Everyone knew Mike Malarchuk at the rink. He was funny and friendly. He was a joker, a real charmer. Everybody liked Mike. Everybody.

I don't think as a kid you can really see the world you're living in. You can't dissect it. You can't comprehend it. Looking back, it's hard to say exactly when things fell apart. There were small hints along the way. Like the time Dad left me in the car while he ran into a store, and he was gone for a while and I got bored. So I went rummaging around in our Gran Torino and found a raunchy magazine—*Juggs* or something like that—and a half-empty bottle of whiskey. Maybe it was half-full. It didn't bother me much. Looking back, you can see the problems you were blind to then.

When Dad was manager of my mite team, the coach's name was Cecil Papke. I spent a lot of time with Cec and his son Murray, who was on our team. They didn't live far from us. I looked up to Cec so much. He was an old-school coach, kind of a Don Cherry type. This was the early seventies, when long hair was the fashion, but Cec made all of us get it cut and combed neatly. He made us wear shirts and ties to all of our games. Cec had coached the Calgary Centennials junior team when he was younger, and to us, that might as well have been the NHL. He'd played semi-pro hockey. I looked up to him. I'd go over to the Papkes' house and play hockey with Murray and just hang out with the family. Cec and my dad were good friends. He covered for Dad all the time— when he would go missing for a few days, here and there, or when he'd get so disoriented he couldn't come to our games. When my dad wasn't able to be my dad, Cec would step in. I don't want to say that Cecil Papke was a father figure, but he was the model for the kind of man I wanted to be. My dad was my dad—I loved him. For a time, he was a great father. But he was also a drunk—a full-blown alcoholic.

There wasn't a specific moment when everything at 8112 163 Street crumbled. I guess it was always kind of chipping away. You hold on to the happy pieces and try your best to leave the worst in the rubble, but the dust of it all clings to you.

My brother and sister saw the worst of it, but they were gone before I was old enough to really understand. Garth, the great goalie, my hero, left to play junior hockey. Terry, six years older than me—a provincial-level hurdler and sprinter—took care of me like a mother, but she married young and left the house before she was twenty. Part of the reason I went to Grande Prairie in the summers was to get out of Elmwood. Life in the raw wild was peaceful compared to the unpredictable chaos at home. I could shoot bears, but I couldn't stop the monster at home.

Jean Malarchuk, my mom, was the toughest, strongest person I knew. She was my best friend. I never saw him hit her, but I know that he did. He lashed out when he was mad. I saw him take things from the fridge, like a tub of cottage cheese or a plate of leftover dinner, and fire them at the wall. He'd throw plates across the room in the middle of dinner. He'd smash dishes on the floor. Mom tried to keep me away from the violent outbursts, but it was impossible when he came home blitzed. If we were lucky, he'd come home late—if he came home at all. Once, I woke up in the middle of the night, hearing a radio turned up loud. I got up and walked around the house, looking for it. It was downstairs, coming from my brother's room, but he was away playing in Calgary at the time. I found Dad passed out in the room, still dressed and shit-faced. He had been listening to a hockey game and fallen asleep.

Nights like that were bearable. Other nights weren't. I've forgotten many things in my life, but I'll never forget the sound of shattering glass. It woke me up. *Smash.* And then another. *Smash.* It sounded like a stack of plates slammed on the ground. It could have been a baseball, or a deer, or a missile crashing through our house. I opened my eyes. Dad was home. It was 3 A.M. and I was twelve. I jumped out of bed and ran to the kitchen in my pyjamas and bare feet. I thought Dad was throwing plates at Mom. I needed to help her. But she sat alone at the kitchen table. I could hear Dad shouting outside. *Smash.* Another window shattered, back in my parents' room. He had taken a hammer from the shed. I ran to Mom and she hugged me.

"I'm sorry, Clint, it's your dad. I locked him out. I had to lock him out. He broke the windows." She'd called the police. Terry was still at home then. She came into the kitchen and we huddled together as he yelled and ranted and smashed.

Dad was gone when the police arrived. Blue and red lights revolved through the jagged glass of the smashed windows. I remember the wail of the siren. I couldn't stop shaking. The cops sat down with my mother and wrote up a report. They said they'd drive around the block to make sure he didn't come back. We pulled each other close in the same bed and tried to stay warm in a room Dad hadn't got to. It was still cold. So cold we'd freeze alone. I tried to sleep but kept seeing shattered glass and my father's rage, so I stayed up and watched the night leave and the room get light. I didn't hate him then. I didn't know what to feel, what to think. This was a man I loved and he was ruining us.

The morning was as cold as the night. I got dressed, ate breakfast and went to school as if nothing had happened—overtired and screwed up as usual.

4

Wobblebottom

SCHOOL WAS NEVER MY THING. THE TEACHERS ALWAYS SEEMED to hate me, and the feeling was mutual. My third-grade teacher was the worst of them. As wide as she was high—probably five feet tall and three hundred pounds—we called her Mrs. Wobblebottom. She patrolled the class with a wooden yardstick in hand, randomly blasting it down, inches from heads and hands. It broke frequently, but she always found another one. We were petrified.

I was a class clown. I was always busy talking, always making jokes and causing distractions. It was impossible for me to concentrate. The numbers and words at the front of the room just blurred together. I couldn't keep up. My head would spin and I was anxious—the shit at home, the buzz around me, the mounds of gum under the desks—everything whirled around in my mind and made my skin creep up my arms and slowly crushed my chest. So I made jokes and laughed and talked and did everything I could to stay outside of myself. Mrs. Wobblebottom didn't understand.

One day, while I was entertaining my classmates, a blackboard eraser whizzed through the air and hit the wall just inches from me. A cloud of chalk dust fell on my head. "Don't take shit from anybody," my mother used to tell me, and I assumed that applied to teachers as well. And I was mad. I grabbed the eraser and threw it back. It hit her in the chest. Chalk exploded on the broad side of the barn door. She came at me and I bolted between the desks. My classmates roared as Wobblebottom's face went deep red—it was like she was going to kill me. I took off down the hall, burst through the doors and raced up the monkey bars. Unless there was fried chicken tied to the top bar, she'd never attempt that climb. I was safe.

Wobblebottom came huffing out and screamed at me. I ignored her. She hollered and threatened, but I'd stay up there forever if I had to. When she finally relented and went to the office to get the principal, I climbed down and ran across the field to my house. Mom had to drag me back to Elmwood Elementary. I ended up in the principal's office, but I didn't back down.

"She threw it first," I said. Mom always had my back on stuff like that. I would tell her what happened at school, and if I deserved it, I deserved it. But if she thought I was just sticking up for myself, she'd go to bat for me. She was pissed about the eraser thing.

I knew I had a unique kind of problem as soon as I started at Elmwood Elementary. The anxiety consumed me. Mom knew about the gum on the desks and how sick it made me feel. All that chewed sloppy shit clumped in mounds made my stomach twist. I wanted to hurl. So many germs and shit. *Am I the only one who sees this? Am I the only one who feels this way?* One day, Mom went to the school before class and scraped the gum from underneath my desk and scrubbed it with Lysol. After that, I kept a bottle of Lysol in my desk and cleaned it myself every day. It helped a bit.

Sunday nights growing up were like a frickin' ritual. The next day was Monday and I had to go to school. I just couldn't handle it. It just stressed the hell out of me. I'd cry. I don't know—Jesus Christ, I must have been the worst kid in the world.

I always had trouble getting to bed. It was something about being alone in my room, alone with my thoughts. My head would just spin. Sunday nights were a train wreck for me. It wasn't depression then—how can a kid that young be depressed? But it was constant anxiety. It never went away. "My stomach's churning," I'd tell my mom. "It won't stop."

Mom would actually have to drag me to class on Mondays. We'd take the sidewalk around the corner to get to school. As soon as she got me through the doors, I'd slip out the side entrance and be at the kitchen table when she got home. Mom took me back again and again. The things that woman did for me. I wish I could have been better for her. With all the shit she took from Dad, I don't know how she found the patience for me.

"I'm stupid, Mom. I don't get it. I can't go back."

"You're not stupid, Clint. You'll get it. Let's go." She said it every day.

But really, my grades were never good. I struggled. I could never focus in class. In the sixth grade they put me in a special-education program. I looked at the kids that were around me—there were about eight of us—and most of them were bad, bad kids. But I wasn't one of those kids who go around picking fights. Usually, I was the one helping out the kids getting picked on. There's no better feeling than punching a bully in the face and making him squeal like a little pig. Some of the other kids in the class had special needs. I thought to myself, *I'm not one of those kids who tease people, and I'm not handicapped. I'm just plain dumb.*

Hockey was my escape. That outdoor rink was the only place I didn't feel anxious. Sometimes I'd play with the older kids, my brother's age, and I'd strap on the pads because I was too young to play out with them. As long as I played net, I could be on the ice endlessly. I'd load my gear on a toboggan and lug it through the field and down the small path to the hockey rink. Mom always knew where I was. That gave her peace of mind.

I refused to take breaks while playing, so most days the ice in my crease was stained yellow—I decided it was easier to wet myself than to take off the goalie gear and interrupt the games. Mom always asked why my equipment was so rancid. She must have known. "Mom," I'd say, "that's hockey."

One of the kids in my grade was Kelly Hrudey. You might remember him from his incredible days with the Los Angeles Kings, or more recently as a commentator on *Hockey Night in Canada*. He was a pal and came to my house a bunch, like a lot of the kids in the neighbourhood did. We were a really sports-minded group.

Kelly was probably the best athlete around growing up. He was just naturally gifted at everything he did. We played on the same baseball team, but never on the same hockey team. He says it's because I was the best in net at the time and no one wanted to compete with me. He learned how to play on the outdoor rinks, just like me. But Kelly didn't even start playing organized hockey until he was about fourteen years old. He started playing a level below A hockey, but pretty soon he was in Medicine Hat as a junior. The Tigers weren't very good. He was facing something like fifty, sixty shots a game. That's when people started to really notice him. Imagine starting organized hockey as a teenager and making it to the NHL and being that successful! Kelly clearly worked hard for his success. He was a a natural superstar, and I envied his ability at every sport he played.

In the summers, we'd play ball hockey all day, every day. We'd play on the street in front of our house or over on the school blacktop. These were massive games that all the kids from the area got into. Sometimes things got violent, as these things tend to do. I don't remember this, but I've been told that during one of our marathon ball hockey games, I got mad at Kelly for some reason and punched him in the face. I don't know, it probably happened. I've punched a lot of people.

When I was pretty young, maybe twelve (everything seemed to happen that year), I remember these people down the street who had something like six kids, and four of them were boys. They were kind of like orangutans. The oldest brother was the same age as Garth. So they made a classic wager: "I bet my little brother can beat up your little brother." They put money on it. The thing was, I was fighting a fourteen-year-old. That's a big difference at that age. It was out in the field behind our house, where most of this stuff happened. It was a full-on fight.

"You can do this," Garth told me. I was scared because the kid was much bigger. But I won. I always won, even against the older kids. My brother made sure I was tough. He was always picking on me, which helped me a lot. I learned how to be an actor, in a way—to roll with challenges and stand up for myself, even if I was trembling inside. Because I excelled on the ice, I was always playing with kids older than me. When

I was twelve, I was playing with fourteen- and fifteen-year-olds. I didn't even have hair on my nuts. They did. It was a big age difference, but I held my own.

That was the same year Garth broke my nose for the first time. He was practising his pitching on the baseball diamond behind our house and he had me catching for him. He was nineteen and brought some good heat. He also had a temper. The ball kept popping out of my catcher's mitt when he threw fastballs and slipping under me when he threw curveballs. "Just hold your glove in front of your face," he said. "I'll hit the glove." That's how he talked to me then. "Just do it."

So I watched him wind up and I put the glove in front of my face. There was a pause, and I thought the ball should have been in my mitt by now, so I lowered it to see what was happening. *Boom*—a fastball, square in the nose. I have a great pain tolerance, but I still remember, when I got up, that Garth said, "Clint, do not cry. Do not cry!"

I wasn't going to cry. But then I looked at home plate and the blood was just gushing all over it. I screamed and started to run. Our house was right there. You just went through the back alley, opened the gate and you were in the backyard. I was scared as shit seeing all that blood. "Don't! Don't! Don't! " Garth yelled after me. "Don't tell Mom!"

She heard the screaming and came out. "Oh my God!" she said.

My nose was almost sideways. I looked like a Picasso painting. "Garth, you asshole!" Mom said. And she chased him around with her sandal. It was the first of many broken noses for me. They used to call me Bent Beak. It got hit so many times it changed shape. My dad had the same look. It wasn't hereditary so much as a lifestyle thing. My nose was like a curved stick.

That was the only time he broke anything, but Garth had always terrorized me in the typical ways that older brothers do. He was just a little more creative at times. When he'd babysit me, he'd make me go to bed at five or six o'clock because he wanted to go outside to play. He'd tell me there were rattlesnakes under my bed and that if I got up they would bite me. I was young—I'd believe anything he said. I'd lie there as long as I could, until my bladder was about to burst. Then I'd run across my bed and leap to the doorway, bolt to the bathroom, pee, and then leap back into the bed, imagining a pit of snakes snapping at my heels. He also told me a bear lived in the basement, so I'd refuse to go down to the cold cellar. This was before I learned how to use a rifle.

That wasn't even the worst of it. When we still lived in Grande Prairie, when I was really young, he and his friends built a tree house and wouldn't let me in. I sat there, pouting at the bottom of the tree, until I felt a warm trickle, like rain. I looked up, and they were pissing on me. They were laughing so hard that one of them accidently knocked a piece of wood off the platform and it smacked me right in the head. It left a big gash, so Garth made me wear a toque at dinner so our mom wouldn't find out—it was the middle of July. When she pulled the toque off my head, my hair was all matted with dried blood. My mother had a unique talent for running after you while removing her sandal in full stride and whacking you on the ass. She got Garth good.

The worst of it, though—the big whopper of all the terrible things Garth did to me when I was young—happened during an expedition some of the neighbourhood kids went on through the Edmonton sewer system. About two miles from our house, there was a ravine with a great big steel door in one of its banks. It was the drainage ditch for the rainwater in the city. We managed to wedge the door open enough to get inside. There were all these tunnels that led to the manholes around our streets. It was all Garth's idea. Terry was there, too. We borrowed a baby buggy, a real one, with big wheels. We had a rope that we could use to pull it along, so Garth went in ahead in waders, and the plan was to get a couple of guys in the buggy and pull them along through the waist-high water, then send it back for the next few—kind of how they did it in *The Great Escape*.

We had everything we figured we'd need for underground exploration, which amounted to a few flashlights. It was all planned out. I was the youngest kid, just a tag-along little brother, so they had me test out the baby buggy. Garth waded ahead and I got into the buggy. He pulled me into the darkness. When the water got shallower, Garth called down the tunnel and told me to get out of the buggy, so I hopped out and trudged along in the black water. When I finally got to the first open area in the tunnel, Garth wasn't there. I called for him, and there was no answer. I was scared. I turned on my small flashlight and searched around and couldn't find him. Then I heard something above me. There was a ladder on the wall, leading up to the manhole on the street. I flashed the light up and caught a full moon. Garth had climbed to the top of the ladder. *Thwack.* He shit right on my head. True story. I had to walk home two miles covered in shit. "Don't tell Mom! Don't tell Mom!" he said. "I didn't mean to hit you!"

5

Stomach Pains

I WAS STILL IN ELEMENTARY SCHOOL THE FIRST TIME THE DOCTORS tried to figure out what was wrong with me. They told my classmates I had ulcers. That's what Kelly Hrudey remembers the teachers saying— that Clint was in the hospital and would be away for a while because he was suffering from a stomach problem.

It wasn't ulcers. That was just how they tried to explain these things back then. My anxiety had become unbearable, and I was always on the edge.

Nighttime was the worst. I couldn't be alone without feeling over- whelmed by panic and fear. I cried a lot, but I never really understood what was wrong. A few months after the night my dad smashed our windows and took off, I could still hear that smash every night in my dreams and would wake up sweating and panicked. Dad was still around then. He'd take off for days at a time and we wouldn't hear from him at all, but then he'd come home sober and sorry and my mom would take him back. Or he'd come really late at night, smelling of booze, and apologize for working late.

I don't think I knew how to deal with my drunk dad—someone I loved and hated at the same time. With my friends, I was funny and loud and competitive and normal. But I was always hiding something.

In the fifth grade, I started to unravel. My head was spinning. It was filled with anxiety swirling around, refusing to leave. I would just cry. I mean, really, just sobbing uncontrollably alone in my room. For a while, I wouldn't go anywhere unless it was with my sister, Terry. I felt comfortable and safe around Terry. She was probably the nicest person in the world. I acted fine when I was around other kids, but the anxiety never went away. I was a great actor.

I don't know if it was depression. I wouldn't describe it as that, exactly. I was just so anxious. I'd try to find reasons in my mind for what was causing it. I'd worry that I was the only person on the planet who felt this way. Or I'd worry that it was really just me here, and no one else was real. Weird shit. No one knew what was wrong.

My mother took me to see our family doctor, Dr. Flook. He was a nice man. He kept asking me what was wrong, so I did my best to explain it. I told him I had taken a knife from the kitchen and pushed it into my stomach—just enough to draw blood and feel pain. I think I was just so anxious and feeling depressed that I thought if I pushed it hard enough, it might end the pain, but then it might kill you, too. It was very abstract at the time. I was young—I had no idea what I was doing. It didn't cause any serious injury, but I think it scared the doctor, because he told my parents what I had done with the knife, and they agreed that I needed to stay under observation at the hospital. He thought I was having a nervous breakdown.

They kept me in the children's ward. Dr. Flook would come in to see me once a day. He'd ask me a few questions about how I was feeling, almost like I had a broken leg or something like that. They didn't do much else. I didn't even see a psychologist. I was kept under the supervision of the nurses. My parents would come and visit—both of them, even though Dad was on his way out of our lives at the time. The incident when the cops were called was the beginning of the end for my parents. But he came to see me in the hospital. I was glad. I still loved him.

The anxiety didn't go away. I had to interact with the other kids in the children's ward. We all had to eat together in one room and it made me anxious. I hated it in there. One night, I tried to escape. I had been crying all night in my room and decided that I'd had enough. All the other kids were sleeping. I crawled past the nurse's desk so she couldn't see me. I made it to the stairwell—we were on the fifth floor—and got through the door without her noticing. I made it all the way down until I found a door that said EXIT, but it had that emergency alarm on it, so I didn't go through it. Instead, I went down another flight of stairs to a door that said MORGUE. That freaked me out, and I ran back up the stairs and crawled past the nurse's desk and into my room. Another night, I got upset again and tried to leave, and they sedated me.

No one knew what to do with me.

I missed a lot of school. My mom would bring my books and lessons from class, but I fell far behind and never really caught up.

The one thing they did let me do while I was in the hospital was leave to play hockey. It was the only thing that seemed to make me happy, so they decided it was better to let me play. My mom would bring my hockey gear up, and I'd get half-dressed in the hospital room and she'd drive me to the rink. My teammates were nice. They didn't say anything to me about being in the hospital. They didn't ask me what "ulcers" were. I just played the game and everything felt fine. Then it was back to the hospital.

I was there for two months, cooped up in this "cuckoo's nest" for kids. I have no idea why they let me out in the end. I have no idea what they learned about me. Nothing really changed. They probably thought, *Forget it, this kid is hopeless.*

6

Empty Bottles

DESPITE MY TIME IN THE HOSPITAL, I STILL EXCELLED ON THE ice. I jumped a level in hockey when I was thirteen. They called me up from the Ironco bantams to the Westgate Chevy midget team. All the other players were fourteen, fifteen and sixteen. These guys could shoot the puck.

It was a tough time for me. It didn't help that Dad was screwing around with the mother of one of the players on the team. Everyone knew about it; the rumours got around. I remember going down the street to play hockey with one of my teammates on the midget team. I rang the doorbell, and his mom answered. She looked at me and said, "You're nothing but a punk. And your mother's a slut." She was a friend of the woman my father was having the affair with. They'd all turned on my mom—and on me, apparently. "I don't want you around here," she said. Somehow my dad and this broad he was screwing came out as the victims.

My parents divorced a year later. Dad had been kicked out of the house for a while, but this time Mom made sure his ass was gone for good. Just as alcoholism is a progressive disease, a bad marriage also festers. And their marriage had rotted away. Mom used to stick up for him. She put up with his drinking as long as she could; she sheltered me from him. (For everything he did, Dad never hit me.) She knew that the man she had fallen in love with was trapped somewhere inside of what he became. Eventually she realized that the man she loved was never coming back.

I was always very courteous to my mom. She never asked me to cut the lawn; I just did it. If I saw her outside doing it, I'd say, "No, no, I can do it." I hated taking out the garbage, so she'd do that. But my room was always clean—spotless, actually. I couldn't stand a mess. That had more to do with the OCD I'd be diagnosed with later than with being a good kid—but still it was a bonus. The same went for my hockey gear. I used to wipe away all the puck marks to make sure everything looked brand new.

It was just Mom and me by then. Terry was married and had moved away. Garth was off playing junior hockey in Calgary. So Mom and I relied on each other. She needed me and I needed her. We sold our furniture to make ends meet because the old man wasn't paying what he was supposed to be paying in support. And we couldn't find him to make him pay. We had a table and chairs. Everything else we sold. We just hung on, together.

Mom had to go back to work to support me. It sounds like a sad old cliché, but it's true. She found work as a secretary in an office downtown after spending two decades raising a family. It was hard on her. I came home one day and found her sitting over this damn typewriter, crying—she couldn't learn to type fast enough.

"I can't do this anymore."

I hugged her. "Yes you can, Mom. You can do this. We can do this. Just keep pounding the keys." We became a team. When I got home from school before her, I'd try to put dinner together for her. She was always grateful, even though the only thing I could make at the time was a bowl of Corn Flakes.

Mom always put me first, even in the tough times. She was one of those parents who always drove the players to games and practices. It didn't matter how early or how far—she'd pick up every teammate in the area and drive us to play hockey and then drive everyone home again. I don't know if Mom thought I had a future in the game or not. She probably knew that I was elite for my age, and she was well versed in the game with all of Garth's success. But I think she just did it because she knew how much the sport meant to me.

I played for the Canadian Athletic Club in AA level hockey—there was no AAA in Edmonton at the time. There was a South Side Athletic Club and Northwest Athletic Club. We played all over the city. I changed the name on the back of my jersey to my mother's maiden name, Henning. Knowing what my dad had done, it was a show of solidarity with my mom. He wasn't coming to games anyway. He probably didn't know, but it was a bold statement for a kid my age to make. I ended up changing it back after a year because it caused all kinds of confusion. By that time, I'd already made a name for myself as a Malarchuk. Garth and Terry both kept their last name, too, so I was on my own with the Henning thing.

We had a routine in the summer to earn extra cash. She'd go to work and I'd get on this old rickety bike I had and ride out to the construction sites on the outskirts of Edmonton. There were pop cans everywhere. I'd take green garbage bags and fill them up and hide them in the bushes. Then I'd bike miles home. When Mom got home from work, we'd drive out and pick up all the bags. We earned a nickel a can or bottle.

That's how I paid for my first pair of goalie skates. At that time, if you played in a community league, they'd loan you the gear for the season. But I had to buy my own skates. I got them from Ken Hitchcock. Long before Ken became a Jack Adams Award–winning NHL coach, he sold hockey gear at United Cycle in Edmonton. They had a lot of used goalie equipment at the store, and Ken always gave us a really good break. He knew a little bit about my background, that I was one of the best goalies in the city and that my family situation was less than ideal. We weren't pretending to be poor—we *were* poor.

I didn't want to play goal to be like my dad. I wanted to be like Garth. He left home to play Tier II Junior A in Kamloops, B.C., when I was ten. Then he played major junior for the Calgary Centennials. We'd often drive down to watch his games. Garth was drafted by the Washington Capitals in the seventh round, 109th overall, in the 1974 NHL draft. The Toronto Toros of the upstart World Hockey Association drafted Garth in the sixth round, eighty-sixth overall, the same year. I was so proud of him. He never made it to the NHL on the ice—it just didn't work out for him. He played in the International Hockey League in Kalamazoo, Dayton and Fort Wayne before retiring in 1977. Garth went on to be a police officer in Calgary and then joined the NHL ranks as a well-respected scout. He was the real father figure in my life. But we never talked about Dad. Never. He was always a topic better left buried in the past.

Besides the skates I bought with the pop bottle money, my most prized piece of gear was an old catcher Garth gave me for Christmas one year. He was away playing in the IHL and had it sent home. The label said it was from Santa. I unwrapped the present under the tree on Christmas Eve. It was a brown leather Cooper GM-12 catcher, the best of its kind at the time, before they had webbing. That night, I went to sleep with the catcher on my hand. I woke up on Christmas morning and it was still on. It was the best gift I'd ever received.

A lot of kids dream of making the NHL, but very few ever do. I realized this when I was young, but I basically said, "Screw that. I'm going to be a hockey player." I'd heard that if you worked hard enough and wanted something badly enough, it would happen. It seemed logical to me. School sure as hell wasn't going to work out, but I was actually good at hockey. So I worked harder than any kid I knew.

There was a contest called Save and Score, run by Lowney's candy bars in 1971. The grand prize was a week at Bobby Orr's hockey camp in Orillia, Ontario. It was a Canada-wide contest. I was ten at the time. The people who sent in the most golden wrappers would win the trip. I saw the contest as my big opportunity. I'd go to the arena with my mother to watch one of Garth's games, but I'd spend the whole time digging through the garbage cans, pulling out every candy wrapper I could find. I must have searched through hundreds of garbage cans across Edmonton. I collected about 2,500 Lowney's wrappers. That was the easy part. The hard part was writing my name and address on each one. I finished in first place by a mile and won goalie equipment and the trip to Bobby Orr's camp.

They flew me from Edmonton to Toronto, and then I had to take a two-hour bus ride to Orillia. It was the first time I had really left home, other than visiting my grandmother in Grande Prairie. Kids obviously get homesick, but for me it was constant. It kept me up all night. The instructors called me the homesick kid. But the guy in charge of the program was really nice. His name was Bill Watters. He went on to jobs in upper management with the Toronto Maple Leafs and as a sports media personality. But to me, he was the guy who went out of his way to help me when I felt alone and scared. He and his wife were incredible to me that week. I'll never forget that.

I started a serious workout regime when I was twelve years old, and I stuck with it obsessively. Aside from spending every minute I could on the ice, I was militant about doing all of the exercises and drills in Jacques Plante's book. I'd do push-ups and sit-ups and deep knee bends. I'd run the stairs, up and down, up and down. When I worked up at the ranch in the summers, I'd do shoulder shrugs and take extra deep strides while carrying ten-gallon buckets of milk across the barn to pour into the pigs' trough.

The work ethic and focus helped get me noticed by the Portland Winterhawks while I was playing midget. But it also took over my life. There was no line separating competitive drive from full-out obsession. I constantly compared myself to other goalies. I feared that I'd be second best. I'd lose sleep over it. *I have to be the best, I have to be the best,* I'd think while working out. I'd think about it while playing. I'd think about it while lying awake in bed at night. Worried, worried, worried—honestly, as a teen, I'd lose nights of sleep over it. *Am I going to lose my starting job? Am I going to sit on the bench?* If I got pulled from a game, I'd double up my workout the next morning. I'd bug my mom constantly. "Do you think I'm better than that goalie? What about this guy?" Whatever I was emotional about, I was obsessive about. It had become a competition.

There was no draft in the Western Hockey League in the seventies. Each of the teams had a region from which they could protect a certain number of players for their roster. The Edmonton Oil Kings moved to

Portland, Oregon, in 1976, but they maintained their territorial rights over Edmonton. A scout from the Winterhawks came and spoke to my mother and me about my future with the team. I was thrilled, but Mom was skeptical about me leaving home. She knew what I was like, still battling anxiety and depression. But there was nothing I wanted more in the world than to be a hockey player, and this was the only way. She believed I could make it to the NHL and be a star. I knew it more than anyone.

I went to the training camp, but I was still young then, probably fifteen. So they asked me to go and play for their Tier II affiliate in Fort Saskatchewan, about an hour outside of Edmonton. At the time, the Alberta Junior Hockey League boasted future NHLers like Keith Brown, Jim Benning and Ken Daneyko. But the star of the league was Mark Messier, a fifteen-year-old playing for the St. Albert Saints. He was a big, powerful skater who could shoot. No one could touch him. He was pretty damn good.

The rink in Fort Saskatchewan was an old barn with chicken wire instead of glass above the boards. We had a tough team. We used to brawl all the time. It was a small town—forget about a stop light; I think it had maybe one four-way stop. We played in one of those typical old-time hockey rinks that sat maybe 1,200 people. But it was always packed. Everybody smoked, so this grey cloud hung over the ice.

To play back then, you had to be half-tough. You couldn't back down from a fight. We had some serious bench-clearing brawls. And when we had a brawl, you had no choice but to get into them. A lot of them happened during warmups. There was only a painted red line separating the two teams. Somebody would skate over it a little bit, or you would steal a puck from the other team—or shoot a puck at them—and it was on. We had a few battles with St. Albert. They were really tough—mostly because they had Messier and he was a man at fifteen. But they had some other seriously tough guys, too. Those games always ended with blood and bruises. At the Fort Saskatchewan arena, both teams left the ice at the same end of the rink, and there was a lobby between the two dressing rooms. We fought with St. Albert back there one time, and the RCMP had to come and break us up as if it were a riot.

The team called this kid up once, a chunky farm boy. We always had to wear dress shirts and ties, but he came to the game in a flannel lumberjack shirt. It was a rough game. So the coach told him, "Okay, you're going to get out there and fight that guy, their goon." The coach meant that the chunky lumberjack farm boy would fight him when it was his turn to go on the ice, but he just leapt over the boards without a stick or gloves and went after the guy. You had to at least wait for the puck to drop! I thought he was going to the dressing room. He could barely skate. And he just went up to this guy and pummelled him.

I played two seasons in Fort Saskatchewan. I was the starting goalie at sixteen, played a lot and did really well. We won the Alberta championship, beat B.C. and then lost to Saskatchewan in the national semi-finals. During the 1978 season, the goalie in Portland got hurt, so I went up and played. I was terribly nervous and far from home. That homesickness stuck with me for so long. But I did okay in my first major junior showing. I picked up two penalty minutes, which sounds about right for me.

We had a few twenty-year-olds on that team in Fort Saskatchewan. After games, we'd all go to the local bar in an old hotel. Glasses of draft beer were forty-five cents, but I was still pretty tame then. I'd sip tomato juice.

Our rink was about an hour from home, so sometimes I would stay at one of the billet homes after games and road trips. Otherwise, I'd trek back to Edmonton to stay with Mom. It was a long haul. At the time, I was enrolled at Jasper Place Composite High School, but I was still such a terrible student. I took ridiculously easy classes like guitar, art and drama.

Drama was always my first class of the day, and I was always late. If I made it on time, I'd be exhausted, so I'd climb under the stage, where all the costumes were stored, and sleep for an hour. Our donkey of a drama teacher didn't like me very much. After a few truancies, he started locking the door. So every time I got in late, I'd have to knock. One time, the class was in the middle of rehearsal, so he opened the door and started poking me in the chest with his finger.

"Don't do that," I warned him. He was kind of hurting me. He was really mad.

"You're always late!" he shouted. "You don't take this seriously. You're always interrupting." And the whole time, he kept shoving his finger into my shoulder. So I smoked him. I just drilled him in the face as hard as I could. He went ass over teakettle.

I was suspended for quite a while after that. I think I was expelled, but my mom went and got me back in. She defended me because the donkey was poking me. I had told him not to. I said I'd drill him, and I did.

I ended up with an extensive rap sheet at Jasper Place. I had a history teacher, Mr. Wey, with these dark horn-rimmed glasses and a bushy mustache. It looked like he was wearing a pair of those gag nose glasses. One day, he kicked me out of class, probably for talking or joking around or whatever. I went out into the hall—I'm pretty sure I'd planned this in advance—put these gag glasses on and walked back into the room a few minutes later.

"Hey, Dad!" I said in a squeaky, nerdy voice. "Can I have the keys to the car?"

Mr. Wey wasn't impressed. "Get out."

"C'mon, Dad, I got a date. I got a date. Give me the keys. You'll like her! She's hot, Dad. She's so hot!"

"Get out of my class, you little punk creep. Get out now."

The class was in stitches, so I pushed a little further. I grabbed the fire extinguisher next to me on the wall. "You're so hot and bothered, Dad. Why are you so hot and bothered? You need to cool off." I sprayed the extinguisher everywhere. It was an old pump-style extinguisher—it squirted out water. I let Mr. Wey have it and then let the whole class have it. Everyone was laughing. They thought it was great.

I got suspended for that one, too.

Years ago, Jasper Place wrote me, asking for a picture for their wall of fame. I don't think I sent one.

7

Butterfly

I MIGHT HAVE BEEN A TERRIBLE STUDENT IN THE CLASSROOM, but I was a scholar of the game.

I taught myself everything by watching the best. Goalie coaches didn't really exist when I was learning the game. The closest I came to having a real mentor in net, beyond my brother, Garth, was Dave Dryden. When Dave played for the Oilers, he lived about a mile from Mom and me. I was about sixteen then. I used to hang out at the Oilers' practices back when they were in the World Hockey Association. I'd just go by myself and sit in the stands. I was trying to learn from them. One day after practice, I went over and talked to Dave while he was standing by the bench. We kind of became friends. Dave was a very nice guy. I visited his house a few times, and he'd always stop to chat with me at the Coliseum. When I'd go down to watch him practice, I'd ask him questions about the game, equipment, the team—everything. He was one of the first guys to have a goalie-mask-and-cage combo, which seemed cool at the time.

I was a sponge. I took in everything Dave said. Here was this NHL and WHA veteran, taking the time to speak to an overeager teenager. He represented huge moral support for me. I'm not sure if he knows how much that meant to me.

I played in a transitional period for goalies. Basically, I was among the last of a dying breed: the standup goalie. Growing up, it was ingrained in your skull—"Stand up! Stand up! Play the angles! Play the angles!" But partway through my NHL career, the butterfly style revolutionized the position. Glenn Hall was the first butterfly goalie, but it wasn't until Patrick Roy in the mid-1980s that the approach to goaltending really changed. When Roy came along and had all his success, I kept thinking, *He's playing it all wrong! He's going down on every shot.* But he was stopping all those pucks. It was unbelievable.

Bernie Parent of the Philadelphia Flyers was always my favorite goalie. The Broad Street Bullies played my kind of hockey. Parent stood up and played the angles. So I did, too. I'd say it worked out pretty well for him, considering he won two Stanley Cups, two Conn Smythe Trophies and two Vezinas. Later, the Flyers' Pelle Lindbergh was almost a clone of Bernie. Looked like him, played like him, wore the same pads. Pelle grew up idolizing Bernie, too. He even got to work with him. He had so much success before he was killed much too soon in a drunk-driving accident in 1985.

I was also a big fan of the great Glenn Hall, who played with the Chicago Blackhawks and later with the St. Louis Blues when I was young. As I mentioned, he was one of the first butterfly goalies, but it would be years before his style caught on. I also loved Vladislav Tretiak. He's the best hockey player never to play in the NHL. Years later, while I was playing for the Washington Capitals, I got the chance to train with him when I enrolled in his goalie school in Montreal. It was a camp for kids, but I showed up like a regular student. Tretiak got a kick out of that. I got to work with the students as well, but mostly I was there to learn from a legend. Standing next to Tretiak on the ice is a humbling experience.

He was teaching the butterfly style. That was the first time I realized how effective it was. I was going from just trying to stand up all the time to learning to switch to a butterfly stance if the angles and shot warranted it. As long as you stop the puck, no one is going to say anything, but back then, if it went in or there was a fat rebound and you were a butterfly goalie, the coach would ask why you didn't stand up. But the coaches had no idea what they were talking about. The majority of shots in games were low, because players didn't have as much time to go top shelf. In practice, all these guys aim for the high glove because they have lots of time. In a game, someone is always putting pressure on them, so they don't have time.

I guess you could say I became a hybrid-style goalie after that, but I never fully overhauled my game to suit the new era of goaltending. I wish I had. But I didn't have the knees for it. They were always bad. You won't see many former goalies who don't grimace when they stand up. Your knees aren't supposed to twist the ways goalies contort them. We usually carry that pain as penance when our careers are done. But my penance should have been covered long before I even made it to the NHL.

When I was seventeen, I helped take the Fort Saskatchewan Traders to the Alberta championships. I stood on my head that season. But in February, my leg started locking up during games. I'd just kick through it and play with the pain. I didn't know any better. I wasn't aware that I had torn cartilage, and each time I kicked through the pain, I tore it a little more. I didn't find this out until after the playoffs, when Garth got me in to see a specialist in Calgary who confirmed that my knee was a mangled mess. I went in for surgery at the end of June, the day after school got out. It went well. The recovery was going as planned—until my knee started to swell up and I got a fever and chills. My leg was like a balloon. I had a staph infection.

They got me on antibiotics right away, but nothing worked. I had to stay in the hospital. Then the infection went to the bone. It's called osteomyelitis, which is basically gangrene. They kept me in isolation in a sterilized room. The only people who could come in wore these *Star Wars*–style gowns. I was in total isolation. When I finally rejoined civilization, people visited for a little while to be supportive, but they had their lives to live. My mom was always there. My buddy Jeff Bulat, who grew up with me in Elmwood, and a couple other buddies would come.

By August, the doctors had almost given up. They said they were going to try to scrape some of this crap off my bone, but if things didn't turn around in a couple of weeks, they were going to have to take my leg off. What started with some torn cartilage was about to turn into an amputation! Either way, leg or no leg, they said I'd never be able to play goal again. "You might be able to skate, but you'll never be able to move around, up and down, like a goalie," the doctor said. "That's just not going to happen."

The thought that my leg—and with it, my dream—might be taken, that my life would never be the same, was debilitating. It felt like my rotting leg was a time bomb ticking down to my brutal execution. Then one day, the doctors tried a new antibiotic and, by grace, it worked. The infection began to lift—I could keep my leg. Nothing was going to get in my way now. The doctor's doubts that I might not be able to play again meant nothing to me. They didn't know the will inside me. I had dreams. If that leg stayed attached to my body, I would take care of the rest. Sure, I hadn't skated in months and my bedridden body was a sack of fading muscles, but no one could outwork me. If anybody could spend an entire summer cooped up like Bubble Boy, with his leg weeks away from being sawn off, and then make a full recovery in time to impress the major scouts, it was me. Sometimes my obsessive personality was a curse. In this case, it was a blessing.

Every summer, it was the same thing. I was pushing, pushing, pushing—*You've got to be the best. You've got to be the best. You've got to be the best.* I mean, who doesn't want to be the best? Maybe some people don't, I guess. But if you're an athlete, your whole purpose is to be the best. If you're going to try to make it all the way, you'd better be thinking that way.

I never gave myself much credit for having actual skill. I always thought my success was all about hard work. I overtrained. In hindsight, I probably limited myself by overtraining. But it was the only way I had of dealing with the fear that I wasn't doing enough. If I ran ten miles, I believed someone else was probably running twenty. If I did a hundred push-ups, someone was surely cranking out 150. The competition lived in my mind. I was terrified of disappointing my coach, and I wanted to never let my teammates down. I wanted my family and friends to be proud of me. I wanted the fans to love me. It always felt like I was being watched—like everyone and everything depended on me. But I guess that's normal for an athlete. We're always being judged.

When I was playing junior, my struggle was not so much with depression as it was with anxiety. The time when I was hospitalized, when I was twelve, I was in a really dark place. Mentally, I wasn't there anymore. Those feelings came in waves, and they would hit me like a cyclone later on. Anxiety was just my normal state of being. I was always on edge. I needed to find a reason why I felt this way, and of course high-level hockey seemed like the perfect reason. I was oblivious to the possibility that it could be anything more than that.

I was in the hospital for just over two months before I was finally released the first week in September. I hit the weights right away. I missed training camp but got back on the ice just before the Traders' season started. *Never going to play again, my ass.* I played the best hockey of my life that year. It was enough to impress the right people in Portland. I ended up with the Winterhawks full time the following season, in 1979.

Portland is a great city for junior hockey. We led the league in attendance. For the first ten years after the team relocated from Edmonton, it sold out a lot of games. And in my first year, we had a very good team. We were coached by Ken Hodge (not the same one who played for the Bruins). Back then, junior coaches were all tough. It was all about discipline. They tried to make men out of you really quickly by yelling and screaming at you. They were all like that back then. Hodge was that kind of coach. He was the kind of coach who was difficult to get to know because he kept his distance. He was tough on everybody, but especially on the goalies. Major junior is a unique situation for a young athlete to be in. It's basically this strange place where you're living the dream, but not really. It's a step up from Tier II and one step away from the NHL. There's a chance that you'll get drafted, but there's also a chance that you're going to blow it, pretty much ending your career.

You're treated well; local people recognize you. And there are a few perks, like actually getting a bit of coin. I can't remember what they were allowed to pay us, but it was something like the equivalent of thirty-five dollars a week today—maybe enough to fill up your gas tank.

All these different things enter your life when you go away to play major junior hockey. The stress level is cranked way up. The possibility of realizing your dream is just an impressed scout away. You have to grow up fast. It was a gut-wrenching combination for me. That first year in Portland, I was so homesick I almost quit hockey altogether. I think I was conscious of the fact that Mom and I had been through so much and I felt like I was abandoning her by leaving. That was tough. I was really close with my grandma, too. I would call them all the time. It was just really tough for me that way—kind of like I was back at Bobby Orr's hockey camp in Orillia. It was a constant feeling that I was a long way from where I was supposed to be. Mom came out to Portland to watch me play a few times, but Dad never did. He was still out of my life at the time.

The only thing that got me through junior was knowing that this was my only shot to make it to the NHL. I had to get drafted. So whenever I started to feel depressed, I did my best to counter it by obsessing about the next game and the next game. It was kind of like a coping mechanism. The crazy game kept me going.

In Portland, I surrounded myself with families. I think it helped fill a big hole in my life. I lived with Dick and Mary Lou Lisk. They were great. We kept in touch with them somewhat. They were a big comfort, considering how much I was struggling at the time. They had a daughter and son who were about sixteen and fourteen. We all got along well. The girl wasn't around too much. The boy and I would kind of hang out and go to movies and stuff. There was another family that I got to know—season-ticket holders. They invited me over for dinners and to hang out. There were three girls in that family, and one of them was a little kid. She adored me. It was cute. She made me feel loved, like I was a big brother.

We were on the road a lot. The travel was insane because we were still treated like a team from Edmonton, even though we were a sixteen-hour drive away. We'd go on road trips for weeks at a time and play everybody—all the way out to Brandon and Winnipeg. We never flew. It was always a bus, just a plain old Greyhound.

On those road trips, we'd be on the bus for hours, all day, and we'd pull into some backwater town at around five in the evening and just feel like shit. But we were a bunch of eighteen- and nineteen-year-olds, pumped up because scouts were going to be there. We were always aware that scouts would be at every game, regardless of how cold and remote the place was.

They made us wear suits and ties every time we stepped off the bus. It didn't matter when or where. Once we got on the bus, we'd change into sweats. But then we'd roll into the next town at three in the morning and have to put our suits back on to check into the hotel, only to take them off and go to bed. Just ridiculous stuff.

The bus stunk on those trips. We'd eat at McDonald's or Kentucky Fried Chicken and places like that. This was before nutrition was really a part of sports. We heard chicken was good for us, with all that protein, so the team figured there was nothing wrong with buckets of Colonel Sanders's finest. We'd eat it, with all that grease dripping off the skin, and be lined up for the bathroom at the back of the bus. Today, junior teams are run almost like the pros. They have meals prepared and ready for the boys as soon as they get on the bus, and it's a spread of good, healthy food. Things have changed.

Being cooped up like that for days on end will make you a little cranky. There would be the odd fight between teammates, which turned into entertainment for the others. We were a good bunch of guys, but these things happen. There was a lot of pent-up aggression. Being trapped on a bus was terrible for my obsession with working out. We only stayed in dingy motels, so there was never a gym to lift weights in. It drove me crazy. I'd do push-ups and sit-ups in the room or on the bus if I felt like my body was rotting away.

I passed most of the time by reading. I think I read every Louis L'Amour western. The Sony Walkman came out around that time, and you could listen to cassette tapes—that was the greatest thing in the world. I listened to a lot of country music—Merle Haggard, Johnny Cash, Emmylou Harris. The good stuff. Country always lifted me up. I was a cowboy at heart. Dreams of rounding up cattle and hunting bears and conquering bucking broncos always lifted me out of my darkest funks. The wild, open country, the twang of a guitar, a good western tale—all of it took me someplace else, someplace better. Then I'd open my eyes and be thousands of miles from home again, with a winter storm beating against the cold bus window. We went through some serious ones driving across the open plains in the middle of winter. We'd be out there with no other vehicles on the road, going thirty miles an hour in a whiteout. One time in the B.C. interior, it snowed so much that these big old pine trees were weighed down with snow and bent over the road like a canopy. It was beautiful, but it was scary, too. We drove through it all.

The longest trip we took was twenty-eight days. We started in Seattle and then went on to Victoria. We had to take a ferry to get there, so we'd leave at three in the morning to catch the first one at nine, and then we played that night. After that, it was off to New Westminster, B.C., and then to Calgary, Lethbridge, Swift Current, Medicine Hat, Brandon, Winnipeg—all the way to the middle of Canada, a couple hours from the edge of Ontario. Our last game was in Brandon, and we left right after the game and drove straight to Portland—two and a half days. They didn't want to stop. We slept on the bus both nights. We didn't have sleepers; we'd just sleep sitting up in the seat, or some guys would curl up on the floor or climb up in the luggage rack. We found ways.

They flew in a driver halfway into the trip because it was against the law to have one driver on such a long trip. They switched him up and we kept rolling. We got home at around three in the afternoon and played a home game that night, after almost a month on the road.

We were a pretty good team both years that I played in Portland, but we never did well in the playoffs. That first season was tough for me. I played well, but I wasn't great. Hodge split the starting duties between

Darrell May and me. At the end of the year, the Vancouver Canucks drafted Darrell. I wasn't drafted at all. My numbers were decent, and people had thought that I would go that year. I was devastated. Totally devastated.

But there were bigger things to worry about. At the time, I was facing five years in prison for assault causing bodily harm.

8

A Strong Defense

I RETURNED TO EDMONTON AFTER THE SEASON ENDED IN PORTLAND and got into a bit of a scuffle with the entire family that lived next door to my mother. These were some goofy neighbours. I had only been home a couple days when one of our dogs went over onto their property. The father chased him with a rake. That pissed me off, so I went over to their house and told them if they ever touched my dog, I'd fry their cat.

Coincidentally, the next day, their cat was hiding under their step and wouldn't come out. It had broken a leg somehow. They thought I was responsible, so one of the sons came over to confront me. He was about my age but he was very big—the whole family was big. I opened the door and he started screaming, "You hurt our cat!" and smoked me right in the face. He hit me so hard I landed on my ass. I saw red. I got up and kicked the living snot out of him. I beat him pretty bad. I was pissed off. You get sucker punched in your own house? And I didn't even touch their cat!

My mother came out and broke it up. The other guy was hurt pretty bad, so she got a first-aid kit to clean him up. Then his mother came over, yelling at us, demanding to know what we'd done to him. My mom tried to calm her down and explain, but she just grabbed my mom's hair and pulled it back so hard she fell over. So I grabbed the lady and said, "Get the hell out of here." I guess I kind of dislocated her shoulder in the process. Just as that was happening, her son-in-law showed up. He jumped over our hedge and charged at me. I don't blame him. If I saw that and didn't see everything, I'd probably do the same thing. I popped him right in the face—*boom*—and he was out cold. Like snoring.

So I got charged with three counts of assault causing bodily harm. I had just turned eighteen, which made the potential consequences that much more severe. My brother Garth was a cop in Calgary then, and he connected us with a great lawyer. At the court case, the whole family showed up, still bandaged from our altercation. But the judge decided I had acted in self-defense and all the charges were dropped. Thankfully, this was long before the days of the Internet, and the Winterhawks never found out. These days, it would have been all over the news.

When I wasn't in court that summer, I was in the gym, determined that I wouldn't go undrafted again. It worked. I improved my goals-against average from 4.53 in my first season to 3.81 in my second. My save percentage went up from .875 to .893. Those numbers may not sound that impressive today, but it was a different game back then.

It was a better year all around. I was still terribly homesick, but I was more comfortable in Portland. I even met my first girlfriend. My life had always been centred completely around hockey. My parents had told me to stay away from girls when I was young. "They only want to mess you up and take your money," Dad told me. Even after he left, Mom continued to warn me. "Just use it for peeing through," she told me when I went to Portland.

One day after practice at one of the smaller arenas in Portland, the team went back to the Memorial Coliseum to drop our gear off. The arena was hosting a big high school basketball tournament. I wasn't a basketball fan, so I was really just watching the cheerleaders. Honest to God, I went down to get my coat from the dressing room when I was leaving and walked right into this cheerleader. She was beautiful. I'm sure it seemed like a pathetic pickup attempt. "Oh my God! I'm so sorry," I said.

Her name was Jodi Bauer. And I was a gentleman, so we ended up going out. So Jodi was the first girl I let my guard down with.

Her dad was a Lutheran pastor. Her family was really nice, and I think they liked me. We'd go to church together every Sunday. I used to go to church when I was a kid, and I was always amazed by the idea of God. I always felt I needed help. I often wondered why I was like this, and whether other people were like me. I wondered, *Is this normal?*

In some ways, I was very confident, but in others I was very insecure. God seemed like a good idea to lean on. I read a lot of Norman Vincent Peale books when I was younger. He was a motivational author who always wrote in a Christian context. You know, he'd pull out inspiration quotes from the Bible, like "I can do all things through Christ who strengthens me." Which means I can do anything I want because God's with me. Just hold the faith. That verse stuck with me. I wouldn't think of it for years, and then it would suddenly jump into my head.

My relationship with God was always very personal. I never felt the need to actually go to church, but I'd pray every night and in the morning. I'd pray during the day when I was stressed. I prayed my whole life.

At the end of the 1980–81 season, I prayed that I'd be drafted. My chance of making the NHL was slipping away. It was now, or it was likely never. I was home in Edmonton when I got the call in June 1981. The NHL draft wasn't televised back then, the way it is today. Players just sat at home and waited for the phone to ring. It was excruciating—like watching water boil, but knowing there's a chance it never will. Everyone thought I'd be drafted, but it was still a shock when the phone rang. It was Maurice Filion, the general manager of the Quebec Nordiques, on the other end. That's how I found out what the next chapter of my life would involve.

Mom was there. Dad wasn't.

It felt like I'd won the lottery. I went seventy-fourth overall, two spots after John Vanbiesbrouck went to the Rangers. It was the year that Dale Hawerchuk went first, to the Winnipeg Jets. Bobby Carpenter,

Ron Francis and Grant Fuhr all went in the top ten. Calgary drafted Al MacInnis fifteenth. Another defenseman, Chris Chelios, went fortieth to Montreal.

My dream was almost a reality. I was going to the NHL. *Holy crap, I'm going to the NHL!* Then the joy gave way to a nervous reality: *Oh shit, this is real. I'd better get ready for training camp.*

9

Training Camp

WHEN I SHOWED UP TO MY FIRST PRO TRAINING CAMP IN 1981, I still had all these illusions about what life in the National Hockey League would be like. This was the big time. This was the show, right? True, but it wasn't the show I expected. If you watch the movie *Slap Shot* today, you probably won't recognize many of the hilarious stereotypes in the modern NHL. But damn, back then—holy shit.

On day one, I walked into the gym for "fitness testing" at the arena. There was a husky guy pedalling leisurely on a stationary bike, smoking a cigarette. I thought he was some trainer testing it out. But there was a guy with a stopwatch standing next to him keeping time! The husky guy was riding this thing so slow, it was like he was on a carousel. His cigarette was just hanging out of his mouth, bobbing up and down as he chatted away in French. The other guys in the room were laughing along with whatever the hell he was saying. I asked someone who the guy was. He looked at me like I was nuts. "That's Moose Dupont. Our captain."

Andre Dupont, a defenseman best known as one of Philly's Broad Street Bullies in the 1970s, was a unique kind of captain. Before one of our practices, I was stretching out on the dressing-room floor, sitting in a split, reaching for my toes. Moose walked in and saw me on the floor. "Hey kid, what the hell are you doing down there? Looking for bedbugs in the fucking rug?" he asked. He was smoking a cigarette again. "Cut it out. You're making me sore. You look like a ballerina."

45

As part of the fitness test at the Nordiques' training camp, players had to run up and down this huge hill at a resort on the outskirts of town. But the vets didn't really care for being tested. One of the coaches stood at the starting point and told us when to take off. We started off in a pack, but a short ways up the hill, Moose and Michel Plasse, the Nordiques' backup goalie, pulled off to the side into the trees and lit up a smoke. It was a long haul, probably a thirty-to-forty-minute uphill run. When the pack came back the other way, Moose and Plasse put out their butts and jogged back to the finish line with us.

I met Dale Hunter for the first time during that camp. It was Dale's second year, but the team put us together as roommates. There weren't a lot of English guys on the team, and we sure as hell didn't know any French, so it was nice to be around a guy you could understand. Dale and I also had a lot in common. He was an Ontario farm boy and I was a rancher from Alberta. He was one of the toughest, hardest-working players I'd ever seen. Dale was probably the fittest guy in training camp—not that the bar was set very high. We also shared the same juvenile sense of humour. Dale was a big-time prankster—he mastered the classics, like putting Saran Wrap across the toilet bowl so some needle-dick's piss would splash back on him or his shit would just squish there against his ass. It worked every time. He and I became really good friends. We would go on to have one of those relationships where we might go years without talking, and as soon as we'd see each other again, it'd be like no time had passed at all.

I was up against Plasse and Dan Bouchard for a spot on the team that first year with the Nordiques. They were both vets and I was a long shot to make the team as a rookie. Bouchard was the established starter, but Plasse had played for fourteen pro teams in four leagues over the past thirteen seasons, so I thought I might have a shot. I really wanted to prove that I deserved to be there.

They dressed all three of us through a few of the pre-season games. During one of them, the coach sent Plasse in halfway through the second period. He played for a few minutes and then, after a whistle, skated over to the bench and pulled a cigarette pack and lighter from behind his goal pad. He handed them to the trainer and went back to the net. He was so used to smoking between periods that he forgot he'd stashed his pack in his equipment.

I had a really good camp. I was probably the best goalie. It really stung when I was one of the last cuts. I knew I had made them notice me. They sent me down to Fredericton in the American Hockey League. With the exception of a couple of NHL games with Quebec, that's where I spent the year.

The Fredericton Express was an expansion team. It was the first pro team of any kind in the city, which was small, probably 45,000 at the time. New Brunswick was a great place to play hockey. The people were really nice. Maritimers reminded me of the farmers and ranchers in Alberta, where I grew up.

But life in the minors wasn't glamorous. We all knew where we wanted to be. My NHL contract was worth $80,000 in the first year, then $85,000 and $90,000 in the following two seasons. In the minors, I'd only make about $25,000. As soon as you'd get called up, your NHL contract would kick in. It was decent money—eighty grand in 1981 would be worth about $210,000 today. Obviously not the exorbitant sums players make today, but not a bad paycheque for a twenty-year-old who, just a few years earlier, had been selling his family's furniture just to get by. Even as a minor leaguer, my $25,000 deal was the equivalent of $65,000 today. It was more money than I'd ever seen. But I was pretty frugal. Some guys spent their paycheques on Mercedes-Benzes or BMWs, stuff like that. I drove an old beater pickup truck that I bought for $1,500. It was puke yellow. It was practical—until the transmission fell out.

As much as I liked the fans and team in Fredericton, I couldn't wait to get sent up. When I got the call for my first NHL game, midway through the 1981–82 season, I was nervous as shit. It was in Buffalo. During warmups, Jacques Richard wired a shot at me, and he could shoot it. I turned my head and the puck hit me in the ear.

The trainer took me into the medical room to stitch me up. The coach, Michel Bergeron, came and looked at my bloody ear. "You can't play," he said.

I was so on edge that I had barely slept the night before. I was a mess all day. I wasn't going through all that just to be denied a start. In the NHL, if you get one chance, you'd better take it.

"I'm fucking playing," I said.

It was a 4–4 tie, but it says a lot about the style of hockey they played back then that I was named the game's second star. Hockey in that era was wide open and exciting, even if it was a goalie's worst nightmare. You could make a ton of unbelievable saves and still let in four goals. There were only twenty-one teams, so the talent wasn't diluted. All the talent in the world was there. In Edmonton, the score would be 6–5 or higher, and the Oilers would win because Grant Fuhr had played great. So it wasn't unusual for fans to see eight goals scored in a game.

Or seventeen, if you were playing the Islanders.

I'd played so well against Buffalo that the Nordiques started me the next game, in Long Island. This was the Islander dynasty that had just won its first of four Stanley Cups in a row. They had Mike Bossy, Bryan Trottier and Denis Potvin. They had Clark Gillies, John Tonelli and Ken Morrow. Billy Smith was in goal. Need I go on? You know the team—it was one of the all-time greats. A year before, I had watched these guys win the Cup on TV, and now I was facing them. It was overwhelming. I felt confident after getting a game under my belt, but I knew stopping the Islanders was going to be a huge challenge.

I was right. Things didn't go well on the scoreboard. We got lit up 10–7. I played the whole game. Bossy got a hat trick—he had four break-aways on me. They scored on breakaways and two-on-ones. It wasn't that I played bad in Long Island; I made a lot of great saves. But the only thing that made me feel good about that day was that Billy Smith let in seven, and he was the best goalie in the game at the time.

The Nordiques kept me as benchwarmer for a little while after that shellacking, before eventually sending me back to Fredericton when both their regular goalies were healthy.

Getting called up for those two games made me work even harder. I wouldn't be diagnosed with OCD for another decade—so at the time, I thought my obsession with working out was just what they call "drive." My teammates thought I was crazy. Back then, goalies hardly ever lifted weights. But I didn't go a day without hitting the gym. I worked harder than any of the guys on that team, in the gym and in practice. I was first one on the ice, last one off. I think that's why our coach, Jacques Demers, liked me. I was a workhorse. In that first year, I played fifty-one games. In the AHL, we would play three games in three nights, and the travel was horrendous. Sometimes we'd play Friday and Saturday on the road and take the bus back to Fredericton to play a home game on the Sunday. Somehow, we just got through those games—I really don't know how.

Our team was terrible. We had a hard time getting players that year. We'd bring up guys from the Fredericton Capitals, guys with day jobs, out of an intermediate league. That's how bad we were. Danny Grant, who played in the NHL in the 1960s and '70s, mostly with Minnesota and Detroit, was the president of the team—he's from Fredericton. He even played nineteen games with us.

I was facing fifty shots a night. It was great for me, though. All the action got me a lot of attention. I was named rookie of the year and MVP of the team.

On a personal level, Jacques Demers helped me out a lot. He was a kind guy. He knew we were young and unsure. Just a few months before, we had been living with billets as boys in junior hockey and now we were young men, out there on our own. He encouraged us.

Jodi Bauer broke up with me by mail from Portland. I'd figured that might happen. The letter said something about how we'd grown apart. Shit, we were *coast to coast* apart—it wasn't going to work. But it hurt. I let it hurt.

Demers saw that I had something spinning through my head at the time. He could tell I was struggling. He pulled me aside one day and asked what was wrong. I'd never had a coach do that before. The locker room is no place to explore hurt feelings and broken hearts. I was embarrassed. "I got a 'Dear John,'" I said, trying to shrug it off. He took me aside and we talked it out. I still can't believe how kind he was.

49

I considered him a father figure. His wife at the time was also really nice. They'd have us over for dinner. I'd have gone through a brick wall for that man.

I also liked that he had a good sense of humour. I was always a clown in the dressing room, so that worked out well for me. Before one of our practices, there was a men's recreational-league game going on. I stripped down to my jockstrap, put on some skates, put a paper bag with holes cut out on my head—like the unknown comic on *The Gong Show,* which was big back then—grabbed a stick, went onto the ice and starting stick-handling around them. All the guys were watching. They were just dying. When I got off the ice, one of the Express trainers warned me that Demers was looking for me and he was pissed. But when I saw him, he just started cracking up. He thought it was hilarious—but warned me that it probably was best not to do stuff like that when the brass was down from Quebec. "If you want to make that team, don't let them catch you doing stuff like that!" he said. "You can do that to me, but not to them!"

Fredericton was a lot of fun, especially because I had a bit of money, was on my own for the first time and was part of the biggest show in town. I was twenty, twenty-one years old, a kid, but a lot of the guys were in their late twenties and early thirties. There was a bar we used to go to called the Cosmopolitan. We called it the "Cos." It was a college town. Lots of fun.

My first couple years as a pro, we had some . . . well, *unique* fans. There was one couple that liked to go to the bar after games. Afterwards, they'd always invite a player or two back to the house for a hot tub. The wife was pretty hot. And the husband liked to watch. At first, I didn't believe it. But then, after a week, another guy would come to the rink and say, "Holy shit, I yadda, yadda, yadda . . ." It was crazy. One of the guys went back for a dip. He felt awful about it after.

"I screwed his wife in front of him. He's telling me to give it to her." He was so broken up about it. His guilt was overwhelming.

"You learn from your mistakes. Don't beat yourself up," I said. "You have to move on."

One morning, I walked into our training room at the rink in

Fredericton, and there was big guy with bushy black hair lying belly down on the trainer's table. In front of him was a stationary bike, which he was pedalling with his arms. He'd basically just invented the upper-body training machine. I'd never seen anything like it. I thought, *Who the hell is this guy?* I mean, *I* was always the first person at the rink.

He got off the table just sweating like a pig. He was built like a house. His arms were the size of my legs. He introduced himself. "Hey, how are ya kid? Rick Dudley."

"Hey, how are you?"

"Yeah, I'm all right. My knees were busted, so I had to get cardio in."

Dudley was a journeyman who had made his way through the NHL and WHA for more than a decade with the Buffalo Sabres, Cincinnati Stingers and Winnipeg Jets. After a season with the Jets, he wound up in Fredericton.

Dudley really liked me because I was one of the few guys who actually bothered to work out. He was always on vitamin pills. Dudley was probably the fittest man I'd ever met. He was stronger than Dale Hunter, for sure, and he was so committed. Even I didn't work as hard as Dudley did, and in terms of his career he had nothing left to prove. It was pretty much over for him. He intrigued me.

We'd climb on the bus for road trips and he'd wear this hilarious Marty Robbins cowboy hat—black with a flat rim all the way around. And he hauled his friggin' guitar on the bus. He'd play and sing for us as we bused through the minors.

In the end, Dudley only played seven games with the Express before he called it quits for good. In one game, Dudley got into a fight and was tossed out. On his way off the ice, he stopped in front of the other team's bench and challenged them all to a fight. There were no takers. They knew his reputation. That was the last game he ever played.

I didn't realize it at the time, but Dudley and I had a lot more in common than I thought. And even though we only spent a handful of games together, he would become one of the closest friends in my life—right until I pulled that trigger.

10

Hitched

OUTSIDE OF HOCKEY, BASEBALL WAS MY LIFE. DAD COACHED Garth and later coached me. It was our summer sport, aside from boxing in the backyard. Dad was a hell of a ball player and he made sure I was, too. For a brief period, I was almost considering making a go at it instead of hockey. I played in an intermediate city league each summer. I could pound it and I had a great glove. I was scouted to play baseball in a minor pro league out west the same year I signed with the Nordiques. They were only offering about $50 a week compared to my $80,000 pro hockey salary, so it was an easy choice. But I've always loved baseball and wondered what it would have been like to have gone and played. I was a shortstop and second baseman. I went to a tryout in Edmonton, and they said, "You're pretty good, you know." I moved on to a second tryout in Calgary, and they liked what they saw. They asked me to come to the rookie camp. I asked about the contract and told them I'd just signed with an NHL team. The scout told me to stick with hockey. I'm pretty sure he was right—but then, you always wonder what might have happened in life if you had travelled down a different road.

I seemed to fall in love with every girl that paid attention to me. I met my first wife at a baseball tournament the summer after my first year in Fredericton. She was from Medicine Hat but was living in Calgary, and I was staying there during the off-season at my mother's place. She was a dirty blonde. I was twenty-one at the time. She was about a year younger. We hooked up and started dating. Six months later, she was pregnant. I was going to break up with her before she told me, but when I found out, I figured that marrying her was the only thing to do. It was the honourable thing. But everyone was against it—my family, friends, everyone. They all said the same thing: "You were about to break up, and then she got pregnant—isn't that suspicious? She wasn't on the pill? Well, why not? You guys are having trouble and you're about to be in the NHL." The thought did cross my mind, but I didn't want to go there. I never confronted her about it.

The wedding was held in Medicine Hat, Alberta, where her parents lived. She was five months pregnant at the time. Everyone at the wedding was mad. It was so intense. It turned into a gong show. My brother, Garth, was my best man. Even as we drove to the church, he tried to get me to reconsider.

"Clint, let's just get on a plane and fly to Vegas right now," Garth said.

"Holy shit, you're nuts," I said. "I don't have a choice."

We made it to the church and I got married. Afterwards, there were pictures and all that other wedding stuff. But my brother took the groomsmen and went bar-hopping. They lost track of time, apparently.

I used the phone at the reception hall to call all the bars in town.

"Is there a group of guys there in tuxedos and cowboy hats?"

"They just left."

So I phoned another one. "They just left."

And another. "They just left."

I hung up the phone, and in walked my brother and the rest of the groomsmen. They'd had a few. Garth knew I was mad but tried to talk his way out of it.

"Hey, Clint! How's it going?"

"Where the hell have you guys been?" Everyone at the reception was waiting for them. We still had the first dance and all that other shit to do.

"Ah, fucking relax," Garth said.

"Fuck you," I said.

"Fuck *you*."

"Fuck *you!*" We got right up in each other's face. My mom saw us shoving and came over.

"You two sons of bitches. There's no way you're going to have a fight in here." She got between us and tried to push us apart. I swung over Mom's head—just, *boom*—and smoked Garth in the face. The fight was on. We went fist to fist.

I ended up on the floor with blood all over my tuxedo. Garth broke my nose, but I put a good gash in his forehead. Ten minutes later, I walked over to Garth with a tall glass of whiskey.

"What the hell, you pouting?"

"No."

I had two pieces of Kleenex up my nose. He had a bloody bar napkin stuck to his head.

"Mind if I sit down?"

"No, shit, sit down."

I sat down. "Good fight, eh? There was a time you'd whoop my ass, Garth. But I got you pretty good."

He took a sip of whiskey and handed it to me.

"Yeah. Shit, you caught me here and here."

"I think you broke my nose."

"It's been broken, what, eight times? Shit, don't worry about it. You're ugly anyway."

I took a sip. "You're ugly too," I said.

My new bride and her family were devastated because of the fight. Her family was over at their table, all upset. I think her mom was crying. "The wedding is ruined!"

Garth got up and sauntered over to my wife and in-laws. "Why the long faces?" he said. "We've all made up! Let's let 'er go and enjoy the party!"

Her dad was angry and incredulous. "What?! You guys are covered in blood!"

"Yeah, and now we're over there drinking and having a great time." As shocking as that was for her family, for Garth and me it was just another fight. No big deal.

Later that year, I had surgery on my nose because it had been broken so many times. After the surgery, I was in a baseball tournament in British Columbia, and our team went into a bar for maybe five minutes before I got hooked by a right. I was so pissed off. I'd just had it fixed and it looked kind of pretty. The bouncers jumped in right away. That's why I don't like fighting in bars—they always get broken up. If you're a real man, I'll meet you outside. I got thrown out one door and the fucker who sucker-punched me went out another door. I went after him and he ran like a jackrabbit.

So I had to go back to the hospital for a second round of reconstructive surgery. It was supposed to last forty-five minutes, but it took three hours. They cut my skin and pulled it back onto my forehead. The doctor told me the bone had splintered. He said if I broke it one more time, I'd likely do some permanent damage. I already had trouble breathing because of it. I didn't bother getting it fixed up after that. There was no point. I'd just keep breaking it.

You could probably guess that I didn't have a very pleasant marriage with my first wife. But the nuptials did bring something wonderful to my life. A few months later, I was in the shower at the Colisée after a Nordiques practice. The trainer told me my wife had called the arena. She was in labour. "You better get down to the hospital."

I rushed out of there still wet, fumbled my keys into the ignition of my old beater truck and sped over to the hospital. My heart was pounding. I was there when she was born. Everything was great. She was beautiful. Everything was beautiful. My first kid, you know. It was so emotional. We called her Kelli Jean Louise Malarchuk. I have to admit that the name came from Kelly Hrudey. I always liked that name, so we just switched it up a bit. We agreed to give her our mothers' names as well.

It was an overwhelming time. I was only twenty-two and so close to fully realizing my dream. And now I had a gorgeous baby girl. The problem was that Wife Number One and I never really saw eye to eye. I wasn't exactly in the NHL yet. I played only fifteen games with the Nordiques in my second year as a pro. I was going up and down between the NHL and the minors, and I worried about her spending. We had a baby to take care of.

If I'm honest, my relationship with my first wife failed for reasons beyond money. I was able to understand this a lot more later on. At the time, I was blind to it. Things were going good, I was doing well, and I'd start feeling anxious and wouldn't know why. I was doing great in hockey, so I wasn't sure why I felt so uneasy. Subconsciously, I'd search for something to worry about. The second most important thing to me was my relationship. So I directed all of my anxiety towards my wife. Struggling with relationships would become a painful and destructive pattern in my life.

11

A Fighting Chance

EVEN BACK IN THE MINORS, I HAD A PROCLIVITY FOR BRAWLING. I had a temper. In practice, I'd always get angry when guys would come in and wire the puck at my head. Once, in practice, one of our forwards, Grant Martin, tried to pick a corner and hit me high in the shoulder. I threw my stick like a tomahawk and hit him in the head. Then I skated over and jumped on him. Grant was actually a really nice guy; I just lost my shit. The next day, Jacques Demers made us roommates on the road.

I did the same thing during a skate at a conditioning camp back home in Edmonton one summer. There were all kinds of different players from junior, college and various stages of pro hockey. I'd played in the NHL and deserved a little respect—you know, shoot low to start. When you warm up a goalie you shoot from far out, you don't just wire a shot from in close—it can cause an injury. The second shooter I faced was this call-up. I think he played junior or something. He skated up past the hash marks in the slot and wound up. The puck came right at my head. I managed to jump and take it in the shoulder, but I fell over and my whole arm went numb. The kid just skated into the corner like it was no big deal.

I grabbed my stick by the knob and chucked it at him. It spun like a helicopter blade and hit him square in the nose. Smashed it—completely broken. He was bleeding all over the place. I skated up to him and pushed my pad against his head. "You little shit," I said. "I hope you bleed to death." All the pros were laughing at him. I didn't feel bad. It was probably bad karma.

The Nordiques called me up during the 1984 playoffs after our season in Fredericton was done. We made it to the second round and faced our provincial rivals, the Montreal Canadiens, at the Forum. The last game of that series became known as the Good Friday Massacre because of a series of line brawls that happened just as the Easter weekend kicked off. It was my first NHL fight. I was dressed for that game, so when there was a bench-clearing brawl near the end of the second period, I was right in the mix. When the teams got back on the ice for the third period, we started brawling again before the puck even dropped. It was bloody. Peter Stastny's nose was busted by Montreal's Mario Tremblay. Our Louis Sleigher drilled Jean Hamel when the linesman was trying to break them up. Louie went in there and clocked him over the linesman's head—knocked him out cold. He lay there for quite a while, and then they just dragged him off the ice. I guess they didn't have stretchers back then. The punch broke Hamel's orbital bone, and the damage to his vision led to the end of his career. I tangled with Habs goalie Richard Sevigny and then pretty much grabbed anyone I could find. When the brawl started, we were up 1–0, but half our team was booted out of the game. We all sat in the locker room and watched as the other half tried to hang on for the win. The Habs scored five goals in the third period and knocked us out of the playoffs.

Thanks to my dad's boxing lessons, fighting was my special talent. Down in the American League, I fought Tiger Williams. We were playing the Adirondack Red Wings during the 1984–85 season, and Tiger was down from their parent club in Detroit. He was in my crease, so I gave him a whack with my stick. He turned around and swore at me, so I asked him if he wanted to go. The play went down to the other end, and when the whistle blew, he came skating back to me. "What did you say to me?" he said.

"I said, 'Do you want to go?'"

"All right."

"Give me a second," I said. I took off my mask and gloves and placed them on top of the net. "Let's go."

We squared off. He was strong, but I didn't think he was a particularly good fighter. It was a decent hockey fight, like any other. I didn't think anything of it at the time, but everyone thought it was the funniest thing. I got to know Tiger off the ice over the years. He was such a character.

In 1983–84, I'd played in twenty-three games with the Nordiques, slightly more than the year before, but I still hadn't managed to fully break into the league. And in '84–85, I didn't get called up at all. The Nordiques had drafted Mario Gosselin, a member of the 1984 Canadian Olympic team in Sarajevo. He was also from Thetford Mines, Quebec. The team gave him every opportunity to become the star. Quebec is a hockey Mecca, and they love their homegrown stars. That's understandable.

I played fifty-six games in Fredericton that year. It was hard to have success early and then have to toil in the minors. I had no idea when I'd get another shot and was feeling like the Nordiques had essentially pushed me out of their plans.

But in '85–86, I played forty-six games for Quebec. I had finally made it as an NHL regular. Back then, goalies didn't play seventy games a year the way they do now, so forty-six was a very respectable number.

My mom taped almost all my games that season (and never really stopped).

It was a great year. Everything went right. At the end of November, I made twenty-seven saves to pick up my first career shutout, against the Boston Bruins at the Garden. It was the first time the Bruins had lost that season. Peter Stastny had a hat trick in our 3–0 win, but he gave me the game puck. It was very kind of him. This shutout was a huge moment for me, because I'd lost my previous three starts. I had spent the previous four years playing sparingly, up and down between the minors and Nordiques. I was only twenty-four, but it felt like my career was slipping by. "The puck's in my pocket now, but it's going on the wall at home," I told reporters after the game.

Three days later, we played the Bruins back in Quebec City, and my mom flew in for the game. I played the best hockey of my life, stopping thirty-three shots for my second straight shutout. Two of my best saves were on Ray Bourque. At the end of the second period, I got my pad across when he had an open net from thirty feet out. In the third, I made the same save on the same play, but I had to do the splits to get across and stop it.

"In the third period, we tried to screen Malarchuk more, but even that didn't work," Bourque said after the game.

When I was named first star of the game, I skated out on the ice for the fans and saw my mother cheering along with everyone else. "It was an indescribable feeling. She came in from Calgary to see me play," I told the beat reporters in the locker room afterwards. "It's the first time she's seen me get a shutout. The last time I had two shutouts in a row like this was in pee wee hockey."

The following season, 1986–87, I established myself as a bona fide starter. I played in fifty-four games, which tied me for fifth in the league. Those two seasons set me up as Quebec's number one guy, while Gosselin was still being groomed. That was when I started to become comfortable as a pro. I was more confident on the ice, while away from the rink, I was more outgoing and fun.

I had a lot of great teammates in Quebec. Michel Goulet and Peter Stastny were both among the best in the game at the time. There were some great personalities on the team, too. Paul Gillis was about my age, and we shared the same attitude about the game. He was incredibly hard-working and a very fun-loving guy, but really low-key. He was one of those guys you could rely on; he'd do anything for anyone. Gord Donnelly was the same way. He could get me wound up, and vice versa, and we'd both laugh about it.

And then, of course, Dale Hunter—he was just a hard-nosed, what-you-see-is-what-you-get kind of guy. He didn't pull any punches. No politics. He'd tell you what he thought. And at times, he'd hurt my feelings. He would say things like "These fucking goalies! How could you not have stopped that one!" But on the other hand, he would say,

"Mallard! Great game!" He was just a good, straightforward guy.

Quebec City was a tough place for an anglophone to play in. I struggled with the language barrier, and there was a lot of pressure on the goalies. But it was a great playing experience. The city had a real hockey atmosphere.

I had a little condo close to the arena. I never had a big, fancy house in Quebec, and I didn't drive a nice car. Even after I'd made it out of the minors, it just wasn't my style. It felt good to be in the city, because hockey was religion and you'd get recognized everywhere. Still, they were respectful of your space. No one ever harassed you.

I think they'll get another NHL team one day, for sure. The Colisée was a real hockey rink, and the fans packed it. Some of the older rinks like that, like Boston Garden, were just great for hockey. The crowds were the perfect size. The atmosphere was loud and intense. It was a first-class facility.

I'd always try to get to bed early the night before a game and then head to the rink two hours before morning practice. I'd warm up, work out, stretch, go over my gear. I was meticulous about my equipment. And I was very strict with my warmup routine. I was always a big stretcher.

The travel was nuts. We'd fly commercial, or we'd charter puddle-jumpers to games that were nearby. I was always exhausted after one of those shitty flights. I look back now and think we were really more like glorified AHL players back then—not in terms of talent, but the lifestyle. On the planes, if you had the window seat, you were scrunched up against the side, with no room to move. Our sticks were in the aisle. The hockey bags and luggage didn't all fit in the cargo space down below, so the extra gear was just crammed in with the players. Now every player and coach gets his own La-Z-Boy–style reclining seat!

We pulled a lot of pranks up in the sky. We had a scout travelling with us once. The poor bastard fell asleep. We put a turban of shaving cream—a massive dome of it—on his head. Then we sprinkled M&Ms and other candies on it. Finally, someone lit a cigarette—because you could smoke on planes back then—and stuck in on top, burning like a candle on a birthday cake. If you fell asleep on the plane, you were a marked man. You'd have your tie cut in half or wake up with shaving cream all over your lap. Dale Hunter and I were the ringleaders. We were pretty cruel. But I will say, Dale was always the catalyst for pranks: putting Vaseline in your comb, baby powder in the hair dryer. He'd clean his ears with Q-Tips and put them back in the box. That one was particularly gross.

The league was a lot different then than it is now. You'd never see some of the shit that went on openly as part of team policy happening today. For starters, there was a back area in the locker room where players could smoke. We had a fridge stocked with beer. After the games, the guys would crack a few and sit in the hot tub.

After practice, it was straight to the bar. Lunch consisted of beers and sandwiches, and then the guys would stay there all afternoon, just drinking beers. The married guys would go home around four or five, and then the single guys would go out.

One time, Van Halen came to town for a concert and wanted to see our locker room after their sound check. A few of us were hanging out at the rink. The season had just ended, so we were just packing our gear up and saying goodbye. The guys from Van Halen came in and pounded back some beers with us. I'm sure they were doing more than beer—not that I saw that. We all hung out for a while and we had a few. I didn't even know who they were at the time, except that they had that one hit song, "Jump."

We had some remarkable talent on the Nordiques. Michel Goulet was easily the most naturally gifted forward I ever played with. He could shoot a puck while off-balance and put it up in the top corner, even in practice. Goulet was just incredible, the most talented that I played with, bar none. But the teammate I admired most was Dale Hunter. Actually, he's also the player I admire most from my entire era. He showed up to play every night, and he was tough—probably the toughest guy in the league who had actual talent. He had skill but could still intimidate and frustrate his opponents. Dale finished his career with 3,565 penalty minutes, second only to Tiger Williams on the all-time list. That's the equivalent of almost sixty games sitting in the box! Despite that, he still scored 323 goals and 1,020 points. That's my kind of hockey player.

There are guys in the NHL today who have never been in a fight in their life. How do you play hockey without fighting? We would have been murdered. It was a goon show half the time. My defensemen always knew that if a player started something with me, they were not to jump in. I could handle myself. "Treat me like any other player," I told them. "I'm not just a goalie. Let me fucking show them." There was no way I was going to be one of those goalies who needed his defensemen to fight his battles for him. And besides, I used to hack the hell out of players in front of my crease. Most of the fights I was in, I started. And I didn't fight the amateurs. I fought the guys who were tough. Guys like Tiger Williams.

There was one game against the Detroit Red Wings in 1985–86 when I busted my ass to the bench for a delayed penalty. There was a scuffle on the way back to my net. One of their guys was shoving J.F. Sauve, the smallest guy on our team. "Screw you," I said. "He's five-foot-fuck-all." As I jumped in, the Red Wings' coach, Brad Park, hollered down to his goalie, Mark LaForest, "Even it up!" The poor guy. I destroyed him.

I never interacted with Patrick Roy, even though one time, in his rookie year, the Nordiques and the Canadiens got into a bench-clearing brawl. The games were always heated between the two Quebec rivals. This one wasn't as bad as some of the others we'd be in; the players were just kind of standing around, and Roy grabbed my sweater from behind. I turned around and glared at him: "Don't even fucking think about it," I said. Roy had a few fights later on in his career. He went on to win a few Cups and earned a spot in the Hall of Fame, but when it comes to bar brawls, I've got more wins.

Chicago was a tough place to play. The old stadium was just nuts. A cloud of cigar and cigarette smoke just hovered over the ice. You could smell the beer, like in a dive bar. I remember standing on the red line before my first game at the Madhouse on Madison in December 1982. The noise was unbelievable. And they were just announcing the starting lineups—the game hadn't even started yet. You could just feel your heart vibrating in the noise. I looked over at Randy Moller. We were both rookies.

"This is unbelievable!" I yelled.

"What?" he shouted.

As loud as I could yell—"This is unbelievable!"

He couldn't hear me. That's how loud it was.

Even though I had made it as an NHL starter, I was still obsessed with getting better. I'd spend eight hours a day working on my fitness. I treated it like a job. I got up in the morning and went to the gym at six. There were mornings when guys would ask if I'd just come straight from the bar. Not quite—I'd had a three-hour power nap. They'd spot me under the bench press and my breath would be so heavy with alcohol that if someone lit a match, we'd go up in flames.

I'd run twelve miles one day, up to twenty the next, then back down to twelve—alternating between twenty and twelve. After running and lifting weights all morning, I'd go over to a local boxing gym three times a week. I did this everywhere I played, from junior on up.

As a result, I think my superior conditioning made up for the fact that other goalies had more skill. I basically willed myself into becoming an NHL goalie. I'm convinced the best save I ever made happened because I was so athletic. There was a shot from the middle slot to my right in the faceoff circle. I have no idea who shot it, because the save was too crazy to really care. Somehow, my left hand got twisted around my back, near my hip on my right side, and I made a glove save. It went right into the glove. The only people who saw it, I think, were sitting right behind the net. It had nothing to do with skill. It wasn't intentional—I just flailed around. Total luck, but a goddamn glorious save. It's one of those memories that sticks with a guy long after his career is over.

In 1987, instead of the usual NHL All-Star Game, the Quebec Nordiques hosted Rendez-Vous 87, a two-game series between a team of NHL All-Stars and the Soviet national team. In fan voting, I was their first choice as goaltender. It was probably one of the biggest highlights of my career. Some accused Quebec fans of stuffing the ballot box, but I didn't give a shit. It was such a thrill to be included. Michel Goulet and Normand Rochefort also made the team, and Nordiques coach Michel Bergeron was named as an assistant coach. The other two goalies were Ron Hextall, who was just a rookie, and Grant Fuhr. The rest of the team included Mario Lemieux, Wayne Gretzky, Dale Hawerchuk, Doug Wilson, Mark Howe, Mark Messier, Glenn Anderson and a slew of superstars from the NHL. Pretty much the best in the world against Russia. It was so cool. I was like a kid watching legends play.

I still remember Mario—he was really young then, in only his third year in the league. He was lying on the trainer's table, smoking a cigarette—just relaxing, having a dart. It was pretty eye-opening to see him smoke like that. I'm sure it was a short-lived thing, as good as he was. Maybe it was a show of bravado, I don't know. But I just remember thinking, *Hey, he's human!* Mario was a really nice guy. There were no TV cameras on him, no special attention. He didn't want it. I'd walk in there and he'd be playing on the ground with someone's kid. You know, just a really down-to-earth superstar. That's pretty special.

Lemieux was the toughest guy to play against. He gave me nightmares. I don't think there's a player now who, as a goalie, you think *Holy shit* the way we did with a Gretzky or a Lemieux. Today, probably Sidney Crosby or Evgeni Malkin can strike the same kind of fear. And maybe Steven Stamkos and Alex Ovechkin. But even they don't really compare to Gretzky or Lemieux. Those guys were the elite of the all-time elite.

Lemieux always went top shelf or faked and went around the net to stuff it in the other side. So as a goalie, you'd want to be way out of the crease when he came in so he couldn't go upstairs. But if he didn't see a place to shoot, he'd go around, stuff it in and make you look like an asshole. He had long arms and long legs. And he never said shit.

When Gretzky came in with the puck, you had to worry about Jari Kurri. He had a rocket of a shot. I thought I had good reflexes. Nope. Once, Gretzky dropped a one-timer to Kurri just inside the blue line. As a goalie, you think, *I should have that.* But the puck was in and out of the net before I even moved my glove. He could crush it.

Gretzky was also a really nice guy. I was amazed by how kind these superstars were. He's an icon, but he always treated me nicely. He was a very classy guy. But I hated him when we played. The referees were intimidated by him because he was so good and he was the Oilers' captain. If you're a ref, what are you going to say back to Wayne Gretzky?

We ended up in a battle with the Buffalo Sabres for the final playoff spot in the Adams Division in 1987. We beat Billy Smith and the Islanders 4–1 in early April to clinch the playoff berth. I stopped twenty-eight shots for the win and had a shutout until 7:43 of the third period.

The win secured fourth place for us and put us in the post-season for the seventh straight year. But with just seventy-two points, it was our first sub-.500 season since 1980–81. I had eighteen wins in the fifty-four games I played, compared with twenty-six wins in '85–86. All things considered, I was damn proud of the season I had. In just two years, I'd established myself as a legitimate NHL starter and been the top vote-getter among goalies for the NHL All-Stars. But I was disappointed in the playoffs because the Nordiques went with their main man, Mario Gosselin.

We surprised everybody that spring by beating the first-place Hartford Whalers in the opening round, four games to two. In the division final, we met our old friends, the Montreal Canadiens, who were also defending Stanley Cup champions. It was a battle. We took the first two games at the Forum but lost the next two back home at Le Colisée. We split the next two, setting up a seventh and deciding game, but the Habs beat us 5–3 to end our season. I saw only 140 minutes of action in the thirteen playoff games we played.

My time as a Nordique was pretty much done.

12

Traded

I ALWAYS WENT TO CALGARY IN THE OFF-SEASON. MY MOTHER had a house there, and my brother had a ranch outside of town. All my friends were there. And so was the rodeo. I spent most of my time hanging around the Stampede scene when I wasn't training for the next season. I also played baseball. In June of 1987, I had just arrived for one of my ball games when my teammates told me I'd been traded. They'd heard it on the radio. So I phoned my mom, and she told me I needed to call David Poile, the general manager in Washington at the time.

It was a huge deal. Dale Hunter and I were sent to Washington in exchange for the Capitals' first-round pick and forwards Gaetan Duchesne and Alan Haworth. The first-round pick turned out to be a kid named Joe Sakic. (I used to tell everyone I was traded straight up for him.)

It was an exciting time for me. I'd never been traded before, so there was a small sense of sadness. But Quebec had slipped the previous year and were clearly in a rebuilding phase. I saw the deal as a new beginning, with excellent prospects for a better situation—the Caps had finished second in the Patrick Division that year. Much as I had enjoyed Quebec, after six years in the NHL, with the previous two being particularly satisfying, I knew it was the perfect time to build off my success.

When I heard about the trade, I went out with the boys to celebrate. We went to this cowboy bar, the Longhorn. After we had a few beers, our waitress came over and said, "Your wife was here looking for you."

"Oh shit," I said. We were in the midst of a trial separation. Our relationship was falling to pieces, and I'd basically had it with our marriage. But our daughter, Kelli, was still so young and I loved her so much, so it was difficult. You don't want to break up a family, but what kind of family were we?

My buddies hid me in a corner of the bar and sat around the booth with their backs to the room, hoping she might miss us and leave. No such luck. Sure enough, she tracked me down. She sat on my knee and started acting all lovey-dovey with me. I knew she hated Quebec, and now that I had been traded, she probably wanted to get back together and start again. Christ.

Whenever I thought about our relationship, I didn't see how it was going to work. And everyone in my family thought we should break up. But we'd already invested several years into the marriage and we had a kid! So in the end, I couldn't fight it. Wife Number One came to Washington. We fought throughout that first season in D.C.

One night, later in the year, one of her friends came to visit us. They were out bar-hopping and came home the next morning. I had been home with Kelli all night and had to get up for practice. I was pissed. Really pissed. After that, I think I just thought, *Fuck it.*

Despite the shit show at home, I had a great season that first year in Washington. I led the league in shutouts with four, which was a lot in the high-scoring eighties. On the ice, everything was moving in the right direction.

I'm not exactly sure why I had more fun in Washington than I did in Quebec City, but it's probably because I felt secure in my position on the team and in the league. For the first four years of my career, I was fighting just to prove that I could be a number one guy in the NHL. Now I had the confidence that I was that guy, and besides, I had been a valued part of a blockbuster trade. My personal life was messed up all year, with my marriage getting closer and closer to its end. I also suffered swirling bouts of anxiety that I didn't fully understand at the time. It'd been with me ever since I was a kid, when I was hospitalized for those two months, and it never really went way. I had just learned to live with it, acting like nothing was wrong in public, but knowing it was slowly destroying my personal life.

So I took advantage of every opportunity I had to let loose and forget the battles going on inside of me. One of the best examples will be forever remembered as "the time we took the horses." During one of our road trips out west that year, we took a commercial flight from Minneapolis-St. Paul to Los Angeles, where we had a five-day break before playing the Kings. Management took us to this fancy golf course for a team-building excursion. We all piled into this little puddle-jumper from L.A. to Palm Springs.

On the flight, Dale and I got to talking. It occurred to me that half these guys had never even seen a horse before, let alone ridden one. So we told them all we wanted to show them how. Almost everyone thought it'd be cool. But when we arrived in Palm Springs, we found out a bunch of our luggage had been left back in L.A., so we were stuck in suits and ties. A lot of the guys changed their minds. They wanted to wait for their bags and then go golfing. But Dale and I were still in. "Ah shit, you guys. Bunch of pussies." And off we went in our suits to track down some horses to rent.

We walked a little ways down the road outside of our hotel and found this small western-themed place, like a little saloon. They had horses for rent. Check! They also sold beer, so we asked if we could take some along. Check! They loaded up our saddlebags. So Dale and I went riding out along the trails, still wearing our dress clothes. We saw snakes and roadrunners and all sorts of shit. It was pretty cool. We started going up a canyon. It wasn't chilly, but we said, "Ah, we're cowboys—we need a fire and some beer." So when we got up to the top, we made a fire, even though it was about a hundred degrees out—we had had a few beers by that point. Later, we rode a little farther up the canyon and found ourselves staring out over the hotel we were staying at. The team was out on the course, playing golf. "Those pussies!"

We charged down the canyon towards the course, hooting and hollering. We had our suits rolled up like bedrolls behind our saddles, and our ties were wrapped around our heads. We rode up and down the fairways. The guys were all cheering. We rode onto the greens and started pulling the pins out. Neither of us are golfers, so we had no idea what we were doing. Then we started jousting, riding at each other with the flags. We rode around, taking out all the flags we could find.

The course marshal showed up and started chasing us in his little golf cart. "The marshal's after us!" But he couldn't catch up. We were turning back as we galloped away, shooting at him with our hands. *Pew-pew . . . pew . . . pew . . .* The guys on the golf course had had way more beer than us, but we looked like we were completely bombed because we were riding around on horses.

When we had had enough, we just dropped the flags and went back to the stables. The cops were waiting for us. We were in big trouble, but our general manager, Dave Poile, paid for all the damage, so we didn't get charged.

Dale was a hillbilly redneck like me—though I prefer the term "cowboy"—and naturally, we roomed together. We'd always get to the airport and he'd say, "Shit, I have to give you my carry-on"—and he'd hand me his toothbrush. We would be on a ten-day road trip, and that shithead would just bring a toothbrush—and give it to *me* to carry in *my* bag. It was all he needed. I swear he just had the one suit and two ties. If it was a really long trip, sometimes he'd have a pair of gonchies wrapped around his toothbrush. We get to the hotel and I'd unpack my clothes and give him his toothbrush and shorts. "Thanks, chum," he'd say. Everything was "Thanks, chum."

Even after our joyride with the horses, Dale and I continued our antics. It was a team-spirit thing. We did the Saran Wrap the toilet seats gag—not a very elaborate prank, but it always earned a laugh. At restaurants, Dale was notorious for standing next to you at the urinal and then just pissing on your foot. You wouldn't realize it until there was a pool of piss on your boot. But he wouldn't just do it to a teammate. He'd do it to any guy. "Oh my, I'm sorry," he'd say. Everybody had jokes, but not like Dale. One time, we stole the doors off Garry Galley's Jeep in the middle of winter. We put it all in the trunk of Dale's car. It was damn cold out. We just wanted him to freeze his ass off as he drove home.

Right before the playoffs, the team was on another road trip. When I came home, my first wife was gone. She had taken Kelli with her. My neighbour had driven her to the airport. He was a really nice guy; he was waiting for me when I got home so he could give me the news in person. "I know what it's like to be a bachelor," he said. He gave me a bag with a bunch of items in it—stuff like toilet paper.

I was pissed off and screwed up. My head was all over the place. I didn't tell many people what had happened, but the team seemed to know. Throughout the playoffs, I roomed with Dave Christian, who had recently been through a divorce. He was great, a huge support.

Even with everything going on at home, I played well down the stretch. After the All-Star Game, I went on a run where I won six of seven games and allowed only ten goals. Our coach, Bryan Murray, was singing my praises. "Clint has to be discouraging teams with all those point-blank saves," he told the press. "There just are no easy goals when he's out there." It was the best season of my career. I finished with twenty-four wins in fifty-four games, and my 3.16 goals-against average was sixth in the league. My counterpart, Pete Peeters, led the league with a 2.79 average.

We finished second in the Patrick Division, behind the New York Islanders. Our first-round opponents were the Philadelphia Flyers, coached by Mike Keenan. Ron Hextall was in goal. We went down 3–1 in the series before clawing our way back to force a game seven. Murray went with Pete Peeters as the main guy in the series. I wasn't in goal for any of our wins and played only once when Peeters was pulled. Dale Hunter scored the overtime winner on a breakaway on Hextall in the final game.

We faced the New Jersey Devils, who had just come off an upset win over the first-place Islanders, in the second round. The Devils were led by rookie goalie Sean Burke, who joined them late in the season after playing for Canada at the Calgary Olympics. He was red-hot down the stretch, single-handedly getting the Devils into the playoffs and then pushing them past the Islanders. Burke was pretty much the story of the playoffs to that point.

Peeters played the first two games of the series for us. We won the first and lost the second. There was concern that he was getting pushed back into his crease too much by the Philly forwards—something that would never happen to me. I got the start in game three. At that point I didn't have a win to my name in seven career playoff games. I needed this chance to prove I could make it happen in spring, when it mattered most.

It didn't work out the way I'd hoped. I allowed two goals in the first period, followed by two quick goals in just over a minute in the second period. In total, I let in seven goals on twenty-one shots before Murray put my ass on the bench. We lost 10–4—the most lopsided playoff defeat in Capitals history. It was brutal. I felt terrible. I'd let the team down and embarrassed myself right when I needed to play the best hockey of my life.

Peeters was back in goal to start game four. But halfway through the second period, he got hit in the mask with a John MacLean wrist shot. He fell backwards into the net and hit his head on the ice. He stayed down for several minutes and they carried him off on a stretcher.

I sat on the bench, getting ready to go. But my confidence was completely shot after getting pulled in the last game. I felt like shit. We were up 2–1, and I could just imagine the headlines if I blew this lead and let the Devils run away with the series.

Thankfully, the nerves didn't ruin me. I stopped the first shot, and then the second and the third, and I felt my confidence rising. In the end, I turned aside all thirteen shots I faced and we won the game 3–1. "I didn't stop too many shots in the last game," I told reporters. "It was a tough couple of days. I was pretty depressed." There was no point in trying to hide the fact that I was nervous about getting back between the pipes after the shellacking I had taken.

"I guess if at any time in my career the pressure was on, that was it," I said. "Any time you lose like that, your confidence is down . . . It was a pressure situation. I'm just glad we won. It was a tough couple of days. It was the toughest moment of my entire career."

It took half a game to go from goat to hero. But my winless streak continued. The *W* went to Peeters. "I don't care who gets the victory," I lied. "I'll contribute anyway I can." It was great to save the game. But damn, I wanted that win.

I got the start in game five, back at home in front of a sellout crowd of more than 18,000 fans. Unfortunately, my redemption tale was over. We lost 3–1. On the third goal, I gave the puck away in the corner to Pat Verbeek, who passed it out front to a wide-open Kirk Muller, who had scored on a breakaway earlier in the game.

Peeters came back and won the next game 7–2. They gave him the start in game seven back at home, and we lost 3–2. Season over.

I was devastated after we lost that series. And my seven-goal debacle haunted me for a lot longer than I let people know.

I went back to Calgary that summer and spent my time working out, hitting the rodeo and having a good time. I considered each to be a full-time gig. Back then, I saved most of my drinking for the summer. That being said, if I was out late, I was always up at six and in the gym. I could still be hung over from a night on the town in Calgary and be on the bench, pumping reps, before sunrise.

My best friend back in Calgary was a one-time rodeo star named Coleman Robinson. He was one of the top riders on the Canadian professional circuit when we met in the eighties. I just rode ponies compared to him. He was the real deal. Everyone in Calgary knew who Coleman Robinson was. He was as well known as I was as an NHL hockey player—rodeo is that big out west. When he wasn't riding, he worked in the movie business for years, arranging for big Hollywood productions to come to Alberta and shoot on ranches or up in the mountains. We'd met back when I played for the Nordiques, and he became one of my closest friends.

I was newly single in the summer of 1988. I'd recently divorced Wife Number One and was eager to make up for lost time. Coleman and I hung out on the Calgary rodeo scene, which always had lots of women around. The rodeo adventures were particularly good. Compared to the rodeo, hockey was tame—crazy tame. Every weekend, I'd be out at the rodeos across Alberta with him, getting in trouble and having a blast. Coleman and I have had more fun than two people should ever be allowed to. He was actually a lot like Dale Hunter, but much more social.

We used to drive around looking for fun in my old beater of a truck. It had all this cow shit in the back from some work I'd done up at my brother's ranch near the mountains. I hadn't bothered to get rid of it. It had been there so long, weeds were growing up out of it. Here we were, an NHL hockey player and a rodeo star, and we were driving around in a beat-up piece of junk. Coleman and I didn't care.

One night, we were driving through downtown Calgary on our way to a Hank Williams Jr. concert. We were sitting at a light when my muffler fell off. Coleman got out, picked it up, threw it into the truck bed and away we went.

All things considered, we had a lot of success with that truck.

Often, the rodeos we went to were out of town. There was a big group of people on the Calgary rodeo scene, and I fit in with them like one of the boys, even though I was playing in the NHL. We would go out in a big group of guys and maybe eight of us would share a hotel room to cut costs. We'd flip coins for mattresses and cram in. But you never wanted to sleep next to a married guy, because they'd always throw a leg over you.

This one time, we stayed at a Marriott. We had a king-size bed and we raided the minibar. Coleman and I woke up nose to nose. We were pretty much cuddling. I opened my eyes at the same time he did—probably because he farted or something.

Seriously, these rodeo guys were characters. They made hockey players look like Boy Scouts. During one of our rodeo excursions in Innisfail, one of our buddies decided he needed some privacy with a buckle bunny in a porta-potty. They were in there for quite a while when we got a brilliant idea. I maintain that I was not part of the crew who snuck up behind the travelling toilet, but I watched the whole thing. It tipped over so fast. *Thwack!* Door first. The guys rolled it over and the door flew open. Our buddy and his girl were both covered in shit. She was furious. He thought it was hilarious. "Best orgasm of my life," he said.

My contract with the Washington Capitals stipulated that, for insurance reasons, I wasn't supposed to take part in any dangerous activities off the ice. It wasn't a rule I intended to respect. I was never a real rodeo rider, like Coleman. But I held my own on old nags. I picked up my first win in Crystal Creek. I did a really good job of keeping my rodeo riding from the Capitals. It was easier back then, before every move you made was posted on Twitter. But I still managed to get busted pretty good once.

I was part of this exhibition ride at the Calgary Stampede that summer. It was a special kids' event where cowboys came and gave demonstrations of their skills. A bunch of elementary school classes had come to see their first rodeo, but all the cowboys thought it had been rained out. I was working the chutes that day. My friend Winston Bruce, the big boss of the Calgary Stampede, was in a bind. He was a buddy of mine, so I told him I'd do it.

"Are you kidding me?" he asked. "You're an NHL player. You can't do it."

"No problem," I said. "I'm in."

The ring was all slop. I'd worn a slicker, the kind of yellow coat the cowboys wear, because it was pouring rain, but I was covered in mud. I rode about eight different horses for the kids, showing them mane and tail, bareback and a lot of fun stuff. I didn't think anything of it.

The next day, I was back at the rodeo when I was paged over the public-address system. My mother was looking for me. I went to the Stampede office and called home right away.

"You better call David Poile," she said. "He just called looking for you. And he sounds mad." I thought I'd been traded or something, but when I called, he just tore into me. "What the hell are you doing?" he asked.

I played dumb. "What are you talking about?" I didn't realize that a photographer had been at the event. A picture of me being thrown off one of the horses went over the Associated Press wires and appeared on the front page of the *Washington Post*. The headline read: WASHINGTON CAPITALS GOALIE, CLINT MALARCHUK—AIRBORNE. I'd been riding bareback in the photo and had just been tossed way up in the air.

"You're flying off a horse that's about ready to kick your head off!" he shouted. "What the hell are you doing?"

Think fast, Clint. Think! "Oh, that's my brother," I said. "They said it was me, but it wasn't." My brother doesn't even ride. He's afraid of horses.

Poile didn't buy it. He was pissed. The contract said I wasn't supposed to do stupid stuff, and by his definition, this classified as pretty goddamn stupid. I could see where he was coming from, but I tried to bargain.

"Look," I said, "I'll sign a waiver." No deal. No rodeo.

13

Capital Crimes

IN THE FALL OF 1988, THE CAPITALS WENT TO TRAINING CAMP IN Lake Placid. For a team excursion, they took us all out on a trail ride one day. As I've said, I'm quite handy with horses, but I told our guide that I was actually the Capitals' stick boy and that this was my first time riding a horse. A bunch of my new teammates were in on the gag with me. I had one of them introduce me to our trail guide. "This is Joey. He used to be pretty good with horses, but he got kicked in the head when he was a kid. He's not right."

I hammed it up like I had a speech impediment. The guide had us riding single file down the trail, looking at the scenery and enjoying nature. Every couple of minutes, I'd go charging off the trail with my horse.

The instructor tried to catch me. "Come on, Joey, come on back here!" Then I'd come crashing back through the trees. This guide was a dude, meaning he wanted to be a cowboy, but he wasn't a cowboy. He looked the part and tried to act the part. But he wasn't a cowboy. He had a rope on his saddle but had no idea how to use it.

"Hey boss," I yelled in my Joey voice. "Can I try your rope? I want to throw your rope!"

He pulled out the rope and tried to show me how to use it. He threw it at a big rock, but the rope coiled backwards and he was throwing it all over the place. He couldn't hit it.

"Okay, okay!" I shouted. "My turn. Give me a try! I want to try!" I took the rope. "Oh, I think you've got this all coiled wrong." I fixed it up, handled it like a pro, whirling it a couple times around my head, and *thwump*—I bagged the rock right away. All the guys stood behind the guide, just dying. No one let the poor guy in on the gag. As I walked away, I just said, "See ya later, bud!" in my Clint voice and gave him a wave.

Washington was a great city. I loved the place. I had lived in the States before, when I played junior hockey in Portland—a beautiful area, but D.C. was a whole new world. There was so much stuff going on. The house I lived in was in the same area as where the original Wonder Woman, Lynda Carter, lived. That was pretty cool.

There were always all kinds of things happening in Washington. One time, the team had a chance to meet President Ronald Reagan. The Capitals had played an exhibition game against the U.S. Olympic team, so we were invited along with them to an event at the White House. Please forgive my attention span, but I viewed the White House trip with the same reverence I afforded Mr. Wey's history class back at Jasper Place Composite High. Our team lined up, waiting for the president. We all wore suits and pretended to be civilized. To me, Ronald Reagan was an actor I used to watch in old westerns. I wasn't really concerned with his politics. To be honest, I was just a dumb Canadian then. I was very new to the country and didn't have the respect that I do now—especially for the leader of the most important country on the planet.

I was at the end of the receiving line, next to a Secret Service agent who was too serious for me to not mess with. First, I flicked the cord attached to his earpiece and knocked it out. He put it back in, and I flicked it back out. He was appropriately annoyed. Then I took off my cowboy boot and started using it as a radio, like Maxwell Smart. The presidential guard wasn't impressed, but I thought it was hilarious.

Dale Hunter elbowed me in the ribs. I turned my head with my boot still in my hand, and there was the president waiting to greet me.

Making the best of an awkward situation, I told President Reagan that I loved his movies, particularly the westerns. "Oh, I enjoyed making them," he said. "It was a good time in my life." He must have thought I was an interesting Canuck, because he stayed to chat for a while—about westerns, ranching, being president, the whole works. "It was a very special time in my life," Reagan kept saying about his days on the silver screen.

"I bet it was," I said. "It sure beat the Bonzo the chimp thing."

"Oh, oh, yeah," he said, almost as though he didn't want to talk about it. He told me how great it had been to get paid to ride horses and have fun back then. And then I kind of ruined it by forgetting that we weren't in a locker room. I asked him about Barbara Stanwyck. She was a hot old cougar back then.

"Between you and me," I said, "you ever take a run at that?"

President Reagan went "No but I sure would have liked to." Then he shook my hand and walked away.

I can't be sure, but I think a lot of my teammates bought my act. At least when I was with the Capitals, they did. I went through a lot of personal stuff, but I attributed all my anxiety to my terrible marriage. If I couldn't sleep or stop worrying about something, it was always my wife. I didn't have a name for my condition at the time, so I just figured that my sleepless nights and bouts with anxiety were tied to my toxic relationship. One of our rookies, John Druce, sat next to me on one of our commercial flights to a game, and we got talking about coping with the pressure of playing in the NHL. He was a few years younger than I was, and I think he was nervous about his future in the show. It seemed weird to me, because he was a great player. His confidence just didn't seem to be there.

"How do you do it?" he asked me. "You're a goalie—you have more pressure than any of us." I started listing off all the research I'd done on coping with pressure. Some book I'd read on psychology or something like that.

"Listen, John, I know what you're talking about," I said, trying to give him some support. The whole time I was thinking, *Holy shit, you think I'm calm? If you could just get inside my skull, you'd know that I'm just trying to hold myself together and keep up a composed front.*

I'd like to think that I helped him. Druce went on to have an incredible playoff run in 1990—he scored fourteen goals in fifteen games, one of the best individual playoff performances ever. It was the highlight of his career. I remember seeing how well he did that spring and feeling really happy for him.

When I played in Quebec and Washington, I was good at making it seem like nothing affected me. You have to remember, Bryan Murray was the head coach, and that man hated goalies. I love Bryan, but he was one of those guys who, if you had a great game but you lost 2–1, he'd say, "Well, you didn't make the big save when we needed it." If you played great but lost, he was tough on you.

We played Pittsburgh on New Year's Day in 1988, and a shot took a bad bounce and went in. I was playing really well and we were beating them by a few goals—we ended up winning 5–3. After the game I was happy, enjoying the win, but Murray came in and chewed my ass out. "You let in a goal like that! Christ!"

It really bothered me. I went home that night scared shitless and consumed with anxiety. We were playing the Oilers the next day—Anderson, Messier, Kurri. Thankfully Gretzky was out. But shit, I barely slept that night. I still ended up playing well and we shut them out 2–0. It was one of the best games in my career. For everything Murray exposed in me—my lack of confidence and overpowering insecurities—he also managed to bring out the best. He motivated me.

Of all the pressures a pro hockey player faces, the constant threat of being traded is one of the worst. Players will never admit it, but it affects them. I remember Mike Ridley, one of my teammates with the Capitals, having a very hard time dealing with a rumour that he was to be traded to Buffalo. During practice, he was in the corner, rapidly shooting a puck back and forth against the boards as if it were a Ping-Pong ball. He kept doing it over and over again. It looked like he was having a nervous breakdown, brought on by the pressure. Some of the guys were laughing at him, but I saw so much of myself in him at that moment. I remember feeling relieved that I wasn't the only basket case on the team. The trade rumours turned out to be unfounded. Ridley played another five seasons in Washington and retired in 1997 with more than 800 games in the league and 758 points.

As it turned out, *I* was the one who got shipped to Buffalo. The day before the trade deadline in March 1989, the Capitals sent me to the Sabres along with Grant Ledyard and a sixth-round pick for defenseman Calle Johansson and a second-round pick. I was surprised by the deal. There had been plenty of rumours that the Capitals would trade one of their goalies before the deadline. Along with Peeters and me, they had Don Beaupre, who had been a starter with Minnesota down in the minors. I figured either of those guys would be the one to go—I was confident that the Capitals wanted me to be their number one guy. But I was a twenty-seven-year-old with a solid track record, and Buffalo's general manager Gerry Meehan thought I was the best veteran goalie available. Daren Puppa, the Sabres' young stud in net, had broken his arm during a game a couple of weeks before, so they were looking for a reliable replacement to get them through the final stretch of the season and into the playoffs.

When Bryan Murray called me into his office before practice that morning, he was fighting back tears. He choked up a bit as he said, "Clint, I hate to tell you this, but we've traded you." He looked devastated. I was surprised to see him so emotional. Bryan had always been hard on me, but he wasn't a heartless bastard. He pushed his players to be the best, and I respected that. He was always a good guy at the core of it. Now here I was, traded—and consoling my coach because of it. He kept apologizing for the trade.

"It's okay, Bryan, I understand," I said. He probably doesn't remember any of this now, but seeing how much he cared really meant a lot to me then. He's a tough guy, and the fact that he was emotional told me that I was a valued member of the team.

Of course, when you're traded, you're in shock. When I was sent from Quebec City to Washington, it was during the draft, so the season was over. I didn't have to pack up my gear and say goodbye to everyone. It really felt like a new beginning more than a sort of ending. But this was different. The trade to Buffalo was totally unexpected. I guess there were rumours, but I'd learned to ignore all that stuff. It's a weird feeling because, on the one hand, it seems like one team doesn't want you but on the other, there's a team that wanted you badly enough to trade for you.

I packed my life into my pickup and made the seven-hour drive to Buffalo. A lot goes through a player's mind when he gets traded. I understand that everyone, no matter what their line of work, has had to change jobs or move to a new city. Everybody starts over. But being traded is different. Most players don't have a say where they end up. And it's a strange, abrupt goodbye. A team becomes your family; you spend days and nights together—weeks on the road. You battle the press and critics together and spill blood as one. And then you show up for an early-morning skate, get called into the coach's office—and it's done. Just like that, you're heading north on Route 220, singing along to Hank Williams Jr.'s "Whiskey Bent and Hellbound" as you pass through Altoona, Pennsylvania, halfway to your new life. I was sad to leave Washington. I'd put together two great seasons with the Capitals, had led the league in shutouts and was finally being mentioned among the game's elite. But I was a piece in a new puzzle now. I arrived in Buffalo excited and ready for whatever came next.

I pulled into the Ramada Inn in Buffalo and met up with Grant Ledyard, who'd been traded from the Caps with me. The team's equipment manager, Rip Simonick, picked up our gear and took it to the rink. The next day, we drove over to the Memorial Auditorium and found our jerseys already hanging in our new stalls. We had one practice with our new team before flying off to Manhattan to play the Rangers at Madison Square Garden.

The Sabres had been on a downswing prior to the trade. Since Puppa's injury, they had won just seven of seventeen games and Boston had knocked them out of second place in the Adams Division. The battle now was to hang on to third place against a Hartford team that had gained a bit of ground on them. Buffalo had a good crop of players, led by Pierre Turgeon, Phil Housley and Dave Andreychuk, but this was just before the arrival of the stars of the nineties, like Alexander Mogilny and Pat LaFontaine.

The Rangers, with a roster that included Brian Leetch, Brian Mullen, Tony Granato and John Vanbiesbrouck—not to mention a couple of surefire Hall of Famers, Marcel Dionne and Guy Lafleur, in the late stages of their careers—were battling my old team for first place in their division. And the Garden was always a tough place to play. The fans knew how to welcome the visiting team: they'd throw batteries at the opposing goalie. Hostile crowds never really bothered me, though. I was always extremely focused during games. As soon as the puck dropped, I was transfixed. I didn't hear the crowd—it was just a hum in the background. I was obsessed with one thing: making sure the puck didn't leave my sight. In front of me, a blur of bodies swirled around, hiding the puck as it moved. Half were with me, half against, but they were all obstacles. Anytime I couldn't find the puck, my breathing would stop until it came back into view. Everything was riding on that black disc. If it got past me, I was ruined. Single-minded obsession is the most critical skill a goalie must have.

That night, in my first game as a Sabre, I shut the Rangers out. We won 2–0—the perfect way to kick things off. I started the next four games, picking up two more wins, a loss and a tie. I was hot. The city loved me; I was the saviour. That stretch was the best two weeks of my life. I'd never felt higher than I did at that point. I felt as though I was on the verge of something huge.

14

Jugular

THE FIRST TIME I SHOULD HAVE DIED WAS A WEDNESDAY. MARCH 22, 1989.
As I prepared for our game against the St. Louis Blues that night, I sat by myself in the locker room at the Memorial Auditorium, staring down at the floor, visualizing myself in net. It was a routine I did before every game. The meditation forced me to focus on one thing: the puck. It quelled the chaos and turned it into a positive obsession. I'd run through stop after stop in my mind—a pad save, a glove save, a breakaway.

After being lost in an imaginary future, I got off the bench and went out into the hallway, beneath the seats slowly filling with fans. I turned to face a cement-block wall a few feet away, squared my shoulders and crouched. *Thud.* I threw a rubber ball against the wall with my right hand and caught it with my left. *Thud . . . thud.* Then I threw it with my left and caught it with my right. *Thud . . . thud . . . thud.* Each time, the ball bounced off the wall faster than it originally hit it. I threw the ball harder and harder against the wall—catch and throw, catch and throw.

It was a routine I had picked up from Vladislav Tretiak when I went to his camp in Montreal. It was essential to getting into the right frame of mind to play. Sometimes, I would throw two balls against the wall, tossing one and catching the other at the same time. I forced myself to learn how to do that. On off-days, I'd pick a number and I wouldn't stop the drill until I hit that number without dropping a ball.

Whenever I did these pre-game drills, people would stop to watch me, but I blocked them out of my head. I'm sure the speed was remarkable to them. But in my mind, it was just one fluid blur. *Thud . . . thud . . . thud . . .* The anxiety became manageable. The repetition slowed everything down and let me focus on one simple thing.

After the drill, I was still tense, but it wasn't debilitating. I finished getting dressed with the team and went out for warmups under the lights of the Aud. The tension stayed with me through the shooting drills, but it was all directed towards the game now. Each shot was part of a countdown. My heart pounded throughout the national anthem. My mind and body were consumed by the beat. *Thud . . . thud . . . thud . . . thud . . . thud . . . thud . . .* And then the players lined up, the puck was dropped, and it all came to a crescendo. Then silence: *20:00 . . . 19:59 . . . 19:58 . . .*

The clock crept past the five-minute mark. It was still the first period and I hadn't faced many shots yet. We were up 1–0. The puck was on the boards in the corner and I was on my post. The Blues' Steve Tuttle, a twenty-three-year-old rookie, charged to the net, looking for a pass. One of our defensemen, Uwe Krupp, was right behind him. *4:45 . . .* The pass came just above the crease—a backdoor play. I slid across the net. *4:44 . . .* Krupp pulled Tuttle down from behind and slid into me, skates first. *4:43.*

It felt like a kick to the mask. There was no pain, but I pulled my helmet off. And then I saw the blood. It spattered red in the faceoff circle. A stream gushed out with every beat of my heart. *It's an artery.* I grabbed my neck, trying to keep the blood in, but it rushed between my fingers. It just kept coming. I slumped forward and it glugged out like a water fountain.

Everything was a blur. I didn't see the white faces in the crowd. I didn't see fans pass out or any of the players vomiting on the ice. I didn't hear Blues forward Rick Meagher turn to the benches and scream for help. All I saw was the blood rushing into a red sea around me. *I'm going to die.* Terry Gregson, the referee, looked down at me. His eyes were huge. "Get a stretcher—he's bleeding to death!"

Our trainer, Jim Pizzutelli, got to me first. He had gauze from the medical kit. He pushed it against my throat, holding me so tight I could barely breathe. The crease was covered in blood. I coughed out, "Jim, it's my jugular."

He was so calm. "Just do what I say."

Years earlier, Jim had been a combat engineer in the Vietnam War. His second week in, he was walking through a village when a truck collided with him and four other soldiers. The impact broke his ribs. It tossed another soldier into a gully, where he was decapitated by a sheet-metal hut. Jim was medevacked out, with the young man's body and head beside him. He studied sports medicine after the war. Now here he was, squeezing his arm around my neck.

"We're going to save you."

"Jim, I can't breathe."

He flexed his grip. "You're not going to breathe until we get you to a doctor."

He helped me to my skates and we made it through the doors behind my net. I was scared as hell. I had no idea how much blood I had already lost. I had seen a television show that said a severed jugular would bleed out in minutes. *I'm going to die.*

My mother was at home in Calgary, watching the game on satellite. I couldn't let her see this happen—not on the ice, not on TV, not like this. They put me on a table in the trainer's room. Rip Simonick, our equipment manager, stood over me and held my hand. I asked him to call my mom. When I first started playing for the Sabres, I saw a chaplain hanging around the arena. I asked Rip to call for him, figuring God might be my only hope to live. But at the one game I really needed him, the chaplain wasn't there.

One of the team's doctors took a towel and pressed it down on my throat with all his weight. He'd let up so I could breathe, and the blood would spout out and he'd press back down.

I still didn't have a sense of time. There was mass confusion. Lots of nurses and doctors came down from the stands, wanting to help. Security had to clear everyone out. Jim started cutting off my pads and chest protector. Rip was still holding my hand as he dialled my mother's number. I didn't want to pass out. *If I close my eyes, I won't wake up.*

The ambulance seemed to take forever, but it was probably only ten minutes. When it finally arrived, they got me on a stretcher and put an IV in my arm. I tried to make a joke: "Put in a couple stitches and let me get back out there." Blood gurgled out as I said it. No one laughed. They were white as ghosts, and I figured it was the end.

Rip said, "I talked to your mom. She says she loves you."

Our team doctor climbed into the ambulance with the paramedics and pushed down on my neck the whole ride to Buffalo General. They wheeled me through the emergency room doors. I was still wearing my hockey pants and long johns—they cut the gear off me. They told me I was going to be okay, and I wanted to believe them. I tried to. They put a needle in my arm and I watched their frantic faces drift away.

Back at the Aud, more than fifteen thousand fans, two teams and all the viewers at home still weren't sure if I would survive. There were reports that two fans suffered heart attacks. At the very least, everyone had witnessed a scene they would never erase from their minds.

The teams left the ice after the accident. The players were terrified. My teammate and close friend Grant Ledyard was freaking out—he sobbed with his head in his hands in the Sabres' dressing room.

No one wanted to play after that, but eventually the word came through that I'd live, so the game resumed. The players went back to the benches to finish the first period. My replacement, Jacques Cloutier, stood in the dark red crease and crouched as the puck dropped and the clock started ticking again—*4:42 . . . 4:41 . . .* He played in a pool of my blood and trembled through the rest of the game.

Before returning to the Sabres' bench, Jim Pizzutelli went to change out of his stained clothes. He pulled off his shoes and realized his socks were soaked with my blood. On the bench, he stared forward blankly as the periods went on and thought about how close I'd been to death. An hour after the game, he sat in the trainer's office and locked the door. He stayed there alone and refused to talk to anyone.

I woke up famous. Not just NHL-famous, but CNN news cycle–famous. The surgery took only an hour and a half, but by the time the surgeon had woven more than three hundred stitches inside and outside the six-inch gash on the right side of my neck, it seemed like every person in North America had seen the accident.

My sister, Terry, was in the hospital room with me. She drove down from Toronto and must have left right when the collision happened, because she was there within two hours, when I woke up. As I feared, Mom had seen the collision on television, had watched me bleed out until the cameras turned away and the announcer lost his composure. "Take the . . . *aww man!* That is the . . . *oh God!* Oh, please take the camera off. Don't even bring it over there. Please. Oh my God. Please take it away. That is terrible. Oh my God, what happened?" Mom saw it all and heard it all. She flipped. My brother, Garth, was at her house when it happened. She called him into the living room. "Something's wrong. Clint's bleeding." He told her not to worry because it was probably just another broken nose. "His nose is always in the way," he said.

Reporters swarmed the hospital. They tried to sneak in, saying they were relatives. A few made it all the way to my room, but we sent the bastards away. The Sabres' physician, Dr. John Butsch, came in and I asked him what the damage was. He was reassuring. "You lost a lot of blood, but you're out of danger. You're going to be fine." The surgeon closed the veins on the sliced side of my neck. The other side would compensate, Dr. Butsch said. They had to repair the severed tendons and muscle. The gash stopped a millimeter from my internal carotid artery. If the skate had sliced just a bit deeper, it might as well have been a guillotine.

I asked Dr. Butsch when I could get back on the ice. He said he wasn't sure because I'd lost so much blood, but it would likely take a while. Other doctors and physicians came in as well, and they told me a lot of different things. Team management shared their thoughts, too.

Everyone had an opinion. Some told me to take the rest of the season off and recover through the playoffs—"Just take it easy for a couple of months." Some said I should retire. But it didn't really matter what they said, because I was going to play as soon as I possibly could. A lot of people thought I'd never come back. I didn't even entertain the idea.

The press kept hounding us, so the hospital asked me to do a press conference. The room was packed. My sister was still there. It was just me and her and the hospital's PR staff.

"When you get knocked off the horse, you get back on," I told the reporters. "It'll be tough to play, but I'll have to be ready . . . I'll be psyched for it . . . I'm anxious to get in there. I'll be happy to play. Something like this kind of opens your eyes. You have a life to live . . . I'm lucky to be here."

There was such a demand from the media that we had to do a second press conference later that afternoon. And that's when I broke down. I don't really know what happened. I wept in front of everyone, with this big bandage on my neck. Earlier, because I was a Sabre, I'd visited with some kids in the cancer ward and posed for pictures and signed autographs. They were so happy and sweet. They were so excited to see me. But it affected me—*I'm alive and going to make it. These kids are still fighting. Some of the kids will die. How scared was I during the accident? And these kids deal with this every day?* Everything flooded out at the press conference. I broke down. I didn't care about the cameras or the recorders. Maybe that's when the shock set in. I let it all out and then pulled it all back in.

I was supposed to stay at the hospital for a few days, but I couldn't get any rest. Even after the press conferences, the reporters kept coming. It was a circus, and it was too much for the hospital to handle. I couldn't stay there any longer, so they released me that night. They took me down to the basement and drove me out a secret exit.

Two days after the accident, I was back where it all started. I called Jim Pizzutelli and asked him to open up the Aud for me before everyone arrived. We walked down the hallway I'd stumbled through, dying, less than 48 hours earlier. I went onto the ice and stood in the blue crease. My blood was gone.

"Boy, we're lucky to be here," I said.

"Damn right," Jim said. "And we're back."

It was nice of him to do, and it helped. But that was the extent of any therapy I'd receive.

That night, the Sabres played the Vancouver Canucks. The team asked me to make an appearance for the fans. I didn't want to do it. I felt like a clown. But they pleaded—told me the people of the city had stood behind me and were concerned. So, during a stoppage in play halfway through the second period, they opened the Zamboni doors. The arena announcer boomed, "Here he is, Clint Malarchuk!" I stepped out. I could have fainted from the standing ovation—I was so weak. I had to leave. I was shaking. My legs felt like rubber noodles. I could feel the stitches. It was like a pinch, a sting. Both teams tapped their sticks on the ice and against the boards as I waved.

I assumed I'd be back on the ice right away, but I had to make sure the stitches wouldn't tear out. I was paranoid that the wound would some-how reopen, so I was careful about turning my head or making sudden movements. But the Sabres knew I was coming back. There was no chance I'd take the advice of those who said I should take the rest of the year off. It wasn't just me being stubborn—I was at the end of my option year. I'd have tried to come back anyway, but financially, I knew I didn't have a choice. As for my body, I was still weak. It takes a while to make up the loss of that much blood. I was probably weak until mid-July, but I didn't tell anyone. And no one talked to me about any psychological effects. I didn't know the meaning of trauma then, but I knew the meaning of being a total pussy, and I sure as hell wasn't going to be one.

I played ten days after the accident, as soon as the stitches were taken out. My first game back was against the Nordiques. Jacques Cloutier started, and then they put me in for the last ten minutes of the game, just to get my legs back. We were winning at the time. The announcer made a big deal out of it: "Now in goal—Clint Malarchuk!" The arena was already going nuts. I got another ovation. I was shaking. The crowd was crazy. There was so much emotion in those ten days. The crowd was so loud, my heart was racing. *I can do this.*

At the end of the game, the guys I had played with when I was a Nordique came up to congratulate me. Mario Gosselin was one of them. Paul Gillis was another. Having our opponents come see me after a game like that was something special. It really meant a lot to me.

Meanwhile, I was the biggest celebrity in Buffalo. Everyone knew my story. People saw me as this macho hockey player, but they'd also seen me break down and knew how quickly I had come back. They thought it was pretty cool. I was a hero in that town. I couldn't buy a meal in Buffalo. Couldn't pay for a pizza. For years, people would tell stories about how quickly I'd returned from almost dying. One of my Pro Set hockey cards had a picture of me with this Kevlar scarf that Rip and I had made after the accident to protect my neck. It looked like an ascot, and I only wore it for a few games. I ended up switching to a high-collar turtleneck reinforced with Kevlar. I couldn't handle that plastic throat guard that dangles off the mask. It was hard on my mobility and vision. Anyway, the back of the Pro Set card describes my injury and says I was "back in action a mere two days" after the accident. The myth was building. The card also notes that I was "winless in 11 playoff games." *Thanks very much.*

My career has come to be defined by that accident. It's my claim to fame. I had a decent run in the NHL, but I wasn't a Hall of Famer. Still, the fact is that I'm probably remembered better than a lot of goalies with similar stats. Even people who aren't hockey fans have seen the accident. I was always proud of that. I got bucked off, but I got back on the horse. I refused to let go.

That season, we met the Boston Bruins in the first round. I played a game or two in the series. I don't remember the goals that went in or how things played out. I just know that I was okay, but I wasn't *great*, whereas before I got hurt I was on fire. And I remember the Boston fans behind my net at the Garden making throat-cutting gestures at me during the game. Back and forth, across the jugular—reminding me to die.

We lost the series four games to one.

15

Night Terrors

THE PUCK SLIDES ACROSS THE CREASE. I PUSH OFF MY POST AS the other team's forward cuts in. My defenseman drags him down from behind and they tumble into me. His skate cuts into my neck.

I wake up.

It was always the same. I'd sit up in bed, clutching my throat, hyperventilating and sweating, my heart pounding. I had the same nightmare almost every night until I eventually stopped sleeping entirely. It happened all the time, but I didn't tell anyone.

I spent the summer after the accident in Calgary, living between my mother's place and my brother's ranch. Garth had about twenty acres outside of town. I was there most days, helping him with the horses. I think he was proud of the way I came back, and I was proud to make him proud. By then, Garth was my father figure. Dad was still alive, but we hadn't talked in years. Not *really.* I think he called me after the accident, but I barely remember talking to him if he did. Our relationship just faded away.

I worked out like a monster that summer because I knew I'd have to prove myself when I got back for training camp. Also, I'd been so weak from all the blood loss and I needed to feel strong again. I'd lift weights, alternating body sections, depending on the day. Then I'd run anywhere from ten to twenty miles. And later, I'd box a heavy bag and a speed bag. There was a boxing gym in Calgary I'd go to three times a week to spar and work out. It was circuit training—the whistle blows and you're doing step-ups; the whistle blows and you're skipping; the whistle blows and you're shadowboxing—it was always right to the next station.

The gym was run by an old boxer named Coco. He was a small guy but seriously tough. A bunch of NHLers trained there, like Doug Houda. There were maybe eight of us who went there. You could spar with Coco; he was really quick and always tagged you good, just to make sure you knew he could beat the shit out of you. He was teaching us, but I knew a few things already. All the other guys were bigger than me, but he put them in their place. But because I had grown up boxing, most times I'd be able to tag him, too. I hit him pretty good once, and he got pissed off and laid into me hard. We ended up fighting. It was a real boxing match. I went home with a terrible headache and threw up. He gave me a concussion, I'm sure. I probably had quite a few of those in my day, but like most guys from that era, I didn't worry much about it beyond thinking, *Holy shit, my head hurts.*

Shortly after the accident, I went alone to see a movie called *Black Rain*. I loved going to movies alone. It was a way to turn my mind off. Michael Douglas was in this one. It's about two cops in New York who get caught up in a gang war involving the Japanese mafia. There's a scene where a character gets his throat cut. I didn't see it coming—it was one of those things where a guy walks up and kills him from behind. There was all kinds of blood. I started panicking and ran out of the movie. I was in the bathroom, throwing cold water on my face. My heart was racing. It was a full-blown anxiety attack. After I calmed down, I made myself go back into the movie, but I was too rattled to concentrate. I couldn't unwind, so I left. Anxiety had always been a big part of my life, but things were getting worse. I knew I couldn't let anyone know. My career would be over if it seemed like I was breaking down because of a stupid injury.

I went to training camp that year ready to battle for the number one position. Buffalo had traded Cloutier to the Chicago Blackhawks in the off-season, but Daren Puppa's arm was fully healed and he was back. Everyone knew Puppa was their guy—they had drafted him to replace Tom Barrasso, whom the Sabres had traded to the Pittsburgh Penguins the season before. But I had been on fire when I was traded to Buffalo, and my stock skyrocketed after the quick return from the jugular injury. The job was open if I earned it.

All through camp, the press kept hounding me with questions. It pissed me off. I thought I was okay, but these people still questioned whether I could ever play as well as I had before the accident. I told them I'd already come back and proven myself, so why was everyone doubting me? They wrote columns questioning whether I should be playing at all. One of the reasons I wanted to come back so fast was to prove to management and coaches that I could still play. But I was still being asked these questions. Everyone kept saying, "Oh, he'll never be the same." That pissed me off. I understand media, though—they're going to play every angle. I just thought, *Screw you guys.* But even though I tried to put the accident behind me, their questions made me wonder. *Should I be back? Am I ready?* The truth was that, all through training camp, I was tentative in the net. I was worried in practice—subconsciously, at least. Scared. We had this one guy, Darcy Loewen, who was a really gritty player. He'd always skate hard to the net, even in practice. I'd flinch every time I saw him coming, even though I tried so hard not to. It was a tic I couldn't afford to have. It exposed me. A goalie who flinches isn't the kind of goalie you want in your net.

My old Fredericton Express teammate Rick Dudley took over as the Sabres' head coach for the 1989–90 season. He replaced Ted Sator, who was behind the bench when the accident happened. I was glad about the move—I really felt like Rick understood me. And our team looked even better on paper than it did the previous season. Rob Ray and Donald Audette were rookies on our team that year. Our other first-year guy was Alexander Mogilny, who had defected from Russia and was the biggest story on our team, if not in the whole league. Mogilny had been on the Soviet team that won gold at the 1988 Olympics in Calgary, playing on a line with Pavel Bure and Sergei Fedorov. He was also part of the Soviet junior squad that got into that bench-clearing brawl with Canada at the 1987 world junior tournament—the "punch-up in Piestany"—when they turned out the lights.

I lived on the same street as some of the players, like Dean Kennedy, a farm boy from Saskatchewan who joined the Sabres in 1989 after spending the first part of his career out in Los Angeles. We made good neighbours. Sometimes in my driveway we'd set up a bale of straw with a plastic steer's head with horns. Dean and I would put on cowboy hats and rope that fake steer for hours. It was an odd site in Buffalo. Sometimes, when I'd get home from practice, I would set up ball hockey games with kids on our street. They'd get home from school in the afternoon, and I'd be waiting with my goalie gear on, ready to play. There'd be kids ranging in age from four to fourteen sometimes. We'd play until dark. There was a pond in the middle of the circle our street made, and when it got cold, we'd set the rink up out there and go play with the kids. Part of me just got a kick out of the joy they got from playing the game. Part of it was an escape. I was a kid again, outdoors, playing the game I loved without a care in the world. It helped ease my anxiety. It was the inactive moments of solitude that haunted me. I had to stay active. I'd play the game nonstop, forever, if I could.

The street hockey always took place on off-days, of course. Never on game days. Especially not when I was playing. Those days were exhausting enough. My stress peaked on game days. I didn't recognize it as obsessive-compulsive disorder at the time. I didn't even know what OCD was. It's not that being stressed before playing a hockey game is particularly abnormal. Every player feels pressure before they play, especially goalies. Lots of players throw up before games. I did it many times. You get so tight and anxious, it's like your body just rejects the tension. It's difficult to say that I was more stressed than other players before games—I can't know how they felt—but I know that it consumed every part of me. I don't think that is normal.

I always had trouble sleeping, especially the night before a game. I'd toss and turn and wouldn't be able to shut my mind off. It was shitty sleep after shitty sleep that season, and it was just the beginning of my battles with insomnia. I'd get into bed and think about how I needed to get a good night's sleep in order to play well in the game the next day. And then I'd get stressed because I wasn't falling asleep, and I'd think about how terrible I'd play because I hadn't slept well. The stress would build and build. Even if it wasn't related to hockey, I would find something else to obsess about. It could be anything: problems in my love life, the new coat of paint needed in the basement, whether the doors were locked and the stove was off.

The season after the accident, it got worse than it had ever been. It's that feeling you get when you have to wake up for something really important early in the morning and you're depending on the alarm to get you up. But what if something happens to the alarm? Or what if you just sleep right through it? *What if . . . What if . . . What if . . .* And you lie there in this crazy haze, your mind spinning in circles. You stare at the ceiling, you toss and turn, you get up and make sure the front door is locked and that the back door is locked and then you check the front door again and then the back door . . . and then, *Oh shit, what about the stove?* The smallest things invade your mind and keep it ticking before the big things return. *I'll probably play shitty tomorrow. If I play shitty, I might never start again.* And soon you're staring at the red numbers on your alarm clock and it's 3:43 A.M. *Shit.* When I'd finally close my eyes and drift into a peaceful place, I'd feel a blade against my throat and see gushing blood—wake up sweating, check my neck, catch my breath and start all over again.

It's weird how the mental affects the physical and the physical affects the mental, isn't it? That never crossed my mind at the time. I didn't understand the relationship. On game days, I'd try to get in a two-hour nap because I'd slept so badly the night before. I was always one of the first guys to the rink. I was nervous once I got there, but it eased a bit. When I was at home and obsessing, I'd let it out. But when I was around people, I'd try to hide it. I'd kind of settle down as I went through my routine in the locker room, just trying to stick with the same system that helped to manage the anxiety. I'd go through the same stretching, check my equipment to make sure it was perfect, stare at the floor in silence and then throw my racquetball against the wall, fine-tuning my reflexes to make sure I was ready to go. Warmups would pass by in a blur. I'd be in my zone unless some dipshit on my team raised the puck and hit me in the head or caught me in the collarbone. Then, right before the opening faceoff, my mental chaos would go sky high. But when the puck was dropped, everything was fine. My mind was obsessed with one thing: the puck. Nothing else crept in.

For an hour or two after the game, I'd still be in that kind of euphoria—and then it would start all over again. It was chronic anxiety. It's difficult to make sense of it. As miserable and debilitating as it was, it was normal for me. That seems so morbid. But it's true.

The season went fine. I wanted to play more, but I was a team guy. Buffalo relied heavily on me as a backup, and I was proud of how I played. In twenty-nine games, I had a 3.35 goals-against average and a .903 save percentage, both of which were pretty good by the standards of that freewheeling, high-scoring era. But I hated every minute I spent on that goddamn bench. I desperately wanted to prove that I had overcome the injury and that all the naysayers were full of shit. More than that, though, I needed to prove it to myself. The accident haunted me, but I wasn't about to admit it. I certainly wasn't going to accept it. I didn't tell anyone about the nightmares or insomnia. I wanted to deny it all.

The best way to do that was to keep my act going on the surface—always instant smiles, instant humour. I tried to keep things light while riding the pine. There used to be a phone beside the bench at the Aud that the trainers would use to call for an ambulance if something bad ever happened on the ice. (What could possibly be that bad?) Sometimes, during the games, I'd call my mother back in Calgary—just chatting away with her as she watched on satellite TV and I sat on the bench. I'd wave to her. Jim Pizzutelli always got a kick out of that.

Even though we were competing for playing time, Daren Puppa and I got along great. Here's the thing about goalie partners: you sit beside them, you work with them, you practise with them and everything. We're all overly competitive, proud men. If you don't want to be the league's best, you have no business playing the game. But at the same time, you're part of a team. And all clichés aside, you care about that team and you take your role within it seriously. Goalies are in a unique situation: if one plays, the other doesn't. Ideally, though, they have the sense to support each other. Of all the goalies I shared the net with, Daren was one of my favorites, even though we were complete opposites. He was really quiet, really reserved, while I was the team clown.

For a while, I didn't think he liked me very much. When everyone else was laughing with me, he just sat there quietly. Then one day, his fiancée, Meg, told me that Daren thought I was the funniest guy he'd ever met. She asked me to be the MC at their wedding at the end of the season. I was really pumped because I liked him, but until then I didn't know what he thought of me.

I was dating a new girl I had met in Calgary during the off-season. She was from a big-time rodeo family. Following my usual pattern, I fell in love with her right away, she moved in with me in Buffalo, and pretty soon we were married. It was better to cover up all the holes in my life than deal with the broken foundation.

My good buddies Grant Ledyard and Dean Kennedy were still on the team. Both of them saw that I wasn't exactly myself but figured I'd be fine. We weren't much for spotting warning signs back then.

The Sabres finished the season with the third-best record in the NHL with a record of 45–27–8, just three points behind Boston, who led the Adams Division—and the league. Mike Foligno was our captain and Phil Housley and Mike Ramsey wore the As. Puppa earned a spot on the second all-star team and was fifth in the league with a 2.89 goals-against average. Dave Andreychuk and Pierre Turgeon led the team in scoring with forty goals each, and Turgeon led us in points with 106. But even as a rookie, you could tell that Mogilny was the rising star of the franchise. The kid was dripping with natural talent. He was also the laziest guy on the team. He had a kind of *screw you* attitude. If it wasn't laziness, maybe it was just defiance. This kid had a wrist shot that just blew you away—it was so fast. But in practice, he'd just skate over the blue line and flick it at the net. He just wanted to get done with practice. He just didn't care.

Mogilny told the team he hated flying, which I thought was bullshit at the time. Later in life, I would come to understood fear a lot more than I did then. I'm sure his phobia was legitimate. But at the time, it just made him seem precious. Because he didn't like to fly, the Sabres got a limo to take him from city to city. Which was luxurious for games up and down the eastern seaboard. But then we'd play in St. Louis or Chicago, and all of a sudden it's a twelve-hour ride in the back of the limo. Limo or not, a half-day drive is a long haul to make between practices and games. He got cured of his flying issue pretty soon after that.

When I first came back after the accident, I'd read in one of the papers that Steve Tuttle was having a hard time, that he was having nightmares and shit. I got Steve's number and tried to call him, but he wasn't around. I told his roommate and teammate Sergio Momesso to tell Steve that I didn't blame him for what happened. I had never really considered the trauma that the accident might have caused the other players involved. Sure, I was the one who had been injured, but being involved in an accident like that has to mess you up. So when the Blues came to town in early December, I wanted to make sure Tuttle knew it was okay. I passed by him at centre ice during the warmups and shouted, "Jesus, you're a cutthroat bastard, aren't you?"

I did my best to carry on my sense of humour, despite the shit going on in my head. At the time, I got along really well with Jim Kelley, a writer for the *Buffalo News*. As he got older, Jim had this white beard going—it made him look like Kenny Rogers. When we were in L.A. on a road trip, I went into the record store and picked up a Kenny Rogers album. I had it all set up. As people were lining up to get on the plane at the terminal, I walked up to Jim.

"Kenny! Kenny Rogers! Oh my goodness, Kenny Rogers!" I pulled the album out of my bag. "Would you sign this for me?"

Shit, he signed autographs for the whole flight. I reconnected with Jim years later. He said, "I'll never forget that, you son of a bitch!"

Jim died much too young in 2010 after suffering from pancreatic cancer. He was one of the good ones.

Dudley used Puppa and me in tandem, with no clear starter really emerging. I didn't mind this because Puppa was supposed to be the go-to guy, but I was making a strong case that I deserved to play. Then, during the 1990–91 season, I suffered a serious back injury that sidelined me for most of January and part of February. I felt a terrible pain in my upper back and neck during one of the games. I managed to play through it, but I knew it was bad. It hurt to skate. It hurt to move. I couldn't even check my blind spot when I drove home. Throughout my career, I was always paranoid about missing games because of an injury. It took a lot to keep me out. I often played hurt. Look at the picture of me clutching my neck when my jugular got cut, and you'll see I had a cast on my hand. I was playing with a broken thumb.

My dad taught me to fight, but my mom made me tough. *Be tough, be tough.* The first time I remember getting hurt in a hockey game was when I was eight, on the outdoor rink near our house. I was playing forward and went into the boards stick first. It speared me right in the gut and I fell down, unable to breathe. My mom was right there, standing on the snowbank above me. I writhed around on the ice, gasping for air. "Clint get up, skate to the box." That was exactly what she said to me. "You want to lie there and get attention? Or do you want to be a man and skate to the box?" So I got my ass up and went to the bench. She instilled character and toughness in me.

I carried that with me throughout my career. If I went down, I didn't stay down. I tried to play through every injury, and if I couldn't, I came back as fast as humanly possible. I took pride in that for a long time. But most of that was rooted in fear. Any honest player will tell you that. A fear of losing your job, of being traded or going unsigned. Or of some damn rookie coming in and taking your job. So you bite the bullet and play hurt.

But this injury was like nothing I had felt before. I was out for much of January, and the team hit the skids, going 1–8–4 with me away. Rick called me up one night and said, "Clint, do you think you can play? I think I'm going to lose my job here." I hadn't played in I don't know how many weeks. I was doing physical therapy, trying everything possible to fix my neck just enough to allow me to function in net. I've always felt this need to please people. It's hard to tell where that came from, but I never wanted to let anyone down. Rick Dudley had earned my respect as a teammate in Fredericton and he had it as the bench boss in Buffalo.

"Rick," I said, "I'll do my best."

I took these shots before I played to completely freeze out the pain. It worked. I played again. I got hot and we started winning. I went 3–0–3 in my first six games back. It ended up saving his job—for the time being, at least. We had a decent year, but the success they had when I was playing didn't get us far. Montreal knocked us out of the first round of the playoffs.

After the season, I went to see a back and neck specialist in Toronto. He said, "You've got a broken vertebra here, buddy. You could have been paralyzed at any minute. And you took freezing? You could have been paralyzed. That's stupid." Oh well. *Be tough, be tough.* Rick thought a lot of that. It was a key moment in one of the most important friendships of my life.

After the season, everyone from the team went to Puppa's wedding. As the MC, I spent a lot of time roasting Duds. All players have stories about their coaches that they probably won't share unless they're in a situation like that. I wasn't too mean—just enough to get the boys roaring. Duds loved every minute of it. He thought I was the most well-adjusted person he knew. He thought I had the perfect timing for jokes and that I had charisma and confidence. Years later, he'd tell me that the night of the wedding, as he sat there getting roasted, he looked at me and thought, *This kid has it all.*

16

Whiskey and Pills

I DIDN'T DRINK A LOT THAT FIRST YEAR AFTER THE ACCIDENT. I relaxed over a few beers with teammates here and there—nothing much. But the next summer, the second after the accident, I really started to spiral. I was going to a lot of rodeos and partying hard, doing everything I could to avoid the shit going on in my head.

When I returned to camp for the 1991–92 season, I was in a bad place mentally. My obsessions boiled inside me. It was just getting worse. I knew I was struggling, but I was too stubborn—maybe too afraid—to ask for help. I was trained to cowboy up. If you get bucked off the horse, you get back on. Get your jugular vein cut, you get back in the game. That's what I did. There was no way of processing the actual depth of the accident. There was no way to get educated, no resources. Back then, we didn't have team psychologists. No one ever asked me anything about my neck injury. And counselling didn't occur to me, either. I thought, *It's just an injury*. I thought the accident was completely irrelevant to how I played the game or functioned in my personal life.

I was doing all of the typical OCD stuff—checking stoves, turning them on and off, water faucets on and off, constantly. Germs were a huge concern, like they were when I was a kid in school who couldn't function unless the desks were cleaned with Lysol. If I opened a door, I'd open it with my pinky. If I shook someone's hand, I'd wash it as soon as possible. I washed my hands a lot.

I'd go to the movies alone in an attempt to shut my head off. It was impossible. Everything was magnified. It was more anxiety than depression at the time. But if my head had ever stopped spinning, I would certainly have been depressed. I was so messed up, so wound up, I just didn't stop long enough to feel it. It's hard to explain to someone who has never felt this way. But some people reading this might be thinking, *Yep, that's me.*

By far, the most damaging obsession I had was my belief that my wife was messing around on me. This was my second wife, of course—another relationship that was doomed from the start. She saw me suffer as I tried to fight a war within me that I didn't understand. And when my obsessions and paranoia peaked, I turned to her and saw nothing but betrayal. It was a constant insecurity in all the relationships I've been in. It was irrational. But then, obsession is the opposite of rational thought. My anxiety was on overdrive after the accident. Not realizing that I suffered from mental illness, I searched for outside causes of the stress that consumed me. Hockey was an easy one. You're anxious in the days and hours leading up to a game. You're nervous; it makes sense. But when I wasn't playing, or if I was playing well, it didn't seem like a logical cause for anxiety. I loved the game more than anything, and as a kid it was the one thing that relaxed me. So I tried to find other reasons for my stress, and they all started with her. *Does she really love me? Am I the best she's ever had? Who does she think about when we're in bed?* Before I'd leave to go to the rink for a game, sometimes I'd ask her these questions point blank. I needed to clear out my mind, to reassure myself. I had to get it out of my head.

I hadn't slept in almost two weeks. The insomnia consumed me. I'd go to the arena and play goal and come home in a red-eyed haze. My eyes burned from lack of sleep. When I got to the rink, no matter how tired or anxious I might have been, I put on the best show I could. On the surface, I was unflappable. No one would say anything.

At the time, I suffered from these uncontrollable tremors where my hands would start to shake. I'd fold my arms across my chest and tuck my hands into my armpits to keep them from quivering. At night, I'd keep thinking, *I have to sleep, I have to get up tomorrow, I have to function.* And then I'd just try to breathe. As soon as I could almost doze off—in my bed, or on an airplane—*boom.* I'd just wake up. There would be about a five-second calm where I'd be kind of dazed. Then the anxiety would overwhelm me again. It was like it heated my whole body, from my waist to my head. It'd get warmer and warmer, and by the time it got to my head, my forehead was hot. By then, I'd be panting like a dog and cussing myself—*Damn, geez, goddammit, I could have been asleep. You were right there, Clint.* Then I'd try to close my eyes and sleep, and the whole thing would happen again. Around six in the morning, I'd just say screw it and get up. I was wasting my time trying to sleep, and if I did manage it, I'd probably snore right through practice.

I was confused and angry and desperate, but I refused to ask for help, even though I was already on pain medication for a bulging disc near my neck. I had no trouble talking to professionals when it came to physical pain. But emotional problems? Hell no.

On January 23 of that year, I started to vomit up blood before a morning skate in Pittsburgh. I hunched over the toilet and puked and puked and puked. The team sent me to the hospital right away. They shoved a scope down my throat and looked deep into my guts and discovered some festering ulcers.

At times, emotional turmoil takes a physical toll. I couldn't hide anymore—my body was demanding help. My hospitalization was in all the papers. Everyone knew about the ulcers, but no one knew what was going on in my head. I remember being so anxious that I couldn't sleep or eat. I couldn't function. My OCD was off the charts. I felt out of my skin, and as an NHL goaltender I'm really not sure how I managed to get by on a daily basis, but people dealing with this kind of thing are incredible at covering it up. It was like I was twelve again, only this time the ulcers were real. The stress in my life was like an ongoing preoccupation that dissipated but then came back and became bigger. Eventually, it would go away again, but it always came back stronger. Soon it would destroy me.

Three days later, one of my teammates threw a Super Bowl party for the players at his house. My wife and I went to the party and I had a few beers with the boys. We went home and I had a bad reaction to the medication I was taking for the bulging disc. I swelled up, was almost convulsing and had a hard time breathing, so I was rushed to the hospital.

At least, that was the story we told to disguise the truth. John Butsch, our team doctor, told the press I'd had a reaction to my pain medication triggered by the beers. That was true—so far as it went. The whole truth is much more complicated.

We did go to the Super Bowl party. I did have a few beers with the boys. And I did my best to act normally, but I was out of my mind with anxiety. One of my teammates complimented my wife's body—he said something to me about how good she looked. Later, I saw him hovering over her. And then they were gone. I searched all over for them. He was gone and she was gone.

I didn't actually see him screwing her. But in my mind . . . I don't know, I just thought, *I'm not stupid.* I didn't really know whether anything happened between them, but I sure thought it did. She was gone for a while. When I finally found her, I was furious. *What the hell was that? You're gone for an hour? He's gone for an hour? And he's telling me how hot you are?* I was so upset. It was still early in the evening, and we were the first to leave the party. Whether it was justified or not, I don't know. We went home and had a massive fight. I was so pissed off at her. I wasn't being rational. I was seeing things in my head—my wife and my teammate—and I couldn't make them go away. It was anger and rage and frustration and fear, all twisting and turning inside of me. It was exhaustion. And I was hurt and angry—feeling mean. *You bitch. You goddamn bitch . . .*

I opened a bottle of whiskey and drank it all. The label on the pain medication said not to take the pills with alcohol because it would cause drowsiness. I thought, *Fuck it. I'm going to sleep tonight. And I don't care if I wake up, either.* I had thought about suicide before, but I don't know that I wanted to kill myself that night. Maybe I didn't care if I did. But I just wanted to sleep, because I hadn't slept in so long.

I swallowed a handful of pills. It's all blurry; a crazy haze. I just remember wanting to close my eyes and make it all go away.

A few minutes later, I collapsed on the bedroom floor.

My wife screamed.

My heart stopped beating.

There were shadows in the bright lights—people watching over me. I thought I was dead, but then I blinked a few times and the world came into focus. *Nurses. Doctors. Hospital.* I tasted charcoal. A sharp, constant pain in my chest. *Shit.* Couldn't close my mouth because there were tubes shoved down my nose and throat. They hurt a lot. My arm was stabbed with an IV and I was hooked up to some weird machines. I threw up several times.

My wife had saved my life. She was a flight attendant and knew CPR. She pounded on my chest and gave me mouth-to-mouth resuscitation until the paramedics got to our house and stabilized me.

I woke up at Erie County Medical Center. Doctors kept asking me if this was a suicide attempt, and I kept saying no. That's when I told them I hadn't slept in days and that my mind was all over the map. One of the doctors I spoke with said it sounded like I had obsessive-compulsive disorder.

The story was buried in the papers as a minor injury brief. On January 28, the *Toronto Star* published a short paragraph between the news that my teammate Pat LaFontaine had been named NHL player of the week and an item saying that Wayne Gretzky had agreed to be part of a strike if the NHL Players' Association voted for one.

Malarchuk in hospital: Buffalo Sabres goalie Clint Malarchuk was sent to hospital yesterday because of an alcohol-related reaction to pain medication. Malarchuk drank alcohol Sunday, which reacted with pain medication he had been taking, team doctor John Butsch said. His condition is not serious.

I was in the hospital for four or five days. A psychiatrist evaluated me and officially diagnosed me with obsessive-compulsive disorder and depression. "You're going through some shit, son," he said. It was the first time the chaos inside me was given a label. We discussed my depression but focused on treating the OCD because it appeared to be the catalyst for my anxiety. He gave me medication and set me up with a psychologist in Rochester whom I'd have to meet with once a week.

I went back to the team shortly after being released from the hospital. It was uncomfortable. Really uncomfortable. I'd tried so hard to hide my problems. Most guys in the dressing room were completely shocked by what had happened. They knew how upset I was at the party and they quickly found out about the pills. *Clint Malarchuk? The dressing-room joker? The game-day monk? The guy who played after getting his jugular sliced? No way.* I was the last guy that they imagined this could happen to. I felt exposed. Like all my deepest, darkest shit was just hanging in my stall behind me.

The press wasn't satisfied with our story. They seemed to think Dr. Butsch's narrative was too tidy and they wanted more details. I explained that I'd been having trouble sleeping, and after having three or four beers at the party, I went home and tried to concoct my own sleeping potion by mixing my pain medication with more alcohol. They didn't know that my heart had stopped. They only knew that I had knocked myself out and woken up in the hospital. But they could see how uncomfortable I was as I tried to answer their questions. "His voice quavered, his forehead sweated, he had a pained expression as he spoke," wrote the Associated Press. I worried that the incident would mar my character. I'd been very active in the community in Buffalo over the past few years, something I always prided myself on as a pro athlete. I believe players have an obligation to the fans who make their dreams possible.

"I think I established myself as a real community man and a pretty big role model to a lot of kids," I told the scrum that day. "And I think anytime you're that, you don't want to be involved in anything with drugs or alcohol. And there's no way I'm a drinker. In fact, it was probably the first time I drank this season." Honestly, it was. I always stayed away from booze during the season.

My first game back was on February 11. We lost 5–1 to Hartford. Three days later, I played poorly and was pulled in a 7–6 win over the San Jose Sharks. During the same west coast road trip, I left the Sabres to deal with a child custody issue from my first marriage. The added stress of that situation compounded my mental state. The departure also raised speculation in the press that my days in Buffalo were numbered. At the time, there was buzz that the Sabres were looking for a new goalie. Puppa wasn't playing very well and speculation about my personal problems made it seem like I was an unstable alternative.

The team's spin about my reaction to the pain medication did little to stop the stories from spreading around the league. Everyone believed I had overdosed on drugs or booze. I knew other players were whispering about what happened. Only a few knew how bad it really was. I certainly wasn't going to tell the world that I basically did myself in by draining a bottle of whiskey and taking a handful of pills. I couldn't have that in print, on the record, for everyone to see. It means you're a coward. That you took the easy way out. That's what I thought at the time, because I still barely understood the reality of depression and anxiety. I'd spent my life battling mental illness without knowing it. I was screwed up without knowing *how* screwed up. More than anything, I was confused by what I had done to myself. I hadn't made a conscious, drawn-out decision to commit suicide. I'd fought away those thoughts in the past and had never taken it this far. I certainly hadn't planned anything. But on the other hand, why would you take a handful of pills and drink a bottle of whiskey? Why would I do that to myself? It was so confusing. It's hard to explain. Anyone who has been clinically depressed—not just blue or sad—will understand what I'm trying to say.

I wasn't going to tell the whole truth. But I also didn't want to be known as some sort of addict. I really wasn't a substance-abuse guy back then. This was just the beginning of my self-medicating with alcohol. I drank with the boys, sure, but I worked too hard to let a good time affect my game. I was too obsessed with playing well to let that happen. And I wasn't some druggy or someone taking Oxycontin all the time. I'd never used drugs, never even tried marijuana. I didn't hang out with that kind of crowd. I was around it, sure, but players were very discreet with that shit. I didn't want anything to do with it. It was so important to me that people knew I wouldn't mess everything up with drugs or alcohol. I'd rather be known as mental-fucking-kooky.

So after a couple of weeks, I went public about being diagnosed with OCD. I told reporters I'd seen a psychiatrist and a psychologist who had diagnosed me. I stuck with the same story Dr. Butsch had told about the bad reaction to my pain medication and gave a bit of context to some of the stuff I was going through. My anxiety had gotten the best of me, and I finally had a name for something I struggled with my entire life.

"It just now got to the point where it was severe," I told the press. "It's under control now, though . . . I feel good and I know I'm getting better. The doctors think I should be able to resume my career very soon."

It was scary. But then all kinds of people wrote in to the Sabres and thanked me for speaking about this publicly. It felt good to know that others felt the same way I did and that I'd managed to help them in some way by sharing my struggle.

But it wasn't even close to being done.

The Sabres sent me down to Rochester in the American Hockey League on a conditioning stint. The doctor I was seeing there had me on Prozac. I remember thinking I was cured, or at least hoping I was. I just wanted to get back on the ice and leave everything behind me.

When you're messed up like that, you can't tell if you're feeling good or not. How do you know what normal feels like? Prozac made me shake. It didn't work very well, but I kept thinking, *I'm on this drug—I must be okay. I have to be okay. I'm seeing this doctor. I'm getting help.* But it really wasn't helping. Eventually, the doctor in Rochester switched me to another drug called Haldol, which is an antipsychotic. It made me feel like a zombie.

We played the Binghamton Rangers in my first game down in the AHL. I shut them out and the fans were chanting my name. I wasn't healthy yet, but I came back strong between the pipes—regardless of what was going on in my head, I could still play the game.

The Binghamton players laughed at me every time I skated by their bench—"Hey, you crazy fucker, take another pill." I was aggressive all game; I chopped guys and I pushed guys. It was pure rage. Near the end of the third, when we were up 2–0, one of the Rangers forwards chirped me during a stoppage in play: "You need a happy pill to make you feel good?" The game was pretty much over and we were going to win anyway. So I thought, *You don't know the hell I've been through.* I took off my mask and my mitts and set everything on top of the net. Then I turned around and pummelled him. I kicked his ass all over the ice. It started a line brawl. When the linesman had us tied up, another of the Binghamton players said something about being crazy. I don't know who it was, but I threw a right hand over the linesman and knocked him on his ass.

I got a shutout, was the game's first star and started a line brawl in my return. I was really proud of that game. Afterwards, I saw Binghamton's goalie, Mark LaForest, in the hallway. Mark was a veteran, too, and we'd played each other many times when he was with the Detroit Red Wings. I pummelled him in a line brawl when I was with the Nordiques. They called him Trees; he was a great guy. During the brawl, he stood at his blue line but didn't come after me. Goalies usually square off in these kinds of things. "Trees, why didn't you come down to fight?" I asked him. "Why'd you stop at the blue line?"

He just started laughing. "I just came down to make it look good," he said. "There was no way I was fighting you again."

I played one more game in the minors before returning to the Sabres' lineup. I felt confident because I'd played well and defended myself—*I beat that dumbass. I smoked him.* Obviously, I wasn't well. But, you know, that's hockey.

My first game back with the Sabres was in Quebec City, where it all began. It was April 14, the second-to-last game of the regular season.

It was the last game I would play in the NHL.

I was anxious before the puck dropped. I was glad to be back but very nervous. That season, the Nordiques had guys like Joe Sakic, Mats Sundin and Owen Nolan.

During a Nordiques rush, the puck came into our zone and Herb Raglan came barrelling in after it. I went out chasing the puck, and this guy went down on his knees and slid through me. I tried to jump over him, but he clipped me at the knees and I went up and over him. I landed right on my head and almost broke my neck. My legs hyperextended over top of me. I was down for a moment and Jim Pizzutelli, the trainer, came running out onto the ice thinking I might be paralyzed. Just as he got to me, I picked myself up and shouted, "You motherfucker!" Jim thought I was yelling at him. He saw the rage in my eyes. I was just looking around for anyone to pummel, so I pushed past Jim and went after the first guy I saw. I dropped my gloves and started throwing bombs. I didn't really care who it was, but it turned out to be Joe Sakic—the twenty-three-year-old future Hall of Famer that the Nordiques selected with the draft pick they exchanged for me and Dale Hunter. He was nowhere near the play when it happened. I'd just attacked Quebec's superstar. "It wasn't me!" he shouted as a linesman grabbed hold of me.

The game got rough after that. There was a line brawl, and a Nordiques fan jumped into our bench and Rob Ray drilled him about twenty times. Quebec lit us up 7–3. I didn't play terribly (five of their goals were on the power play), but I wasn't spectacular, either.

Afterwards, the Nordiques fans wanted blood. They were mad at me for going after Sakic, and at Ray for going after one of them. They surrounded our bus and rocked it back and forth as the driver tried to pull away without killing anyone. It felt like they were going to tip it over.

After a terrible start that cost Rick Dudley his job, we finished third in the Adams Division and faced Boston in the first round. I ended the season with twenty-nine games played and a 3.73 goals-against average. The Sabres called up rookie goalie Tom Draper in the playoffs and played him ahead of Puppa and me. He played very well, but we lost in seven games.

It was clear that I was on the way out of Buffalo. In June, the NHL held an expansion draft to stock the new teams in Ottawa and Tampa Bay, and the Sabres left me off their protected list. I was the most experienced goalie on the market, with 338 games played, a 3.47 career goals-against average and twelve shutouts, but I wasn't one of the four goalies chosen. The Ottawa Senators chose Peter Sidorkiewicz and Mark LaForest—Trees hadn't played in the NHL since 1989–90. Tampa Bay took Wendell Young and Fred Chabot (who was traded back to Montreal). I didn't mind at the time because I still hoped to stick with the Sabres. But in August, the Sabres picked up Dominik Hasek from Chicago. He would go on to do quite a few noteworthy things in Buffalo. We didn't interact much—we only really crossed paths in training camp.

I drank a lot that summer. When I returned to Buffalo for training camp, I was terrible. I was known for doing well in the pre-season because I always showed up in shape and ready to play. I was hoping to do well in camp, but my head wasn't right. I was a step behind, and everyone knew it. Buffalo put me on waivers before the season started, but no team picked me up. Before one of the practices near the end of training camp, John Muckler, who had taken over as our coach when Rick Dudley was fired a third of the way into the 1991–92 season, called me into his office. I sat down. John was always a straightforward guy. He looked me in the eye and said, "Clint, I think you can still play in the NHL. But not for us."

I didn't say anything. I was broken, but I was impressed with his honesty.

"You've got two options," John said. "Rick Dudley wants you down in San Diego, in the IHL. And the Canadian Olympic team would like you to play for them."

For the first time in my life, hockey wasn't the most important thing. My problems had consumed me. I couldn't do the Olympic thing, because I'd be in Europe all the time and I wanted to be able to see my daughter, Kelli. Meanwhile, I still had a good relationship with Dudley. It was the only option left.

I packed my bags and went west.

17

Can't Do This

THE SAN DIEGO GULLS WERE MADE UP OF A BUNCH OF FORMER pros who had found themselves on the last legs of their professional careers for some reason or another. At the time, the American Hockey League, with sixteen teams, was the primary development league for the NHL. Buffalo's main farm team, the Rochester Americans, were in the AHL, for example. The International Hockey League, in which San Diego played, was a mix of NHL farm teams and independents. We were in the latter category, and we had a stacked team with a few ex-Sabres, including Lindy Ruff, Scott Arniel and Dale DeGray. Rick Knickle and I shared the goaltending duties. The Sabres picked up most of my $230,000 salary.

Several articles were written about my condition when I arrived in San Diego. It was a novelty to have an athlete talking about this kind of stuff. After getting over my initial fears, I was okay with sharing. I framed the move to San Diego as a positive development. "It's great weather, always sunny after all those gloomy winter days in Buffalo," I said. "My health has come a long way. You have your good and bad days."

But I was just as screwed up in San Diego as I had been in Buffalo. I remember thinking, *I'm on this medication now. I must be doing better.* I'd seen all these doctors. They'd put me on Prozac and then switched me off it because it made me shake. They'd put me on this other stuff, called Haldol, and then one called Orap, which is like a tranquilizer.

You're hoping and thinking you're doing better, and believing maybe you are. But you don't know because you've been screwed up in the head so long. You've got nothing to measure your state of mind against. It didn't seem the drugs were working, because I wanted to sleep all day. I'd lock myself in our bedroom and wouldn't leave unless I was going to the rink. I didn't leave the house. I hardly left my room. I cried constantly.

My second wife and I weren't divorced yet. She was pregnant, but the marriage was doomed. She saw me at my craziest. She actually suggested that I see an exorcist—she wasn't kidding. She even tried to arrange a meeting with a priest. My mom told her she needed a lobotomy.

The suicidal thoughts wouldn't stop. I didn't care whether I was dead or alive. If I was hit by a car and killed, I'd be cool with that. That's where my mind was at the time. I probably hadn't slept in God knows how long.

I'd call my mom mostly and she'd just say, "Hang in there, Clint. Hang in there." It was like every day was Sunday night before returning to Elmwood Elementary. She was dragging me back to life.

One desperate afternoon, I dropped to my knees in the bedroom and prayed: *God, either fix me or take me.*

The Sabres called me back up to the NHL in late November. Hasek had pulled his groin, and I was flown across the country to back up Puppa. There were rumours that Buffalo was trying to trade me to the Ottawa Senators. At the time, I had a 2.35 goals-against average, with six wins and no losses with the Gulls. On the ice, life was good. Off the ice, life was hell.

It was weird being back after being dismissed. The team's strength coach, Chris Reichart—a good friend—picked me up at the airport. I basically sat on the bench, and then the Sabres sent me back to San Diego. I stayed at Chris's house that night. I broke down there. We went for a long walk until about three in the morning. "I can't do this anymore," I told him. "I can't do this."

The next day, Chris drove me back to the airport, and I cried the whole way. I knew I was going back down to the minors—but I wasn't crying because of that. The tears just came and I couldn't hold them back. I was so depressed.

Chris was such a good man. He didn't know what to say or what to do, but he tried. What do you say to a full-blown lunatic?

Let me tell you, I'd rather have a broken femur or a broken back, any physical pain, than that depression. Clinical depression is just—I mean, I asked God to take me. Kill me. I didn't have the balls to do it myself. But feeling the way I did, I didn't even want to live.

When I got back to San Diego, my wife was gone. She just packed up and left—she wouldn't answer my calls or anything. Shortly after that, we had a game against Salt Lake and I allowed four goals on the first five shots of the game. Duds yanked me just over a minute into the second period. I sat on the bench with my head going a hundred miles an hour. I remember thinking, *I can't do this. I just can't do this. I don't think I'm any better. I may be worse.* Everything was caving in on me. It felt like I was having a nervous breakdown.

I went into Dudley's office after the game. I was crying—sobbing, really. I was a mess. "Duds, I'm done," I said. "I quit. I know you brought me here to give me a chance, but I'm just getting worse."

"Okay, Clint," he said, "I understand. I don't care about hockey. We're going to get you some help."

He could have said, "We'll just get somebody else. You're thirty-one years old—away you go." Instead, he called in the team doctor and promised that the organization would be with me while I got the help I needed.

Dudley saved my life that day.

We met with Don Waddell, our general manager, who was also very supportive. I took an indefinite leave from the Gulls. They had the team physician arrange for me to meet with a specialist at the University of San Diego who turned out to be one of the nation's leading experts on obsessive-compulsive disorder.

I met Dr. Stephen Stahl at his office in La Jolla. By this time, I was so sick of doctors, and it felt like he was the hundredth expert I'd seen about this shit.

We sat across from each other. He asked me about the prescription my doctor in Rochester had given me. I was staring at him, thinking, *You're full of horseshit. You know nothing.*

"Prozac, first. Then he switched me to Haldol. Then Orap."

"Haldol?" he repeated. "When was this?"

"I was in Buffalo."

"And you were playing hockey?"

"Yes."

"And you're a goalie?"

"Yes."

"That stuff will make you . . . ," he paused. "I can't believe they had you on Haldol."

Basically, I was having pucks shot at me at a hundred miles an hour while I was a zombie. I was trying to play NHL hockey on a schizophrenic downer. Dr. Stahl didn't say much more, but I could tell he was thinking, *Holy shit.*

He scribbled in his notebook and handed me a prescription for a drug called Zoloft and told me to come back in a week.

"Aren't you going to talk to me about my childhood?"

"No," he said. "Why?"

The psychiatrists and psychologists I'd seen in the past had all followed the same pattern. They'd all wanted to interrogate me. Yeah, I had a bad childhood. Who didn't? I got tired of it—*Yeah, my dad did this, my dad did that . . .* You know, who really cares?

I just wanted someone to fix me once and for all.

"Clint, your problem is a chemical imbalance," he said. We're going to get you on the right medication to fix that."

Nothing changed that first week. I stayed inside the whole time—I was in one of the sunniest cities in America, and I just wanted to sit in darkness. I was consumed with my marriage. *I know it's not good. She doesn't understand; I don't understand.* It seemed there was no way to fix it. I was away from the team the whole time. I didn't skate or train at all.

"I've struggled with the problem ever since I was diagnosed last

January," I told reporters. "We're using this week to try to get things stabilized, then we'll take it from there. This disease has affected my career, my life and my marriage. I've tried to make a go of it while being sick, but the problem is that when you're on the medication—most of them—you can't play hockey. At least, you can't be a goalie."

It was the same week after week. No change, but Dr. Stahl kept telling me to stick with the Zoloft. It would take some time to kick in, he said. I'd see him once a week, week after week. I figured the outcome would be the same as it always had been. I wasn't skeptical; I was desperate, and hope was fading.

And then, after six weeks, I woke up and—swear to God—walked outside and wanted to be there. I mean, it was San Diego! I wanted to be outdoors. I wanted to go to the rink. I drove to Dr. Stahl's office for our meeting.

"The depression's lifted," I said. "I've never felt this good."

He said, "Great, let's give it three more weeks," and upped my prescription. I was starting to see a little light. Dr. Stahl said if the drug was working, the depression would ease up. Then we'd see what it'd do for the OCD. I returned to the team around then. It felt great to be back on the ice. The game meant something to me again.

It took nine weeks to finally understand—maybe for the first time ever—what normal feels like. I wasn't depressed. I wasn't obsessive. Stahl told me I was a special, special case. I was dealing with such extreme OCD, and the drug usually only gets you about 60 per cent better. I thought, *I'll take it!* I could have kissed him.

"Good, good," Dr. Stahl said. "We've just got to keep you on it."

I did a feature interview with the *Los Angeles Times* that revealed the reality of my ongoing struggle more candidly than I had allowed myself to do in the past. I explained my obsessions and anxieties. About watching a TV show with an unfaithful spouse in it and becoming convinced that my own wife was doing the same. Or hitting a bump while driving my car and becoming so convinced that I'd hit someone that I'd circle back to look for the body.

"Ultimately, I want to keep playing," I told Rachel Blount of the

Times. "But I want to be happy, too. I would love to be able to resurrect my career and get back to the NHL. I dream of beating the odds and coming back and having another year or two in the NHL. But I can't lose my life doing it. It's been a struggle all my life. It's been so much pressure that I just want it to stop. Sometimes, I wish God would come down and take it all away."

After those nine weeks, I really enjoyed life for the first time in I don't know how many years. It was as though God had come down and touched me on the forehead and said, "Have fun now, son." For the first time, it seemed, he'd actually answered my prayers.

I played exceptional hockey when I returned to San Diego. The game felt natural again. I did an interview with CNN about my battle with mental illness. I did an interview with Prime Ticket. Mental illness in pro sports was rarely discussed back then, but I felt like I needed to share my story.

I was haunted by thoughts of all the things that could have been. There was no question that my play had been affected by my mental state or that my successful return to Buffalo after the breakdown had been limited by the prescription drugs I was taking at that time.

My goal now was to make it back to the NHL and prove that I belonged there.

18

Sin City

AFTER THE SEASON ENDED, MY CONTRACT EXPIRED. THE YEAR IN San Diego had been a success—the Gulls had led the IHL with sixty-two wins and 132 points and reached the Turner Cup final—but staying on was not an option. The team had become affiliated with the expansion Mighty Ducks of Anaheim, and they needed my roster spot to develop talent for the parent club. Besides, Rick Dudley had taken a new job coaching the Phoenix Roadrunners. It was time to move on.

The Canadian national team was still interested in me, but it wasn't an Olympic year. Meantime, the IHL had placed a new franchise in Las Vegas, and the team's general manager, Bob Strumm, asked me to come and be one of the team's marquee players. I was in the middle of my second divorce. I had a little girl and a little boy in my life. My son, Jed, went with my wife when she left me. He was still just a baby, and I didn't get to see him very often. Kelli had recently moved to Australia with her mother. She came to visit when she was out of school. She was about nine at the time. We drove together from San Diego to Vegas to meet with Bob to discuss the possibility of my future with the Thunder, and then continued on to Alberta, where I always spent the off-season. After everything I'd been through in the past few years, it was nice to have my little girl by my side again. On the last leg of our trip together, I asked Kelli where she thought I should start the next chapter in my career.

"Las Vegas," she said.

"Why?"

"Because I like it there," she said.

I thought about it for a moment. "You know what? I like it there, too."

Kelli went back to Australia shortly after our trip across the western part of North America. She would have been five or six when she and her mother moved there. It was a tough void to overcome. My baby girl was a world away.

For an obsessive-compulsive person, Vegas probably seemed like one of the worst places to wind up—booze and cards, 24/7. I was never much of a gambler, though. But Vegas is a city built for insomniacs—at least if I couldn't sleep, I'd have company. And the ranch life appealed to me. It reminded me of the life I loved back in Grand Prairie when I was a kid. There was something peaceful about the vastness beyond the bright lights.

I wanted to enjoy going to the rink again. It was something I'd started to get back near the end of my time in San Diego, when Dr. Stahl had me all figured out and the pressure of playing was no longer amplified the way it had been by OCD. I was so happy to feel normal, and I didn't want to mess it up. But then, that would have been too easy.

I drank a lot in the summer of 1993 and never really stopped. It got out of hand. I was distraught about leaving my two-year-old son, Jed, behind in Calgary. I was still going through an ugly divorce, and Wife Number Two was keeping me from seeing him. I struggled that summer. I was crying hard as I was driving out of Calgary. The city was my security blanket, and here I was, leaving, not knowing what the hell I was doing with my life. When I crossed the border into Montana, I stopped at a liquor store and picked up a bottle of vodka. I was feeling crappy. The next thing I remember is waking up at a rest stop just outside of Vegas. It was dark, and I could see the bright lights reaching up into the sky. I can't remember much about that drive.

It was the week before training camp, and we had some ice time the next morning. The problem was, there's no last call in Vegas. So I drove to the strip and found a bar in one of the casinos. I just sat there as the gamblers filtered around me, and I drank and had a good time.

Suddenly, I was feeling tired. I went out and started my truck at maybe four or five in the morning. Then I remembered we had ice at ten. At this point in my drinking career, I didn't even notice the hangovers. I was out all night and looking for happy hour at lunch the next day.

After about three or four days of that, I knew I couldn't live in this goddamn town and drink to drown my sorrows and still play hockey.

The Thunder flew to Regina for training camp that year. I sat in the hotel, craving a drink. *I can't keep doing this. I need help.* There was a phone book in one of the drawers. I flipped through it and found a number for a local chapter of Alcoholics Anonymous. A kind voice answered.

"I don't know how this works," I said. "I'm from out of town."

"Stay there. We'll have somebody pick you up," the man said. "In fact, we have somebody who just called from your hotel. We'll pick you both up, if that's okay."

A few minutes later, there was a knock at my door. It was one of the other players. He'd been sober for less than a year. We went down to the lobby together, a van picked us up and I went to my first AA meeting.

They went around the room with the typical introduction: "Hi, I'm Fred and I'm an alcoholic." My turn came. I took a breath and said, "Hi, I'm Clint. This is my first meeting. And the jury is still out. I'm not sure."

Everybody told a story. I didn't share mine. They all had pretty devastating tales, but it was nothing compared to what I'd been doing to myself.

Back in my hotel room that night, I lay there awake, thinking about whether I wanted to admit to yet another failure in my life. Then I thought of my dad. There was really no choice. I went back the next night. "Hi, I'm Clint and I'm an alcoholic."

I didn't have another drink for eight years. From that meeting in Regina, eight straight years. It's hard, but I don't think I suffered from the same kind of addiction that other alcoholics have. It was a self-medicating thing. I think I overindulge more than most people do, and my problem was rooted more in that than in dependency.

I was just ready to change my life. I was going through my second divorce, I felt that I had really been helped with my OCD in San Diego and I was getting a new lease on life. The medication was giving me relief, and things were going well in hockey. I wasn't obsessing as much as I had been—I was functional. I looked inside and said, *You know what? You're just giving yourself one more problem to deal with here. You have to deal with this divorce and your kids and all that. But you can do it.* I realized I couldn't afford to screw things up by drinking myself to death, just to deal with being lonely and getting a divorce. Eight goddamn years without a drink. Incredible, until they were gone.

Hockey in Vegas was an anomaly back in 1993 when the Thunder opened their first season in the IHL. For the future and fading stars who had come to the desert to play a winter sport, it was an unfamiliar, glitzy world. Bringing the game to Vegas was a unique and exciting challenge. The team's owners—the father-and-son duo of Hank and Ken Stickney—knew how to sell an experience to the fans. They both owned baseball teams in the California League, even though Ken was only thirty, and co-owned the Triple-A Las Vegas Stars of the Pacific Coast League. At the time, few who called the City of Sin home could tell a hockey puck from a urinal puck, so we weren't selling just the league to fans—we were selling the entire package.

Bob Strumm strung as many blinking lights on his new franchise as he could. My photo went up on a billboard in town. It was so cool— to be on a billboard in Vegas, where you'd find celebrities like Wayne Newton and people like that. We played out of the Thomas and Mack Center at the University of Nevada, Las Vegas, where the Runnin' Rebels were consistently one of the top teams in men's NCAA basketball under controversial coach Jerry Tarkanian.

The lights went dark before every game and our team skated out under spotlights. Songs like "Bad to the Bone" and "The Boys Are Back in Town" pumped through the PA system. After every home goal, fireworks exploded at centre ice. The Zamboni was sponsored by Caesar's

Palace. The advertisements along the boards advertised venues like the Girls of Glitter Gulch, a nearby topless bar. After each period, one of the girls from Glitter Gulch carried a ring card around the ice announcing the next frame.

Strumm had been the general manager of the Canadian team that won the world junior championship in 1982. He brought in NHL veteran Butch Goring to be our coach. Our best player was a seventeen-year-old Czech named Radek Bonk who was considered one of the top NHL prospects in the game. Bonk had played a season of professional hockey in Czechoslovakia before coming to North America to get more experience and raise his stock in advance of the NHL draft. He did all right: 87 points, 42 goals and 208 penalty minutes in 76 games. In the 1994 NHL draft, he went third overall to the Ottawa Senators.

We also employed one of the craziest hockey players I've ever met. Kerry Toporowski came to us from Indianapolis partway through the season. I once asked Bob Strumm to name the toughest player he'd ever had play for or against his team. We're talking guys like Stu Grimson and "the Missing" Link Gaetz. Strumm said, without question, it was Toporowski. He was one of those guys for whom the adrenaline just took over—their eyes roll back in their head and they don't feel pain. I'd like to nominate myself for that category, too. I know what it means to go to Mars or Pluto.

When I met Kerry, I knew I wasn't that screwed up, because this guy could tear a planet apart. No disrespect to him—or to Rick Dudley, who was a member of the same club—but it's very comforting to know you're not the only kook. Of all the guys I played with, Kerry was the craziest. A lot of tough guys are predictable, but Kerry went to a different place. He was a good guy to have on your side.

During one line brawl with the Houston Aeros, I skated down the ice to fight their goalie, Troy Gamble. He kept his blocker on when we fought, which added six inches to his reach, and he was drilling the blocker into my forehead. The fans in Vegas were pushing against the glass, shaking it like it was going to come down. Then I just destroyed Gamble. I probably got him with ten straight shots before the refs jumped in. After the brawl, Kerry started taunting their bench, challenging them all to fight.

After the game, I saw Troy walking by.

"Hey, how you doing?" I asked. I was always friendly with the guys I fought. It's an unwritten hockey rule: you bond after spilling blood.

Gamble just shook his head.

"Ah, fuck man," he said, "why did you do that?"

"You took chunks out of my head with your blocker," I said. "I had a right." Another rule in the unwritten code.

We finished first overall with fifty-two wins against twenty-nine losses—eleven of them in overtime. Almost every game was a sellout, with an average attendance of 7,185—an impressive number for an expansion hockey team in the desert. The fans embraced me there. Including preseason and playoffs, I played fifty-five games, earning thirty-four wins with a 3.36 goals-against average. But I also got involved in the community, doing a bunch of charity work. It was right up my alley—I've always loved to do that kind of stuff. I was on the board of the Nevada Foundation for Child Cancer. I would go to meetings in my jeans and cowboy hat when everyone else dressed in suits. I'd put my feet up on the table. They deferred to me on a lot of questions for some reason. I always gave the same answer: "It's all about the kids, man. It's all about the kids."

Once a week, I'd go to the hospital to visit the kids and bring them all kinds of souvenirs from the Thunder. I considered it part of my job as a hockey player. You have a direct avenue to help people, and you're automatically a heavy hitter with the kids. I used to try to recruit guys to come with me. Most didn't want to—they were too uncomfortable. It was a harsh reality that a lot of these kids weren't going to make it.

I got to know a lot of parents who were going through an unthinkable reality. These poor kids were always tired, usually doped up on pain medication or a cancer treatment, so you'd bring gifts, and the next thing you know, they're sleeping. I spent a lot of time talking to parents next to their brave little kids and became friends with a lot of them. Far too often, their kid would die. The funerals were so difficult. It's hard to not be grateful for the life you have at times like that. And that unquenchable pain—no parent should ever have to go through that.

I stayed in touch with several of those families.

One of the kids I visited was named Brian. He was fortunate to survive his battle with cancer. His dad was a cop in Nevada at the time, but he ended up being the speaker of the state assembly. I got an email from him maybe a decade after we met in the hospital. He told me Brian ended up playing roller hockey. We exchanged a few heartfelt emails. Being able to connect with these kinds of people is one of the things I cherish most about the opportunities hockey afforded me, even after my NHL days were done.

After my first season in Las Vegas, my agent, Daniel Sauve, started to get interest from NHL teams. The Boston Bruins were one of them. They were looking for a veteran goalie, and my success with the Thunder hadn't gone unnoticed. It wasn't a sure thing, but it was interest nonetheless. The thought of going back to the NHL excited me—I wanted to prove that I was strong enough to make it back. But at the same time, I was afraid of drifting back into what I'd overcome. I was pretty content in Vegas, and truthfully I worried that I couldn't handle the pressure cooker. I was afraid things would go south if I left this comfort zone.

I was a hockey player in the minor leagues—of course I wanted to be back in the NHL. Of course I wanted to prove those fuckers wrong— to prove that I belonged. But I was going to AA at the time. I had things together. I was loving life. My shitty second marriage was over. I had a whole new deck to play with in Vegas. Finally, I was getting things right. The thought of losing it all by trying to get it all terrified me. Normally, any player in the minors would leap at a shot at the show, with no hesitation. But I wasn't normal. I went to Strumm and told him my situation.

Strumm and I had a great relationship. He knew I could have left, but he also knew that I had a special connection with the Vegas fans. So Strummer said, "Listen, Clint. This is what we'll offer you. As long

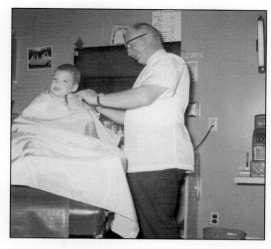

My first haircut.

My first season as a goalie, with the Elmwood mite B team back in 1970. This picture was in the local paper. Notice my stylish sweater.

A team photo with my Elmwood mite A team. We practised and played outside most of the time. My dad was one of the coaches. He's on the left.

My photo with the Ironco bantam AA in Edmonton in 1973. I'm second from the far right in the bottom row.

My older brother, Garth, gives me a baseball trophy. I always looked up to Garth. He was a father figure to me.

Holding a Cooper GM12 catcher, a Christmas gift from Garth. The best gift I ever received.

Making a save on Christmas morning while testing out our new hockey net. Look closely and you'll see a string attaching the puck to the ceiling.

With Bobby Orr (*left*) and Mike Walton at hockey camp in Ontario. It was my first trip away from home, and I was terribly homesick the entire time.

One of the many masks my mother made over the years. It was fibreglass. Every mask I wore until the mid-eighties, even as a Nordique, was made by her.

Terry, Garth and me, sitting in front of our mantel of trophies. We went through a lot together. I was lucky to have older siblings like them.

My team photo with my midget AA team, the Canadian Athletic Club from Westgate. I'm third in from the left in the bottom row.

Before I made it to Portland, I played Tier II with the Fort Saskatchewan Traders when I was sixteen. We played about an hour outside of Edmonton. It was just Mom and I living together at the time.

Wearing my cowboy hat on my first day of training camp with the Portland Winterhawks.

Corralling the puck as a junior in Portland. I played two seasons with the Winterhawks. It was a great hockey city.

Making a sliding save with the Winterhawks.

Kicking out a save with the Winterhawks. I'm wearing one of the masks my mom made for me.

A team meeting with the Winterhawks during my first season in Portland.

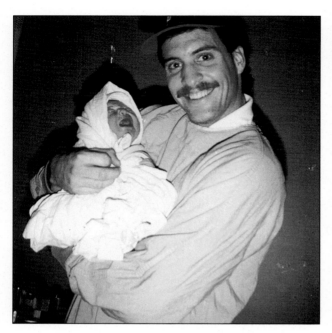

Welcoming my beautiful daughter Kelli into the world.

Quebec City was a great place to play hockey. The Nordiques had passionate fans, and I got to play with stars like Michel Goulet, Peter Stastny and my partner in crime, Dale Hunter.

I was selected for the 1986–87 Rendez-Vous All-Star tournament, one of the highlights of my career.

I played only a couple of seasons with the Capitals, but I had a lot of fun. We had a great team with great chemistry, but we never had luck in the playoffs.

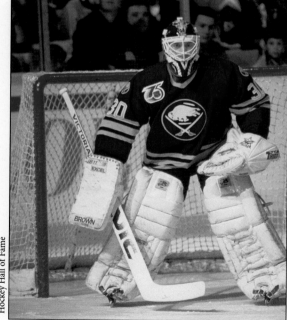

I was at the height of my career when I joined the Sabres in 1989. But in just a couple of weeks, everything would change.

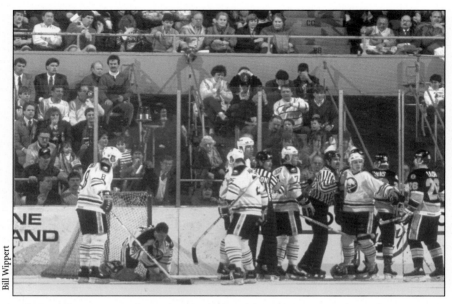

The accident on March 22, 1989. I was rushed off the ice through the doors behind me. If I had been at the other end of the rink, I might have died.

My return to the Buffalo Aud after the jugular accident. The crowd gave me a standing ovation during a stop in play. I was still weak from losing so much blood.

During a TV interview while I was playing in Vegas, I showed the reporter how to make a horse rear up. I landed safely in a crouch.

Up in lights at a Vegas casino, where I was signing autographs after I'd joined the Thunder.

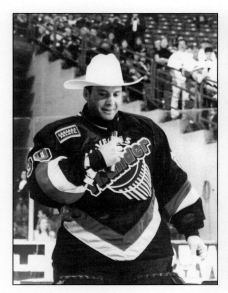

Making a speech after my last game. I was proud to retire as a member of the Las Vegas Thunder.

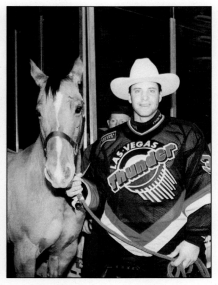

Hanging out with Ace, who was given to me as a retirement gift by the Las Vegas Thunder.

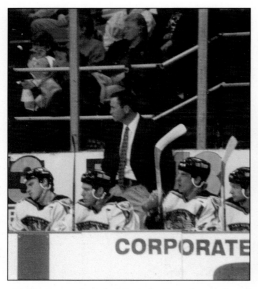

Taking my place behind the bench as a head coach in Vegas after my playing days were done.

All suited up on the day I married Joanie, on our ranch in Nevada.

Joanie and me on our wedding day. We were married at Lake Tahoe in front of a small group of family and friends.

Stretching before an alumni game in Vegas.

Garth, Mom and me.

Taking care of a foal on
our ranch in Nevada.

A day at Lake Tahoe with my three wonderful kids, Kelli, Dallyn and Jed.

Riding a mustang on our ranch.

A little kiss for a foal on our ranch. We're always welcoming new additions.

A checkup with one of my clients, in my second profession as an equine dentist.

Joanie and me at the Calgary Stampede.

Chasing down a
steer on our ranch
in Nevada.

Left: Christmas has always been a big event for us. Even Santa gets into the cowboy spirit.

Above: Instructing U.S. Army troops on horsemanship. These soldiers were being deployed to Afghanistan to hunt for Bin Laden in the mountains on horseback.

Working with a new generation of goalies at High Altitude Goalie Camp in South Lake Tahoe, California.

as you can play, we will match." My salary that first season was around $40,000—a lot less than I'd made in my NHL contracts. They offered $130,000, figuring that would be what an offer from the Bruins might look like. It was a huge raise and a considerable sum for the minor pros. The deal was to play for another season or two and then transition into a coaching or management role with the team. Strumm knew I was thinking about my future beyond the game, and coaching was part of my plan. I looked at that opportunity knowing that my body was about to fall apart. I was in my mid-thirties, my back was bad, my knees were horrible. All things considered, this was my chance for a second life in the game. I don't have to prove shit to anybody anymore, I thought. I was happy.

Strumm sweetened the deal by offering me a signing bonus. I asked him if he could pay it out in horses—a strange request, but if I was going to build a life in Nevada, I'd need a proper ranch. Strumm agreed to throw in two horses that year and another horse for every year I played with the Thunder after that. I think it might have been the first pro contract with livestock involved. A local reporter asked me about the odd request. I told him that I was going through a nasty divorce and that if she wanted to take half of what I owned, I knew which half of the horse she could have. The quote went over the wires and ended up in the *Hockey News*. I don't think she was too pleased.

Later, when I would look back on everything, I'd always get stuck wondering what could have been, thinking I should have tried one last time. But after two or three years of madness, the truth is my mind would have crumbled under the anxiety of a return. Did I really want to come back? Sure. Could I have survived? I'll never know.

I bought a beautiful ranch on the edge of Las Vegas. I invested in sixteen emus because they were a hot item at the time. Emu oil was in high demand. I had their fat boiled down into this oil and packaged under the Canuck Ranch brand name. We'd sell it to drugstores, athletes, sports teams.

The ranch had an amazing roping arena. It was paradise. I had a bunch of roping steers and put up lights so we could rope at night (it was so hot during the day). The National Finals Rodeo, the NFR, was always held in Vegas. I invited all those great riders out to rope at my ranch. Rod and Denny Hay, two brothers, almost missed the finals at the Thomas and Mack Center because they were roping at my house. It was like a hockey player being late for a game in the Stanley Cup final because he was playing ball hockey on some fan's street.

I met my third wife while I was in Vegas—she was working in the promotions department at a radio station that I did an interview at. We hit it off right away, and once again, it didn't take long before we were married. It was the first time I actually had a great connection with the person I married. She was lovely and we were really good friends.

We had more big names come through Vegas during the 1994–95 season. During the NHL lockout, Alexei Yashin, the young superstar from the Ottawa Senators, played twenty-four games with us. Manon Rheaume, the first woman to play in an NHL exhibition game, played with us, too. She was very good, but it was a big jump to face the speed and strength of the shooters in men's pro hockey. Rheaume played only fifty-two minutes in two games with us, but she packed the arena.

I finished that season with thirty-eight games and fifteen wins to my name. It was the last full campaign of my career.

19

Dad

MY DAD CALLED ME UP ONE NIGHT IN VEGAS. I HADN'T REALLY spoken to him in about twelve years—he had left, and that was it. My parents divorced and he was out of my life. He didn't see me play junior in Fort Saskatchewan. He wasn't there when I made it to the Portland Winterhawks. He wasn't there for my first NHL game.

Later, when I played against the Edmonton Oilers, my family would always be there—Mom and Garth, and Terry, if she was in town. They'd come down under the seats after the game to meet me when I left the dressing room.

Sometimes, my dad would show up. We'd be down near the bus, in the parking area underneath the arena, and he'd be hiding behind a pole, kind of sticking his head out.

"I didn't want to bother anyone, Clint," he'd say. "I just wanted to say hi."

That always got to me because he was there when I learned to skate, and when I first put on the pads, and when I first stopped a puck—but he skipped out on so much more. He didn't come to Fort Saskatchewan or Portland or even Fredericton. Damn, it would have been nice to have a dad then.

So I make the NHL and all of a sudden he's hiding at a game in Edmonton from the family he tore to pieces. He tried to get in touch with me more as my career went on, but it always seemed that, the more success I had, the more he wanted to be part of my life. I don't know if that's fair; I never knew his heart—but that's the way I took it.

Before he called that night, we'd lost total contact. I couldn't tell you the last time we'd had a conversation. He wanted to apologize.

"Clint, I'm sorry. I'm so proud of you."

He was crying. I couldn't tell if he was drunk, but I assumed he was. He said he was sorry over and over again, between sobs. It really made me uncomfortable.

"Listen, Dad," I said. "Listen. It's okay. I forgive you."

I hated him for what he had done to my mom, but I was an adult now, and as far as we went, I'd moved on.

He was crying still.

"I'm so sorry, I'm so sorry. I should have stayed with your mom," he said. "I fucked up."

"As far as I'm concerned, Dad, I forgive you." He was in a bad way, so I bought him a ticket to come down to Vegas.

When I was young, he always made sure I wore a sharp shirt and tie to games. It was a matter of self-respect and pride. He came off the plane in Vegas in this baggy old suit that wasn't his, and he had this short, fat tie on. He was missing most of his teeth. He was in his early sixties, but he'd aged so much, I barely recognized him.

Dad was all over Alberta through that lost decade. I think he'd married a couple of times. I know he had gone up to the Yukon and hooked up with a native woman. He bragged about how he taught people in Whitehorse how to plant gardens—as if they didn't know how. He ended up working as a handyman for room and board at a motel in northern Alberta.

We spent five days together. We got along really well and had some decent talks. He told me he wasn't drinking, but I knew he was. He'd stashed some booze in his luggage, and I could smell it on him. I didn't care, but it was like he really wanted me to believe that he wasn't drinking anymore. Maybe he thought it would make me proud of him. I don't know.

He cooked barbeque one night. It was really good; he put the vegetables in tin foil. We sat there eating dinner and then he reached into his mouth, gave a twist and pulled this rotted tooth out.

On his last night in Vegas, we sat on the porch at my ranch, just talking and staring at the stars. He was on again about how sorry he was for everything he'd done, saying how much he missed everything he'd lost along the way. He was well lit; I could smell the booze on him. He carried so much guilt, and he knew that he would never be able to make amends for the pain he had caused.

"I loved to dance," he said. "I loved to dance with your mother." He picked up a broom leaning against the wall, turned it upside down and slowly waltzed around the porch—twirling and twirling, singing softly to himself.

I realized then how much I'd lost. It was his fault, of course. He'd fallen into the bottle. I looked down on him from the edge. There were so many years lost to his disease. I think that's why I softened, knowing how rough the struggle was.

My mother tried so hard to love him. She tried to forgive him for the booze and the rage and the violence. She really loved him. She forgave him over and over until the guy who used to take her dancing fully became the monster inside him. It was the infidelity that turned her hurt into hate. When she hit the wall, she hit it hard. It was too much. I can't and won't blame her.

I really tried to hate him, too. I didn't understand it, because I was young. He's your dad. You can't just hate him. Maybe that was what screwed me up first. There was so much love and anger, confusion and fear. And this attempt to understand hate.

And here he was, this drunk sketch of a man—my dad, again. Waltzing with a broom on my porch. "I loved to dance with your mother," he said. "I'm sorry. I'm sorry. I'm sorry."

20

Retired

BY THE END OF THE 1994–95 SEASON, MY BODY WAS BREAKING down. I was in my mid-thirties and I knew I couldn't keep my game up to the standards I demanded of it. The Thunder offered me a position as assistant coach and assistant GM, so I retired and took the front-office position.

I wasn't completely done playing yet. In March 1996, the team asked me to suit up for one more game, and they put me in for the final five minutes of the first period. I turned away two shots, and when the period ended, my playing days were officially done. It was emotional. The Thunder retired my jersey right then and there, in a ceremony before the second period started. My mom, sister and brother-in-law made the trip from Canada to be there. My buddy Coleman Robinson came out, too. My dad wasn't there.

During the intermission, they pulled out a red carpet and brought my family down to the ice. There was a highlight video on the big screen, showing my best saves and footage of me picking up the horses the team had given me in my first season in Vegas. They presented me with a roping dummy and a cowboy hat, and then Coleman brought out this beautiful horse. It was a high-dollar rope horse—probably the fifth the Thunder had given me, but easily the finest one. I called him Ace. He's still alive, even though he's well over thirty.

Being an assistant coach wasn't that bad. I'd played with a lot of the guys on the team, so I already had a relationship with them. Chris McSorley was the head coach, and the players didn't really like him all that much. The two of us even clashed at times. Once, there was a trade rumour about one of our players, Ken Quinney, and Quinney came to me to ask about it. He'd been a teammate of mine in Quebec, and we had a good relationship. I told him he was on the block. Afterwards, I had a meeting with McSorley and Bob Strumm, the general manager. Strumm said, "Clint, you need to learn how to lie. In this business, you can never tell a player something like that."

Strummer saw my body language change the moment he said it.

"What? What the hell did you say?"

"Well, you have to learn to stretch the truth, Clint."

I was leaning over his desk now. He could see the anger rising. I went off.

"Are you kidding me? You want me to lie? I will not fucking lie. If that's what you think running a hockey business is, you guys have the wrong guy to do that. When Quinney came to me and I told him the truth, he lit up the scoreboard. Screw you guys."

I was livid. And I might have overreacted a bit. Strummer kept trying to talk me down. He's a guy that I love and respect. We're great friends. But I don't believe in lying to people, so I got my back up pretty quick. I'll tell you what I think, I'll tell you the truth—but I'll never screw you over with a lie. Later, I realized what Strummer meant. I should have said, "Ken, I don't know."

I was assistant coach until March 1998, when they fired McSorley and I took over as head coach for the last nineteen games of the season. I loved coaching, but one thing I refused to do was to sacrifice the good relationships I had built with the players. They would come into my office and I'd sit them down and tell it to them straight. The minors are unique, because you have guys coming in from all different levels of the game. Players were always shuffling up and down between the NHL and the IHL, so a lot of talent came through the Thunder. Curtis Joseph, already established as an NHLer, played a handful of games for us in 1995–96. Goalies Manny Legace and Tim Cheveldae shared the net a couple of years later. Pavol Demitra and Ruslan Salei joined the team in 1996–97. Sadly, both died in the tragic Lokomotiv Yaroslavl plane crash in 2011 that killed forty-four people.

In Vegas, I was in way over my head as a head coach, but my relationship with the players helped, and I hired a good assistant coach, Rod Buskas, who was very supportive. And Strummer was good, too. He was an excellent GM.

Being a head coach is fun because you're in control and you get to bring guys in and work with them on a personal basis. I liked to find out what was going on with my guys. I wanted to know what made them tick. "What's going on with your life? You married? Have a girlfriend?" I wanted to know because of all the shit that I had gone through. I didn't just want to be their coach—the game is nothing. I wanted to know the person. A lot of my old players still email me. I think that's why.

I don't know if that makes you a good coach. But I know that my players loved me. They went to the wall for me. They knew that if I gave them shit, it was from the heart.

In the minor leagues, whatever your job description, you end up doing a bit of everything. Sometimes I did color on the broadcasts of the Thunder's games, though my personality proved a bit too colorful for the gig. We only had about six games on TV each year. One time, John Van Boxmeer, my old teammate with the Quebec Nordiques, was in town coaching the Long Beach Ice Dogs. I kept calling him "John Van Pap Smear." I'd say, "There's a close-up shot of John Van Pap Smear." I was just joking around. I'd say it so quick, I don't think people realized. Tim Neverett was doing the play-by-play, and he was having fits. "You can't say that!" he said.

"Timmy, we're in Vegas," I said. "No one is watching this shit!"

I never told John about that. He might be offended by it, but it was funny.

In 1998, I was near the end of my player/coach contract in Vegas. Wife Number Three and I had a beautiful baby girl named Dallyn, and we were looking for a bit of a change from Vegas. The Idaho Steelheads in the West Coast Hockey League recruited me to come coach their team. It was a lower-calibre league, but we went out to visit and I took one look at the place and thought, *This is God's country.* It was beautiful—rolling fields and forests. Just gorgeous.

Back in Vegas, Strumm called me into his office and showed me what the owners were willing to give me to return as coach. It was an ungodly low number. The Las Vegas Thunder had been very good to me through those years. But I was also very good to them. I went above and beyond what they asked me to do as a community ambassador, because that was just me. I had a great career there. The fans loved me. Maybe the team thought I was so hooked on Vegas and the organization that they lowballed me. I mean, they lowballed me hard. The offer was for about $35,000. I had a wife and a baby—and two other kids to support. At the time, the lowest salaries for coaches in the league were somewhere around $80,000. "Fuck that," I said. It was insulting.

Strummer called me, trying to smooth things over. The owner called me, too. They bumped it up to $70,000. I told them to screw off. "After everything I've done?" I said. "I'm done." It wasn't a matter of money anymore. It was a matter of principle.

"You're one step away from coaching in the NHL," Strumm said. And he was right. A move like the one I was considering would be a demotion. But I didn't back down. Strumm had done a lot for me and we would always be good friends. But the team's second offer was a case of too little, too late. I called up the Steelheads and took the job. There were no hard feelings. I know Strummer was just doing what the owner told him to do.

Wife Number Three and I packed up and moved to our own private Idaho—a beautiful five-acre ranch in Nampa, a rural area with few houses and lots of farmland. On our first day in the new house, our neighbour came up to greet us. He was about eighty, dressed in overalls and a Carhartt jacket.

"You might have seen me on the news," he said.

"No . . . why?" I asked.

"Well, I shot some guy," he said.

"Um—really. Well, that's cool," I said. "What happened?"

Apparently, some kids had stolen beer from his fridge in the barn. I could see the barn from our doorstep.

"I heard their pickup truck take off down my lane, so I loaded my shotgun," he said. "I was shooting at them, and I guess I got one."

"I'm a pretty good neighbour," he added. "Just don't steal my beer."

"This is my kind of neighbourhood," I said, kidding. "I'm a country boy myself. I'd have shot him in the head."

"I was aiming for the head!" he said.

Sure enough, later that day, I turned on the TV and there he was, on the news. The old man had actually shot a kid for stealing his barn beer.

The Steelheads were only in their second year when I took over as coach. They had a brand new rink called the Bank of America Center. It seated about 5,200, and we always packed it out. The fans were great. We had a mix of really green young kids and older guys who just wanted to keep playing the game. Matt Loughran was the general manager. He was a great guy—very blunt, a straight shooter. After the first season, the owner told me they wanted to fire Matt and have me take on the dual role of coach and GM. The owner thought Matt was too confrontational. I said no way. Matt was a great guy who told people exactly what he thought. I respected that. He deserved better than to have the owners go behind his back and offer me his job. I wasn't going to be part of it.

Loyalty is all that matters to me. If you're an honest person, I'll be your friend for life. I don't waste time with people who are fake or people who are trying to use you to get something. I don't care about people who are afraid to say what they think. That was always what I liked about Matt. No way would I stab him in the back.

It was fall or winter—I can't remember the month. One afternoon, I got a call from my mother.

"I've got some bad news, Clint," she said. "Your father passed away."

It was a heart attack. He was sixty-seven and he was alone, living in a motel in some small town in Alberta, working as a handyman. That's how he got by in the end. He'd get free lodging while doing odds and ends in these motels. He was in Vegreville, he was in Bonnyville—all these different towns, doing the same thing. He was basically a vagrant.

I didn't go to his funeral. There was no reason to go up and see relatives I didn't know. No one from my immediate family was going. There would be no one there for me to share his memory with. I don't think my brother and sister ever made amends with my dad. My mother certainly wasn't going to the funeral.

I don't think I saw the worst of him. I know my brother saw different things, worse things, but I don't know what exactly. My sister did, too. We never spoke about it. Neither of them wanted anything to do with him. I know he called them here and there. He called me, usually when he was drunk, and he just spat out stuttered apologies. "I get it," I'd say. "I understand. Quit apologizing. You're killing me." Now I knew what alcohol could do. I knew how he lived and how he had been brought up.

I forgave him when he came to Vegas. We had formed a relationship, somewhat. We had made amends. I'd let go of my anger—I just felt sorry for him. He had problems. We had our problems. He wasn't at any of my weddings. But when my dad wasn't drinking, everyone loved him. He was funny and friendly. He coached hockey and baseball. He was there for kids. He did a lot. At one time, my dad was pretty involved in my hockey—through those early years, at least. Other stuff was going on, but he was always there for hockey. He really was.

I got off the phone with my mother and went for a long walk in the field by our ranch. I remember crying.

I had my own wake for him. "God, please understand," I prayed. "He wasn't a bad man. He was a sick man. Please take him to heaven. My dad was a good man."

After a couple years in Idaho, the Steelheads got a new GM and I was in limbo. I loved coaching, and I knew I was good at it, but it's hardly a stable profession. It's the harsh reality of being a coach that your job always depends on the guy above you. The team wouldn't tell me whether they would resign me for the 2000–01 season. I was so pissed off that they wouldn't just give me a straight answer. So I knew I needed to find a backup plan. There was an equine dentistry school about an hour away from our place in Idaho. I had always worked with horses and thought it might be smart to put some of that knowledge to use. So when the Steelheads still hadn't given me an answer by August, I drove over and signed up. Forget hockey; I was going back to school. The Steelheads called me shortly afterwards to talk about the job. There was no respect. I said, "No way, I'm already signed up for school—I'm done."

It was a three-year program, but I got it done in one. At the same time, I worked as a consultant with the Prince George Cougars of the Western Hockey League. I'd fly out there and work with their goalies. And I had a full-time horse dentistry business running out of Idaho. I was the first horse dentist/goalie consultant the world had ever seen.

I'd go out to B.C. to work with the Cougars' goalies and consult with team management. During one of those trips, I went out to a bar with a few of the coaches. I was drinking Diet Coke—I still hadn't touched alcohol in eight years.

I went to the can, came back and picked up what I thought was my Diet Coke. My taste buds quickly told me it was somebody else's Crown and Coke. *Shit, I just had a drink.* I smelt it and tasted it again—yep, definitely Crown and Coke. So I looked to my left, looked to my right and thought, *Well, guess I'm going to have my first drink.*

Damn, eight years. *Well, guess I blew that one. That's it.* It was like a shutout streak was over, or a run of consecutive games started. That's how I thought about it.

I thought maybe I could handle it now. After all, it'd been eight years. Clearly, I had self-control. So I ordered another one. And another. And another. I got liquored up pretty good.

I went out the next night again. Of course, these people didn't know about my issues with alcohol. I was there for a week, and I went pretty hard there—fell back into it. I went home to Idaho and thought I could handle it. And I did, at first. I didn't go drinking every night. I wasn't hung over every day. But it's a progressive problem. It's a disease that festers and builds. I had seen it happen with my dad—how he drowned in the booze and couldn't see clearly. He could see how he had pulled us in with him. But even when the lessons of the past stare you right in the face, it doesn't mean you're immune from making the same mistakes. I don't know if I was drinking because my dad was gone. I think I had dealt with that and didn't carry it with me consciously. But I was definitely drinking because of him—because his disease was my disease. Because he couldn't deal with his life and probably couldn't define his demons. I knew what OCD and depression were. I understood alcoholism. I've wondered if mental illness haunted my father like it haunted me. I'll never know, because he never did. Different times, different realities, different lives. Same problems.

The haunting had faded, but it always comes back stronger and louder and fiercer each time. I could see them clearly now—obsession, depression, booze—but it didn't matter. The demons were circling back. This time they wanted all of me.

East

AFTER TWO YEARS OF MY LIFE AS A HORSE DENTIST AND GOALIE consultant, my old friend Rick Dudley called me up one day in 2002. He was the general manager of the Florida Panthers at the time, and he wondered if I'd be interested in meeting with Mike Keenan about the team's vacancy for a goalie coach. I had applied for a position with the organization before, but it was already filled. When it opened up again, Duds gave me a shot at impressing Keenan, who would be making the choice.

I flew out to Florida, nervous as anything. I walked in thinking, *This is Iron Mike—this is going to be tough.* It was just him and me in the interview. But it went unbelievably well—we just clicked. We talked hockey for a while and then went out to dinner. Turns out I had him at hello. They offered me the job a couple days later. They hired me on a consulting basis at first, so I shuttled back and forth between Idaho and Florida. It was a critical moment for my career. I'd be working with Roberto Luongo, one of the best young goalies in the game. You can't get a better client than Lou. We hit it off right away.

The Panthers were a bad team. Essentially, Luongo *was* our team. He was all we had. He faced an ungodly number of shots every night, and Keenan expected him to stop them all. When I decided to become a coach, I promised myself I wouldn't forget what it was like to be a player. Some coaches forget what it's like to play. Getting yelled and screamed at, getting ripped in the papers—it's difficult for people to understand the amount of pressure these guys are under. Often, we forget that many of them are just kids.

How do you know what you need to do with a guy? You form a relationship. That's my coaching philosophy. I have to build trust. To know what makes them tick.

I think my guys knew that I really cared. I wasn't just doing drills. They knew that when they played badly, I felt bad for *them,* not for me. Well, I felt bad for me, too—I'm human, and I want to win. But I really cared about my guys.

There's so much pressure—from fans, media and management. When you get your ass reamed by the coach, or by the local columnist, it hurts. At least, it hurt me. That's why I wanted to be the guy who remembered how it felt, how it tore your soul out.

Players all say it doesn't bug them, that they never read the papers. Bullshit. They all do. You know it's there, and the curiosity can't be avoided. You want to know what's being said. That's why I think having a coach who can relate to what you're going through means a lot. When I played for Washington, Bryan Murray was tough, and it stung. He was a great coach, and I like him, but at the time—especially with all the shit I was going through—it really messed me up. For most coaches, that kind of feedback is rarely personal. But as a player, you're thinking, *He hates me.* And now you're struggling because you're worried that the coach wants you gone. Sometimes, if you're part of a staff, there's not a lot you can say because you can't undermine the head coach. But you *can* say, "Look, things aren't going great, you're getting your ass chewed, but you're a good player, a good guy. Keep your head up." I can tell a kid, "It's not personal. He's just trying to give you a kick in the ass."

So when I started working with the Panthers' goalies, I believed a huge part of my job was to be a buffer. Good old Iron Mike was notorious for being hard on goalies. I get that coaches whine about goalies because most of them have never been goalies, so it's tough for them to empathize. Head coaches have a lot going on, and when things don't go the way they need them to, it's their job to ask why. But a goalie can't afford to be caught worrying about that shit.

It was inevitable that I would have a run-in with Keenan. Louie hit a rough patch in mid-November through December. After each game, Keenan would get on me about him.

"You talk to your boy?"

"Yeah, I talked to him."

The next day, the same thing. "Goalie, you talk to your boy?" (That's what he always called me—"Goalie.")

"Yes, I talked to him."

The next day: "Talk to your boy?"

"Yes! I talked to him!"

Keenan was the head coach and was under a shitload of pressure. I know he couldn't keep track of the number of times he'd asked if I was doing my damn job, but it got annoying very quickly.

He asked me again after the morning skate the next day. Luongo wasn't playing poorly, but he wasn't magnificent, which is an expectation that has followed the poor guy since the New York Islanders took him fourth overall in 1997.

Once, when we were trailing after the first period, Keenan came into the coaches' office between periods and laid into me.

"Your boy there, did you talk to him?"

"Yeah, I did. And you know what? Go fuck yourself. Worry about your team, your job, and let me worry about the fucking goalies!"

The room went quiet. It was very early in the season. Part of me was just completely fed up with being asked if I was actually doing my job every goddamn day. But the other part of me realized he had a million things on his mind, and yeah, he has a right to expect the best from his players. Also, it's Mike Keenan—you know what you're getting. Cut him some slack. He was stressed because we were a terrible team and Louie was everything for us. I regretted the outburst immediately. I was certain I'd be fired.

The whole time this was going on, I never went to Louie and said, "Hey, holy shit, Mike is concerned with your play." Even after I told Mike off, I didn't want to lay that on my goalie's shoulders.

We lost the game. Keenan and I didn't talk afterwards, and I was sure I was about to get the axe. The phone rang in my hotel room just after 1 A.M. It was Keenan. *Shit, here we go.*

"Hey," he said. "What do you think of your goalie?"

"I think he's fucking good," I said. "What do you think of your team?"

"Ah, we're horseshit," he said.

"No shit."

"We okay?"

"Yeah, we're okay," I said. "We're good."

And that was it. After that, he and I were golden. A short time later, we got pounded 12–2 in Washington one night and hopped on a plane to New Jersey right after the game. The team checked into the hotel around midnight. Keenan said, "Goalie, meet me down here in fifteen minutes."

He trusted my opinion on our goalie. He didn't want to talk to anyone else about the game. We talked at the pub for about five minutes, and then we were just bullshitting over beers.

After Florida, Keenan always kept in touch, whenever either of us was looking for work or if something new started. Out of the blue, I'd just get an email: "Goalie, What are you doing? –Keenan."

I love Mike Keenan. He was always entertaining to work with. He and Duds used to go at it. Hockey is no fun when you're not winning. Especially when you're as competitive as Duds and Iron Mike.

I could see the same kind of competitive determination in Roberto Luongo. I could just tell he was going to be one of the best goalies of his generation. He was a great student, a great kid. His work ethic was incredible, which is something I could relate to. I used to have to send him off the ice. We had a great relationship.

He had great lateral movement, but he was never set. He could get from point A to point B faster than anyone, but he was never square and set for the shot. He worked so hard on that and was always receptive to my criticism.

We spent a lot of time together, on and off the ice. He was kind of a quiet guy, but he had a great sense of humour. I don't know how he handled the shit he went through with Vancouver, but I'm not surprised that he has come out on top. Not too many people could have done what he did with all the unfair criticism he received as a Canuck and the drawn-out situation with Cory Schneider.

Goalies are a different breed. I know how much confidence factors into it. I understand the pressure that these guys are under. I'm in a position where I have two guys I take care of. I observe who is down, who is up and what they need to get back on track. I think people underestimate the amount of pressure goalies face. My self-worth was dictated by the quality of my last game. And that's not right. If you have a bad game or let in a bad goal, you're still a good person. But we don't think that way. The focus on your play becomes microscopic. You can't help but fall into that trap. Maybe when you go home and have a wife and kids and a life away from the rink, you can get out of it. But on the ice, your self-worth is based on how you play and what the coach and the media think. It's not right, but that's the way it is. And my job as a goalie coach is to help them get past that. I try to soften it for them. Tell them, "Hell, just go out and work hard. Don't take what the coach says personally." Trust me, there isn't a physiological mindfuck that I haven't battled with. I can relate to it all.

Some goalie coaches really upset me. They focus entirely on the technical components of the position but don't address the psychological side. By the time a goalie gets to the NHL, they know all the technical stuff. They already have skill. Sure, you can always fine-tune, but you can't overhaul the way a goalie plays the game. The mental stuff is what goalie coaches should be most concerned about.

Coaches understand goaltending more than they used to. It's a part of the game that has really changed over the past couple of decades. When I was in Washington, sharing the net with Pete Peeters, the coaches weren't sure which one of us should start in the playoffs. Our goalie coach told me that one of the assistant coaches, Terry Murray, was worried about my ability to handle pressure because I used to isolate myself before games. I'd sit away from everyone else in the corner and be really quiet, thinking about the game. I really liked Terry, and I don't want to rip him. But when I found out about that, I was upset and surprised. They were worried about me because I was sitting by myself and staring off into space? That's what goalies do! What are you talking about? That's not something you should discourage! The goalie is concentrating. He's focusing. It's the most essential part of the position. The goalie coach shouldn't have told me what Terry said, but he should have explained to Terry how goalies work.

There are some goalies who deal with the pre-game pressure by laughing and goofing around with a nervous energy. There are others who need to isolate themselves. I did both. I really needed to get centred and do all that mental stuff.

Consistency is all mental. We all learned the physical stuff growing up. You can play well in one game, two games, three games—but how do you do it for forty or fifty in a row? That's what separates the good goalies from great goalies. It takes remarkable mental resilience to achieve that kind of consistency. It's the realm of guys like Patrick Roy and Martin Brodeur. If you were to take all the goalies in the NHL right now, I'll bet their physical skill level is pretty much the same. There are a few elite exceptions, like the recently retired Miikka Kiprusoff, but the majority are on the same level. Only the ones with the toughest mental approach to the game rise above the others.

To be honest, I think all goalies have OCD to a degree. The difference, I guess, is in how much they let it overtake their life. But the mind of a goalie is certainly obsessive. Think about all the stress at the NHL level. Your mind can do a lot of talking. When a goalie gets the wrong kind of shit stuck in his head, it becomes destructive in a hurry. And boy, can I relate to that. A goalie is going to go through some slumps, but if he doesn't have someone there to cushion the blow and advocate for him with a coach who's yelling and screaming about how much of a screw-up he is, that's only going to worsen the pressure the goalie feels. A goalie can have a shitty month or even a shitty year. The job of a goalie coach, as I see it, is to be there to take the heat from the head coach and get the guy back on his game.

In hockey, the easiest guy to point at is the goalie. You learn how true this is after playing a few years in the NHL, and if you're going to get anywhere you just learn to ignore it, play through it, do whatever you have to do to stay focused. Because nobody—coaches, media, fans, anyone who hasn't been an NHL goaltender—gets it. They don't understand. And you can't expect them to understand, because they've never done it. I'm sure quarterback coaches and pitching coaches can relate to what I'm saying. Everyone's saying your guy threw the wrong pitch, made the wrong pass. Well, they don't understand and you can't expect them to.

A good coach consciously reinforces what he wants the player's unconscious mind to do. You're constantly putting thoughts in your goalie's ear: *Keep this going. Just think about one game at a time. Don't worry about the next one.* You've got to fortify the notion that it's just one game. As a goalie coach, you have to keep them thinking day to day, game to game, period to period, puck to puck, save to save.

The job isn't just about working with the starting guy, though. Being a backup is one of the toughest roles in the game. Every situation is different. The backup could easily be in the minors tomorrow, but there's always the possibility of an injury to the starter and suddenly he becomes the number one guy for five months. But even then, the team might trade for some hotshot down the road. So you just tell them to keep doing what they're doing. And if they've been playing well, they might worry that they're just getting lucky. You have to put a stop to that. Goalies can't control anything but the way they play. Play like it's your last game and don't worry about anything else. At the end of the season, I'd often talk with my goalies about the pressure they felt during the season. With the spotlight temporarily off, they could see the bigger picture. All the negative headlines, the jeers from fans, the impossible expectations of coaches—they just distract. My goalies would often come to an important realization: *Are you kidding me? I wasn't that bad.*

"No, no you weren't," I'd say. "But welcome to the NHL."

Florida was a lot of fun. It was a great coaching staff—we just clicked. We all had a good sense of humour. One night, we went to a bar and ran into Michael Moorer, the boxer. I didn't recognize him, but our assistant coach, Steve Ludzik, did. Ludzy was a huge boxing fan. He was also a fan of winding me up. When I wasn't paying attention, he went over to Moorer and asked him to have some fun with me. I was wearing a cowboy hat and boots, like I usually do. Moorer came over to me at the bar and said, "You're a long way from home to be wearing a hat like that." I had no idea who this guy was. I turned to face him. He was big, dressed in this black turtleneck with gold chains around his neck. I took my hat off and set it on the bar, getting ready to throw a punch. Then all the guys started cracking up. They stepped in and informed me I was about to fight the former heavyweight champion. I'm glad they told me before I did something stupid! He could have hurt me pretty bad. Moorer and his bodyguard hung out with us for the rest of the night. (I'm not sure why a guy that tough would need a bodyguard.) We went to a few more bars. Nobody messed with us.

Even at the rink, we knew how to have a good time. Winning was serious business, but everything else was open season. My office at the arena was across from Dudley's. One day, the owner, Alan Cohen, was in there talking to Duds, who could see me from his desk. So I did a striptease behind the owner's back, peeling off the layers until I was completely naked and lying across my desk like a pinup girl. Duds had to bite his lip to keep from cracking up.

I knew he'd get my humour. He's one of the most serious guys I've met, but he's also one of the quirkiest. When Duds was coaching in Buffalo, we'd check into these five-star hotels and he'd be all dressed up in a suit, but he'd always have these gross old sneakers tied to his bag. At least he had the decency to keep them separate from the rest of his clothes. He was always a fitness fanatic. He put in a post-game workout area with stationary bikes in this empty loft section at the old Aud. We were one of the first teams to do that kind of stuff. Now everyone does it. Remember, when I first started in Quebec, our post-game routine involved a fridge full of beer and a hot tub. When we were in San Diego, he had the team doing all this plyometric stuff. None of us had even heard about that stuff back then, and we were professional athletes. The man has always been a step ahead of everyone else.

Duds also hated flying. We'd zigzag across the continent on these small chartered planes. Management always sat at the front of the plane (the way coaches do in minor hockey when teams travel by bus). But Duds always sat at the back of the plane, just sweating the whole time. Some of those flights were rough. We'd hit turbulence and hear him freaking out in the back—"Fuck! Get this thing down!" He'd just snap, gripping the headrest in front of him. The veins on his neck would bulge. I was worried he'd punch a hole in the wall and we'd all get sucked out.

I've never backed down from a fight, but I think one reason I always respected Duds was that he could pound me if necessary. The stories about his physical feats are boundless. One of the best is that he ripped a water fountain out of the wall when he was coaching the Detroit Vipers back in the mid-nineties. There was water pouring everywhere. It flooded the hall.

In Florida, one of the drawers in my desk was jammed because Duds picked the desk up and slammed it when he was angry. It was this huge, heavy desk that I probably couldn't lift. The drawer was jammed after that.

One time at a Panthers rookie camp, a couple of players came out of the dressing rooms and were fighting in the hall after being kicked out of the game. I guess this pissed Duds off, so outside the dressing room he flipped over a pop machine and it smashed. It was the size of a refrigerator. There were cans of Coke and Sprite rolling down the hallway. Later, I was walking down the same hall with him and passed the pop machine.

"I think that thing just shook a bit," I said.

The thing is, for a big guy who played a physical game, Rick hates goon hockey. He played tough but never coached like that. He has an intellectual approach to the game. He was smart enough to know what he had to do on the ice to stay in the league, and smart enough to see that he needed a different approach to be successful as a coach or general manager.

Rick has one of the sharpest hockey minds out there. He watches more hockey, at all levels, than anyone I've ever met. As general manager of the Tampa Bay Lightning from 1999 to 2002, he built the team that won the Cup in 2004. He builds teams, and then he gets bored! He was a huge part of everything the Chicago Blackhawks have achieved, including their Cup win in 2010, after he left his job as assistant GM to take over the Atlanta Thrashers. But he gets little credit for that. He's always on the go, building a winner and then moving on to the next challenge.

Most importantly, though, he's always had my back. If it weren't for him, I'd never have had the chance to share this story.

22

South

MY THIRD MARRIAGE LASTED SEVEN YEARS, WHICH WAS A RECORD for me. We didn't have any huge fights or an explosive end. It was just one of those things where life slowly pulls you apart, and you realize that, for all the good it brought, the relationship was just coming to an end. We had a beautiful daughter, Dallyn, who would always bind us together. But my wife and I weren't in love anymore. In fact, it wasn't until we decided to divorce that I had the chance to find out what head-over-heels, knock-you-on-your-ass *love* actually felt like.

And the 2004 NHL lockout is the reason I found it—because that's how I met Joanie Goodley.

The Florida Panthers sent me to San Antonio to work with the Rampage, their farm team in the American Hockey League. Joanie was the skating director and figure skating coach at the arena where the Rampage practised. She had just moved to Texas from Minnesota to take the job and be closer to her parents, who had retired nearby.

I noticed her right away. It was impossible not to. She was stunning. She was in her late thirties when we first met, but with no exaggeration, she looked at least a decade younger. And she had the sweetest, kindest heart. I had never met a woman like Joanie before. She was perfect.

There was an office in the arena with a window that looked outdoors. One day, before we'd really met, I was walking out to the parking lot with a group of coaches and, passing the window, I looked up and saw her. She was in the arena pro shop talking to a friend. I just stopped and stared. She looked up at me.

"Wow," I said. She read my lips through the window.

The next day, I went into the office to apologize for coming off rude—but really, I was just looking for an excuse to talk to her.

"Not at all," Joanie smiled. "It made my day."

Soon we were dating. We hit it off like nothing I'd ever experienced before. Joanie brought the best out in me. I was kind and caring and thoughtful. She became my best friend. Six months later, that February, I proposed to her at the San Antonio Rodeo. She had been teaching at the skating school all day, and I picked her up and surprised her with a last-minute date to the rodeo. Joanie loves horses almost as much as I do. (Her mom had always told her to move to Texas and meet a nice western cowboy. She couldn't have expected that when she did, he'd be from Canada.) At the rodeo, I took her down through the stables. She already knew I had studied as an equine dentist, but she didn't know much about it. She thought I was lying. As we walked through the barn, a lady led her horse in. I stopped her.

"Excuse me. I'm a horse dentist—do you mind if I take a look inside your horse's mouth?"

"Sure," she said. "No problem."

So I did a quick check. "Oh, my—I found something on his tooth," I said, and pulled Joanie over to take a look.

There was a ring around one of his canine teeth—I'd managed to slip it on without Joanie noticing.

Joanie was completely surprised. I pulled the ring off the tooth, got down on one knee and asked Joanie to marry me. It was probably the first successful proposal that involved a horse's tooth.

"What if the horse had swallowed it?" she asked me later.

I hadn't thought of that.

Everything was perfect. Even though the NHL players were locked out and the future of my job with the Florida Panthers seemed a bit uncertain, circumstances had led me to San Antonio and Joanie. I'd been in several terrible relationships in the past, but Joanie was different from any woman I'd ever met. And she had an incredible family. I got along really well with her parents. And she loved that I loved my mother, though they hadn't met yet. After Dudley met Joanie for the first time, he looked at me with a serious face and said, "Don't screw this one up." I promised him I wouldn't.

Over the years, I've lost a lot of money to divorce—legal fees, alimony and child support. It almost wipes you out. My illness affected my relationships, for sure. My ex-wives were living with a man who was going a hundred miles per hour. I was incredibly obsessive and jealous. Looking back, I realize it was mostly my fault, though I don't think they understood what I was going through. And I can't blame them for that. Very few people understand mental illness, and when you're married to someone who suffers from a disease you can't see or comprehend, it's almost impossible to empathize.

I have three wonderful kids from those three relationships. There are a lot of things in my life I would change if I could, but while my first three marriages weren't with the right women, I wouldn't change a thing if it meant not having Kelli, Jed and Dallyn in my world. They mean everything to me.

As soon as my life seemed to be more perfect than I ever thought it could be, all of the jagged, broken pieces of me started to fall apart. I was on Zoloft at the time, but I hadn't seen a psychiatrist in years. The last doctor I had seen about my condition was Dr. Stahl, way back in San Diego. I thought I was cured and stopped taking my medication as frequently as I was supposed to. It was a gradual decline; I didn't feel myself slipping.

When Joanie and I first started dating, we talked to each other about our pasts. She knew I'd been married three times and had three kids. She told me that she had been living in Minnesota for years with this terrible guy who fancied himself a bodybuilder but was actually just fat. It had been a terrible, very abusive relationship. But all I heard was "bodybuilder." *So she's into bodybuilders.*

My mind was drifting into unstable territory. I'd gone through this in every relationship I'd ever been in. With Joanie, it wasn't that bad at first. But it grew and grew and got really bad. This guy became an obsession to me.

A couple months after I met Joanie, I went on a trip to Toronto, and the airline lost my luggage—with my medication in it. I didn't have it for four days, by the end of which I couldn't function. As the days went on, I started to panic. The night before my flight home, I had an anxiety attack. I couldn't leave the hotel room. It's difficult to explain to someone who has never gone through it. But I wasn't capable of thinking clearly. I couldn't sleep. My flight was at 8 A.M. and I tried to go to bed, but I just lay there awake, spinning—*Can't sleep, can't sleep, can't sleep.* I can't remember much of this shit; it's part of the fog. At one point, I got up, took a shower, pulled on my boots, packed my bags and sat on my bed. It was probably midnight. My flight wasn't for hours. I just sat there on the bed. I didn't watch television. I just sat there and panicked about missing my flight.

Morning came and I couldn't leave the hotel room. I didn't want to go to the airport. I didn't want to go to the lobby. I missed my flight. This will sound ridiculous to most of you, but anyone who has ever experienced this kind of fear and confusion will understand how debilitating my anxiety was. Because of my past experience, I knew I was sliding—and quick. When it does come, it comes quickly. And now it was day four without medicine. I had my wits about me enough to tell myself, *You have to get a plane tomorrow. Get your goddamn self together.*

It was kind of like in that movie *What About Bob?* when Bill Murray couldn't get on an elevator or walk down the hall. Everything was "Baby steps, baby steps"—so he'd take little tiny steps. My experience wasn't far off from that. But really, it's hard to explain OCD. Why does somebody wash their hands constantly? They're clean, right? But no, they're not— they never are. When I was a kid, I always wanted reassurance from my mother—*Do you love me? Do you love me?*—and she'd say, "Yes, of course," and for some reason that made me feel relieved. But only for a short time. I was like that with my relationship with Joanie at this point. We'd only been together for a few months and I was constantly worried—*Are you mad at me? Are you mad at me?* And I'd be so relieved that she wasn't, until I started worrying again that she was. They call it the doubter's disease. It's the things that you really care about that make you obsessive.

Joanie called me. "Did you miss your flight?"

"Yes."

"What are you doing?"

"Sitting in my room." I was terrified. She could hear it in my voice. It was the first time she really understood my demons.

She told me to walk downstairs in five minutes. She called the airline and booked me on a new flight. She called the concierge and told him I was coming down and that he needed to get me into a cab. She walked me through the process of getting to the airport. She called me every fifteen minutes to make sure I had arrived at the airport, made it through security and to my gate. She made sure I boarded the plane. Joanie got me home.

When I got back to San Antonio, Joanie took me to the hospital to get my medication adjusted. I was paranoid; I didn't want to see another doctor. At first, I refused to go, but Matt Loughran, my friend from Idaho who was now in charge of the Rampage, helped Joanie convince me to go. When we got to the hospital, the doctor said there wasn't really anything he could do for me. It would take a while for the medication to fully work again because I'd been off it. I started freaking out. My eyes had that crazy glare in them. Matt had never seen me like this before. I stormed out of the hospital and started pacing back and forth across the parking lot.

I was in a rough state for a few weeks. I was drinking then, and I started drinking more to calm myself down. My OCD lives more within my emotions than as physical manifestation—say, turning the lights on and off. I became paranoid that Joanie was lying when she told me she loved me. Or that I really wasn't a good coach and my job was slipping away.

My anxiety kept me up at night. The insomnia was coming back, so I went to a doctor in San Antonio, who gave me some pills to knock me out. The pills made me groggy—I always felt dazed when I woke up. One morning, I stumbled into Joanie's bathroom and bashed my chin on the counter. There was a huge gash and there was blood all over her mint-green vanity and matching bath towels. She was at work at the time. I didn't want to deal with going to the hospital, so I found some thread and a needle in her drawer and stitched myself up.

When Joanie came home and saw my mangled face, she tried to get me to go to the hospital, but I refused. I didn't want anybody's help. I wouldn't budge, so Joanie called Steve Ludzik—my old teammate, who was now the head coach of the Rampage. He and his wife were a huge support for us at the time. They invited us over for dinner and planned to have one of their friends who was a doctor come over to stitch me up. I showed up at the house looking like Dr. Frankenstein's monster. The Ludziks' plan worked. I let the doc take a look at the gash, but I insisted on removing the thread from my chin myself. He was amazed that I could take the pain and that I knew how to stitch up my own wounds. He said I had done a good job, all things considered, but he needed to fix me up with the suture kit he'd brought or the gash would get infected.

Joanie and I married a year later. Joanie's parents came to visit us at our ranch in Nevada, so we decided to make it official that weekend. We went up to Lake Tahoe and got married on a cliff overlooking the lake. In addition to her parents, her two sisters flew in to surprise her, and my daughter Dallyn was there. I met a few people in town earlier that day and invited them to come up. But I didn't tell my mother we were getting married. I was so embarrassed about being married four times. My mom had liked Wife Number Three, but I don't think she liked the others. I figured she would decide not to like Joanie because my track record proved that, inevitably, the whole production would fall apart. I didn't want her to think, *Oh, here we go again!*

The wedding was close to perfect in every way, except for my mother's absence. I regret that. She's been the biggest support in my life, and I love her more than anything. Eventually, she and Joanie became great friends. Of course they would—they were both perfect and they both loved me! If there's a lesson in this, it's simple: always invite your mother to your weddings, regardless of how many you've already had.

We bought a ranch in Gardnerville, Nevada. It was in a beautiful location, on the edge of the mountains, surrounded by golden sagebrush. I envisioned the riding arena and the corral and the tack shed. I could picture how high the trees we planted would grow over our perfect, happy years together in this desert paradise.

I did my best to manage my illness this time. But I had taken the same medication for years—the same dosage and everything. You don't realize when it isn't working anymore, and it's embarrassing to admit that you still have the disease. You don't want to admit it to yourself, let alone anyone who can actually help. Drinking seems to make the obsessiveness and anxiety go away. You have a little more to drink here, a little more to drink there, and soon drinking is the only way to feel normal.

Joanie could see that I was slipping. She tried to help me and swore she'd stay beside me through everything. But she couldn't have known just how bad it was about to get.

23

Open Wounds

ON FEBRUARY 10, 2008, FLORIDA PANTHERS FORWARD RICHARD Zednik had his neck cut open by the skate of teammate Olli Jokinen while the Panthers were playing the Sabres in Buffalo. It was a freak accident. Jokinen tripped after being tangled up with Sabres forward Clarke MacArthur. His leg kicked up and the blade cut into Zednik's external carotid artery. Zednik grabbed his throat and skated for the bench, leaving a trail of blood behind him. The training staff stabilized him until he could be rushed to the hospital, where he underwent emergency surgery that saved his life.

My phone starting ringing and didn't stop for a week. The accident couldn't have been more similar to mine, and reporters wanted to know my reaction to the gruesome scene. Suddenly, everyone was talking about my injury again. I replayed the story over and over.

"It brought up a lot of things I never really wanted to think about again," I told the *Columbus Dispatch.* "I thought about it probably every day for a year or two after it happened to me. It's been more fleeting in recent years, but this brings it all back. I didn't sleep last night. Not one single wink. I thought I was over it."

I was working as a goalie coach for the Columbus Blue Jackets at the time. The Panthers didn't renew my contract after the lockout season, when Dudley was replaced as general manager by Keenan and Jacques Martin took over as head coach.

I was pissed about how the whole thing went down. When Martin was hired after the 2003–04 season, it was clear that he and I didn't connect. And Martin had told Keenan he wanted his own guy. Keenan told him he could do what he wanted but suggested he ask the starting goalie, Roberto Luongo, who he wanted to work with. Luongo really liked me; he and I had a great relationship.

And during the lockout season, I dropped all my shit to go and coach in San Antonio—which I thought was pretty honourable of me to do. In 2005, we held a prospect camp up at Teen Ranch, near Orangeville, north of Toronto. Duane Sutter and I ran it. Keenan and I got to talking about my next contract during the camp. He had to leave before anything was settled, but I told him I wasn't worried about it. I'm a handshake guy and so is Mike. But it's not a league where you can rely on a handshake. You can't depend on anything unless you sign on the dotted line.

Keenan called me on June 30, the last day before my contract expired. He said, "Clint, you're done. We can't bring you back."

I thought he was joking. I said, "Okay, Mike."

He said, "Seriously." And then it hit me. *What?* I was shocked.

The news came so late, all the other jobs for the upcoming season were filled. So I was out of hockey for about a year, working as a horse dentist and chiropractor in Garnerville, Nevada. We probably saw about two thousand horses each summer. It was busy, but I missed hockey.

Doug MacLean, the general manager of the Blue Jackets, had been the assistant coach in Washington when I played there. He gave me a shot with Columbus in 2006. Ken Hitchcock—the guy who sold me my skates when I was a kid—was the head coach. Hitch is one of the best people in the game. He's a brilliant coach but also a wonderful man.

Pascal Leclaire was the main man between the pipes in Columbus—a great goalie whose career was cut short because of bad luck with injuries. He was one of my favorite guys to work with—we connected very well. But MacLean was a lot like Keenan when it came to goalies. If a tender let in a bad goal, he'd kick open the door up in the press box or throw a chair. He'd yell at the Zamboni driver if the ice was bad. He'd probably yell at the popcorn guy if there were too many unpopped kernels at the bottom of the bag. But I mean that in a nice way. He was a great guy, just very passionate and demanding. I could relate to that. So my role with Pascal was to help take the pressure off. I used to pull a lot of pranks and chirp him. I used to tap reporters on the shinbone with my stick when they'd come in the room after practice—it really hurt if you hit it right—and Pascal always got a kick out of that. We joked around a lot. He knew I had his back, no matter what happened. I'd go to war for that kid any day. He was loyal to me and I'd always be loyal to him.

I was probably closer to Pascal than anyone else in the organization. But even he had no idea what was going on inside my head at the time. I hid everything from the team. When the press kept calling after the Zednik injury that winter, I didn't let on that the memory of the accident still haunted me. The nightmares came back. It just kept getting worse. I knew something was wrong, but I didn't want anyone else to know. I didn't want to put a big spotlight on it and expose everything all over again. I felt ashamed at having gone back to that place, for being unable to overcome myself.

It wasn't all bad. I actually had a brief NHL comeback with the team when Pascal got hurt on a road trip out to Vancouver. I strapped on the pads to replace him in practice. I was pretty good. With this new hockey gear, you don't feel the pucks hitting you! And it's light! I was facing NHL shooters in an NHL practice—it was 1987 all over again. The players were trying to bury it on me. Hitchcock was watching, so they didn't let up. I thought, *This is great! Go ahead, Rick Nash, shoot it!* I was kicking pucks aside. Gary Agnew, one of the assistant coaches, came up and told me to stop going down—he thought I was going to have a heart attack or something. I was panting pretty hard, but the competitive side of me just came out. I had so many guys come up to me after that and tell me how amazed they were that I could still kick out the rubber. "Holy shit, you can still play!" It was great. I felt like I could sign a million-dollar contract and make the comeback official. I was sore for about a week, though.

Shortly after that, I suited up for another practice in St. Louis. It didn't go as well, but all things considered, I did pretty good.

Even so, I decided to stick with coaching.

2 4

Open Bottles

IN COLUMBUS, MY ALCOHOLISM REACHED THE POINT WHERE THE people around me couldn't see the OCD because my drinking appeared to be my most obvious problem. It was just a mask, of course—a way to cover up a more deeply rooted issue. But that's basically the textbook definition of alcoholism, isn't it?

The private obsessions persisted.

Joanie stayed back at our ranch in Nevada during the season while I went back and forth to Columbus, because I was on a consulting contract. I'd be there for two or three weeks at a time. Not knowing where she was and what she was up to drove me crazy. It was an old, irrational fear creeping up on me. Sometimes, I would call her fifteen or twenty times a night. She had no idea what was going on. I'd pick a fight with her, just trying to have something to argue about. Anything.

"Where are you?"

"I'm at home."

"What are you doing?"

"Nothing."

"What do you mean, 'nothing'? What are you hiding?"

She'd hang up and I'd call back. "Why don't you want to talk to me?"

"I do!"

It was the same dance, over and over.

In the spring of 2007, towards the end of my first year with

Columbus, we went on a road trip that took us through Nashville. Joanie got a call from a taxi driver. I was piss-drunk in the back seat.

"I have your husband," the driver said.

"What?"

"He is hurt and bloody, but he is all right."

I had gone out on my own and gotten hammered at a bar. Then I had talked myself into a fight with a group of guys. I held my own, but there were three, maybe four of them. Somehow, I managed to get my ass into a cab. The driver found Joanie's number in my phone because I was a bloody, incoherent mess. She told him where I was staying and made sure he got me there.

The next morning, I went to the rink with my dress shirt covered in blood. I'd only brought one shirt on the trip and didn't have time to buy a new one. My eye was swollen like a grapefruit. The Blue Jackets sent me home to Nevada.

Joanie picked me up at the airport. My face was still swollen. I knew then that the drinking was out of control and my job was on the line. But I also believed it was a problem I could fix on my own.

That summer, my drinking just got worse. I spiralled out of control. My head would spin as I thought about the possibility of losing my job, losing Joanie, losing everything that meant anything to me. I believed that people were out to get me.

Joanie's ex-boyfriend, as I've said, was a bodybuilder. They had a terrible relationship. She hated him, but I still became obsessed with the idea that Joanie would leave me for a bodybuilder. "Tell me you don't love me so I can get on with my life," I told her.

My mother kept telling her not to worry about it. "That's just how he is. You have to get used to it." I have to admit that, as much as I love my mother, that was an enabling philosophy.

This part of my life is difficult for me to talk about. Obsession is an embarrassing issue. But we've got to push through. We've got to get this shit out. It's important to admit to insecurity so deeply rooted that it calcifies in your core. I had jealous thoughts so poisonous, I could feel them burn through my veins. It overwhelms every rational part of you.

Growing up, it was family and hockey. My family was fucked; hockey represented hope. Thank God I was good at it. I had to be the best. I'd do anything to get there, goddammit. I'd get on the ice first, leave the ice last, make sure that no one could put in the same time or effort that I did. I'd win by default.

I used to ask my mom—honest to God—at thirteen: "Do you think I'm better than that goalie? Do you think I'm better than *that* goalie?" I'd lie awake at night, staring at the ceiling, worrying that some other guy was better than me. I had to be the best. *Have to be the best.* In junior, the backup goalie would have a good game and I couldn't stop worrying that he might be better than me. I'd get up and do a double workout the next morning.

Whatever I was emotional about, I was obsessive—and competitive—about. Relationships were impossible because they became the thing I was emotional about, obsessive about, and competitive about. *Who is she really thinking about? Who does she want to be with? Who else has she been with? Am I better? Am I stronger?* Taken on their own, these are normal feelings. You're lying if you say you haven't had them before. The problem is when these questions become all you can think about. Consider the average level of insecurity as a one or two on a scale of ten. True obsession hits ten and doesn't relent.

Back in Buffalo, when I wasn't in a relationship, as I left the house I'd do all the regular OCD things—checking the stove, locking the door, going back and checking again, going back . . . and so on. That was the easy shit to deal with. Then, when I met my second wife, it all changed. I was at the rink, worrying about whether or not I was the best lover, the best husband, the best man. With a game to play, I couldn't afford to have to think about this shit. The only way to get it out of my head was to ask her, every day, before I left the house: "Are you sure you love me?" I couldn't leave until I was certain. Then I'd be out of my mind and I could play the game. It was about the competition. Not the sex—the competition.

When I had a handle on things, I could recognize those thoughts as irrational. I'd still have them, but I could push them aside and not give a shit. But without proper medication, I couldn't turn them off. It was a voice in my head that just kept talking and wouldn't let the issue die. *Was he better in bed than me? Was he more built than me? Was he funnier than me?*

That two-year span, when things fell apart in Buffalo and I was sent to the minors, I never stopped feeling that nagging insecurity, that constant voice in my head—driving me to insomnia, driving me to insanity. I was on my knees, praying—*God, I can't make this stop. Either take me or fix me.*

The feelings haunted me with Joanie, too. There was nothing between her and her ex-boyfriend, the bodybuilder. But I couldn't shake the idea that she secretly loved him. I couldn't stop thinking she was disappointed that I wasn't a juice monkey, too. If she didn't think I was pretty great, she wouldn't have stuck by me through this shit. I recognize the logic in that. But of course, the logic didn't click. I was driven to the edge all over again. The voice would never stop.

So that's it; there you go. That's obsession. Embarrassing and ugly—the worst parts of a man, unrelenting and taking over until you lose control completely.

25

I'd Never . . .

A COUPLE OF MY LOCAL FRIENDS, WACO AND DAVE, WOULD COME over to ride and rope in the arena. We'd drink in the barn all day and night. As long as I could drink and ride, I'd be okay. I wished I could drink and ride forever. For a while, the voices in my head would stop and let me relax. I'd drink almost thirty beers a day. When we got short on beers, we'd go and get more. But when the parties ended, the thoughts raged back. Only I'd be drunk *and* irrational. "I just want to die," I'd tell Joanie. "I just want to kill myself."

Once, I sat in the tack shed and told her I was going to do it. I said I'd rig a gun to the door, so that when she came in, a string would tug at the trigger and blow me away.

The next morning, I'd always crawl back. "You know I'd never do that. I'd never do it. I love you," I'd say. But later that night, it would return "I just can't stand being in my head. I can't live like this."

I made it about Joanie. I used her as a crutch. I'd laugh and joke around with my buddies, but I'd fight with Joanie when we were alone. Her parents told her I needed to go to rehab. There was no chance I'd be doing that. I had already gotten the help I needed. I felt I could handle this on my own. I wasn't going to some corny adult summer camp where we held hands and talked about our problems. I was a cowboy and I could deal with this myself.

It had been years since I'd actually checked in with a doctor. They say your body can build a resistance to the medication when you've been on it for a while, but I didn't really understand that at the time. When the prescribed dosage didn't set me straight, I'd turn to booze to take the edge off. *Just need beer just to slow my mind down a little bit.* But a few beers with my ranch buddies always turned into a dozen. Eventually, they'd go home and I'd polish off the entire case on my own. Joanie could always tell when I was lit because she'd hear Johnny Cash playing loudly over the speaker system we'd installed in the barn and outside the tack shed. When I was good and drunk, I'd be angry all over again. It was a cyclical thing.

Joanie kept telling me to go and get my medication checked again, but I refused. I was afraid of being committed again. I was afraid of the weakness it showed.

"I don't need that," I'd say. "If anyone finds out about that, I'll lose my job. I'll never get another job in the NHL again. I can handle this myself."

The fits of rage came in cycles. I'd go from being myself to Jack Torrance—I'm talking full-on Nicholson in *The Shining*—in a matter of minutes. Looking back, it's a hazy period in my life. There was usually a two-hour period in the middle of the day when I seemed fine. That's when Joanie felt okay to talk to me. When she saw my mood turning, she knew she couldn't get through to me.

When things got really bad, I became emotionally and verbally violent with Joanie. I was never physical. I would never hit her, but my rage-filled words certainly left unseen bruises. I became irritable over the smallest things and completely erratic. The only thing predictable about me was that I was probably drunk. She'd call our friends to help, and they'd come over and try to calm me down. Whenever someone else would show up, I'd try to downplay everything. "It's nothing. I've got it under control. It's just a fight. We're having a rough time. It's going to be okay. I'll be fine . . ."

It was almost convincing. My acting was as good then as it always had been.

One of my good friends in Gardnerville was Brian Peck, a local veterinarian I had met through the equine dentistry practice when I was still married to Wife Number Three. He'd bring his kids over to the ranch for dinner and we'd go out back and shoot rifles at cans and targets I'd set up. We got along really well, and I trusted him. He was the guy Joanie called the most when things got out of hand. I told him about my OCD and depression. He could tell that I was slipping—you can only throw them off for so long before it becomes obvious that there is more to the problem than you're letting on. Brian knew my bullshit as good as any of them. But the Torrance-esque episodes were getting more frequent and out of control than before.

After one particularly bad fight with Joanie, Brian sat with me at my kitchen table and I broke down. I started sobbing. I told him there were voices in my head and I couldn't get them to stop. They just kept swirling around inside of me—these obsessive thoughts, *my own voice,* telling me terrible things about Joanie. Brian told me I needed to get medical help. "That's the first step, Clint," he said. "We have to get you in to see someone."

I refused. It was embarrassing to be in this place again. Medication wasn't going to help. Some jackass doctor wasn't going to help. *I don't need help. I'm strong enough to fix this.* But the only way I knew was to drown my anxiety and depression in booze, and that was a whole other problem.

Brian was good friends with the district attorney. I didn't know this at the time, but he actually called his friend and asked if he could get an officer to come and arrest me. Brian didn't want me to go to jail; he just wanted to force me to get the help I needed. The district attorney told Brian there was nothing he could do. Unless I was caught breaking the law, the cops just couldn't go out and arrest someone because they needed help.

The truth is, I broke plenty of laws. It was a miracle, or a curse, that I wasn't arrested sooner than I was. It's hard to count all the times I'd go into bars just looking for the biggest guy in there, hoping he'd take a swing at me. I guess it was jealousy or insecurity, but I felt the need to beat everybody up to prove to Joanie that they might be big and on steroids, but guess what, they can't beat me. I'd come home messed up, with blood on my knuckles.

The breaking point came in the summer of 2007. Joanie had been visiting her parents back in San Antonio, and I was supposed to pick her up at the airport in Reno. She went to San Antonio to get away from my increasingly destructive behaviour and to get some advice from her parents, who were always great at dealing with this kind of stuff. But alone in Nevada, my obsessive thoughts were back and my head was spinning. I wanted to fight someone, someone bigger than me. I needed to get the rage out. So on my way to the airport, I pulled into a random hard-core gym in Reno. I'd never been there before, had no idea who would be inside, but I figured it'd be someone big. I wore my cowboy hat and boots. I went to the front desk and said, "I'm not working out. I just need to talk to somebody." The person at the desk said okay and let me in.

I found these two juice monkeys. One was bench pressing, the other was spotting. I stood next to them. They were both wide. One was shorter than the other—a Mexican guy, stocky and tuned to the max. The other was a six-foot, three-inch white guy, a lot bigger. They both had arms as big as cantaloupes, but all fatty, too. I was forty-six years old and in decent shape, but nowhere near the mass of these guys.

"Could you lift that much if you weren't all juiced up?" I asked.

They looked at me, confused. "What the fuck?" the bigger one said.

"We're not on juice, man," the shorter guy said.

"Liar," I said. "You're a fucking liar. You're flat-faced lying to me, you don't fucking take steroids. You goddamn goof."

The big guy got off the bench.

"What are you, a fucking cowboy?" the smaller Mexican guy said. He shoved me in the chest.

"That's assault, man," I said. "You pushed me. Now I have a reason to kick your ass."

"Fuck you, cowboy."

I drilled him. He stumbled backwards and hit the mirror and dumb-bell rack. The big guy tried to grab me. I elbowed him, but he got his arms around me. The other guy grabbed a ten-pound plate and slammed it into my face. It caught me flat across my nose and eye. If he'd gotten my nose alone, it would have ended up where my ear should be.

I went spastic. I threw a high elbow on the guy holding me and caught him under the jaw. He fell back onto the bench. I was so pissed off at the little shit who used the plate, I grabbed him by the strap of his tank top. "You piece of shit." And I whaled on him.

The other guy didn't get much involved after that. I never hit him again. It was the middle of the afternoon, and there were only a few other people in the gym. But the staff and everyone else were around us now. I took off. I ran out the front door before anyone could grab me. I knew they called the police because I passed a cop car with wailing lights as I was driving away.

My face was messed up. My nose was broken, I was covered in blood and my eye was already black. I drove to the Reno airport and waited for Joanie in my truck.

"What the hell happened to you?" she said, seeing the bloody mess of my face.

"See what you made me do?" I said.

I blamed everything on her. She didn't know what to say. She went through a ton of trauma with me. She was thinking, *I made you do this? This is my fault. I'm bad for you.* She went through a lot of stuff because of me. It was only going to get worse.

After I started that fight with the two juice monkeys at the gym, Brian convinced me it was time to see someone. He arranged for me to go to the hospital in Carson City to see a doctor. Our friend Waco McGill came with us, probably because Brian knew how violent and unpredictable I'd become.

The first time we went, the waiting room at Carson City Hospital was packed, and I told them there was no way I was going to sit around and wait for some shithead intern to dick around with me. We waited and waited and waited until a nurse finally called us up to the check-in desk.

"The doctor will be a couple of hours," he said. "We're going to have to get you a full psychological evaluation, and we'll probably have to keep you in the hospital overnight."

"Jesus Christ," I said. "If I had a broken leg, you'd run me up to emergency. I'm losing my mind and I have to sit here? Just give me the proper medication. I'm not staying overnight."

You could see it in the nurse's face—*Red flag on this guy. We're going to have to commit him.* There was no way I was going to go in to see a doctor who was going to try to commit me.

"I've got to make a phone call," I said.

I walked out of the room, headed down the hall and bolted for the exit. Brian and Waco thought I'd just gone to call Joanie. Eventually, they realized I wasn't coming back.

The next day, when I had settled down and seemed rational, they convinced me to go back to the hospital—for Joanie's sake. Brian set up an appointment and everything. I was in a better state of mind and realized he was right, so I agreed. But again, the waiting room was packed and I was pissed off right away. "This is a waste of fucking time," I kept saying. "We're just going to sit around and wait. If my leg was broken or some shit like that, they'd see me right away, but they don't give a damn about me." We waited for a little while, and then Brian asked the nurse at the desk how much longer it would be. He could see that I was starting to turn. The nurse said it would still be a bit. I was done with that shit. The staff at the hospital had my name in their records and thought I was dangerous. I told a security guard to go piss up a rope or something like that and took off for the parking lot. Brian and Waco ran after me. They were as pissed off as I was that I couldn't get some decent help.

I don't think they realized that the hospital had called the cops. I didn't really know until I saw the lights way up the road as we drove away. A couple of cop cars were heading in our direction. *Ah shit,* I thought. *They're going to put me away.* We were riding in Brian's Dodge Ram 2500 and I was sitting in the back seat. When he hit a red light, I opened the door and bolted. Brian and Waco tried to stop me. "Come back! Where are you going?" But I wasn't about to get locked up. I took off for some bushes on the other side of the ditch.

The cops passed Brian's truck, but one of them did a quick U-turn and pulled him over. Sure enough, they were looking for me. Brian told him I'd taken off at the hospital and they were looking for me, too. He promised to contact them if he and Waco found me again. With my cowboy hat and blue jeans and boots, I was pretty easy to spot, so I held the hat behind my back and ducked my head down as I darted through the trees and shrubs. I was completely paranoid, borderline delusional.

It was dusk, so I figured I just needed to hide out until it got dark. I had to hide down in some friggin' bushes like Commando Clint. I wound up in a parking lot. I got down on my stomach and army-crawled between the cars so no one could spot me. I turned my cell phone on and called Joanie.

"The FBI is after me," I said. "They're after me. They're trying to lock me up."

She had no idea what I was talking about, but I couldn't talk long because I had to keep moving. I hung up and barrel-rolled into another ditch.

Brian and Waco were in contact with me, but they had a cop tailing them, so they couldn't stop to pick me up. I told them I would find my own way home. I hid inside some bushes, lying on my stomach. There were a bunch of cop cars driving all over the place, flying past me.

I called Joanie again and told her the FBI was still on my tail. "I'll get home," I told her. "I'll get home."

When the heat was off, I snuck out to the main road in Carson City and hitched a ride back to Gardnerville, about fifteen miles away.

When I got back home, I looked through my window and saw Joanie and Brian sitting at our kitchen bar. Something crazy clicked in my mind. *Holy shit, this whole time—Joanie and Brian.* She was cheating on me with my friend! Just one look was all it took to convince me.

In reality, they were trying to figure out where I was. It looked like I'd lost my mind. Brian told Joanie she needed to get out of the house. I was unhinged. "He's going to come back here," he warned her.

They didn't see me coming. I charged through the screen door—ripped it down completely. Their white-as-ghosts shock confirmed my suspicions. Everyone ran. They were afraid of me. I went after Brian, swinging for his face. Joanie screamed at me to stop, but I wanted his blood. He ran around the couch to get away from me. I went one way and he went the other. I nearly caught him a few times—just kept swinging and cursing. He was on one side of the couch, I was on the other. We went back and forth around it. I threw the television remote at him. And when I got close enough, I took a swing and missed. Joanie kept screaming at me. Brian tried to calm me down. I got tired—*so goddamn tired.*

Then I realized Waco was there, too.

I don't know what happened to me. I don't know how to explain how quickly my mind flipped into believing my wife was cheating on me with my friend. The cops didn't come after me. I guess they figured I'd made it home and didn't want to deal with any more headaches. Waco took Joanie to a family friend's house to stay for the night. He took the guns out of my house, but he forgot about the ones I kept in the tack shed out back. I went into my room, fell on the bed and passed out. Brian slept on the couch, but I was so out of my mind I didn't even know he was there. Every hour or so, he'd wake up to the sound of me yelling into my phone, "You've ruined my life, Joanie. You ruined my life!" And then it would go quiet. I'd just fall asleep, until I'd wake up again and leave another seething message on her phone. This was the pattern. My rage would build to a point where I'd rant and rave for two or three hours and then just crash.

In the morning, Brian checked to make sure I was still breathing. Then he left me there, unconscious in the tattered pieces of the life I'd torn apart.

26

I Might

THE BARREL OF THE GUN TASTED COLD AND METALLIC, LIKE BLOOD. I sat on the shoulder of an empty road in the desert and thought about the peace of death. It was a horrible notion, but it was the only thing I could imagine taking away the chaos. It was going to destroy me one way or another. So I had the gun in my mouth and was searching for a reason to not pull the trigger.

It was October of 2007. I was starting my second year as the Columbus Blue Jackets' goalie coach and was back home in Nevada before the season kicked off. After a summer that nearly ruined my marriage with Joanie, in which I thought the FBI was trying to chase me down, and in which I had tried to beat up one of my closest friends, I still had farther to fall. I was drunk and depressed and obsessed with irrational things. I was nearly beaten.

My last call for help was to Rick Dudley as I sat in the truck with the gun in my hand. He was the only person I knew who understood where I had been and where I was heading. He'd done so much for me as a coach and as a general manager. Rick was a huge, strong man. But he was one of the most compassionate and caring men I'd ever met, too. Rick understood mental illness. He knew I didn't want to behave the way I did.

When I was out in San Antonio, he told Steve Ludzik to be careful because I'd turn into a monster if I ever went off my meds. When I heard that later, I thought, *What a compliment. Absolutely.* I didn't think it was a negative thing. At five-eleven, maybe six feet, I'd go up against a six-foot, five-inch beast and not even bat an eye. It was important to me. It never bothered me that I was only six feet and 195 pounds while another guy was six-four and 280. I'd take that guy on any day. I was really proud of that—I was cocky about it. It never crossed my mind that I could get hurt—*Fuck you, I can take you down. I've got nothing to lose.* This was the person I became whenever I'd lose control. Duds understood that mentality, crazy as it was. He was also the only person I was afraid of. I knew Duds could kick the shit out of me if he needed to.

Joanie often called him when I got out of control. When I was sober and had a handle on things, I told her to dial his number if it ever seemed like I was losing myself. He always knew how to talk me down. "You better not screw this up with Joanie," he'd say. He knew that I'd lucked out with her, and he knew how quickly I could ruin it. His was the only voice that anchored me in sanity. Over the past couple of days, Joanie could see that I was spiralling out of control. She called Dudley and asked him to come and intervene. He knew things were getting dangerous, but nothing could have prepared him for this. I dialled his number.

"I just want to say goodbye," I said, and I told him about the gun in my hand.

Rick begged me to wait. He said he'd be there in a day and made me promise to wait for him to get there. He was the assistant general manager of the Chicago Blackhawks at the time. That's not the kind of job that gives you time off to go hug a buddy who's feeling down, but Duds got on the first flight he could—and he hates flying. He drives pretty much everywhere.

When he showed up at the ranch, his first thought was that I was a full-out madman. Dudley had never seen me get this bad—and he'd seen me in San Diego, where I was a beaten man. The pain was going to do me in, and he knew it.

I was embarrassed that I needed him to come out. I tried to play it down when he arrived. I said that it was just Joanie getting me all worked up. Duds didn't buy it. At dinner, I made sure we all sat down together and tried to have a nice, regular time—but Dudley could read the act in my eyes.

Joanie had called psychiatrists over and over again, trying to find one that had time to see us. It was a frustrating, infuriating process. No one was willing to take me on, and every time we went to the hospital, we'd wait for hours to see some emergency-room doc who knew nothing about mental illness.

She had managed to book an appointment when Rick arrived. We drove to Carson City to meet with the doctor, but right when we got there, the nurse told us he had been called out of town. She handed us a brochure and said good luck. Just then, Joanie's phone rang. It was another doctor's office. They had an appointment open up, if we could make it there in the next thirty minutes. We rushed across town.

After we checked in and sat down in the waiting room, I started to get paranoid. There was no way out of this appointment. I believed I'd see this doctor and he'd try to have me committed to some sort of asylum. My chest started pounding. *No fucking way.* I told Joanie and Duds I was going to the bathroom and I'd be right back. Then I walked into the hall and bolted. No one saw me leave. I took off, walked to a main street and hitched a ride back to Gardnerville.

It took Joanie and Rick a few minutes to realize what happened. Having checked all the bars in Carson City, they figured their best bet was that I'd hitched back to Gardnerville. They searched all the bars in town looking for me. They went into one bar, and Duds asked this guy if he had seen a guy with a black eye and a cowboy hat. The guy thought he said "black guy in a cowboy hat" and told Rick no, but he'd seen a white guy in a cowboy hat. Rick was confused for a minute. I'd been looking for a bar that was showing the Blue Jackets game. It was about 4 P.M. in Nevada, which made it 7 P.M. back in Columbus—game time. My job was to coach the Blue Jackets' goalies, and dammit, that's what I was going to do. This bar didn't have the game on TV—but now Rick and Joanie knew they were right on my tail.

They were right. I wound up at this place called Center Field's, sat at the bar and had them turn on the hockey game. The place was basically empty. There were a couple of guys sitting at the bar, the bartender, and me. The others started messing around with me. One of the guys had the remote control and kept flicking the channel to a baseball or basketball game. Then he'd flip it back and, after another little while, change it to another station. It pissed me off, but I tried to play nice. At first, I was bullshitting with the guys, so I guess they thought it was all in fun. When I'd had enough, though, I turned to the tool with the remote.

"Joke's over, buddy," I said. "One more time and I'll come over there and pull your little panties over your ass and spank you in front of your girlfriend there."

I was half-joking.

I guess things got a little more heated than I thought, because unbeknownst to me, the bartender called the cops. The Blue Jackets game was still going on. I was having a few beers, feeling like I'd resolved our little dispute, when in walked a police officer.

"Excuse me," one said. "You have to leave."

"What for?"

"Well, we have a complaint here."

"What? That wasn't a real threat!" I objected. "I told him I was going to pull his panties down and spank him in front his girlfriend."

"Now you're trespassing," he said. "You need to leave."

"Fuck that. These guys are joking around. Everything's cool—no problem."

That's when Duds came running in. He was too late.

"I'm not leaving," I said. "It was fun for a while, and then you pulled up. Now it's not fun anymore. I'm just going to watch this game."

"Sir, you have—"

I didn't resist. Everything was cool. I was leaving. But by the time we got outside, a few more cop cars had shown up. And a cop on a motorcycle. He came up and got in my face. Joanie had gotten out of the car and was trying to tell the officer that I just needed my medication. One of them shouted at her to back up, or she'd be arrested. Duds did his best to calm the situation down. He could see where this was heading. They had me up against the wall, searching me, when the cop who was on the motorcycle got up in my face, talking shit.

"Fuck you," I said. "Take your gun out, you little piece of shit. I'll do you up right here."

With that, the cops were on me. A couple of them took me down and gave me a mouthful of concrete. "You're going to jail!" one shouted as he struggled to keep me pinned. They tried to pull my arms together behind my back, but I wouldn't let them. They weren't strong enough; I was proud of that. They knelt on my head and torso, trying to get my arms behind my back. "Fuck you," I said. "Try it!" I was on Pluto.

Then one of them laid his boot into my rib—just drilled me like a soccer ball. Duds took a step forward and one of the cops pulled out his gun and said he'd shoot Rick if he took another step. Joanie screamed at them to let me go. They told her to stand back or she'd also end up in jail. She pleaded with them to just let me take my medication, but no one would listen.

I was a full-out madman now. Once that adrenaline starts flowing and I feel justified, I fight to the death. If I pass that point, there isn't much room for reasoning with me. They kicked me a few times, but I couldn't feel anything; I blocked the pain out with rage. One of the cops on top of me had his gun drawn. There was this little laser attachment on the top. I chomped down and bit it off. Eventually, they got the cuffs together and shoved me into the back of a squad car.

"You fucking goddamn motherfuckers," I shouted, kicking at the door.

They had me. I saw Joanie's terrified face through the window as Duds tried to console her. *Shit.* I tried to play nice and told the cops driving me away that I was messed up on bad medication and needed to get some new meds. The cops just ignored me and hauled my ass away from Joanie and Duds.

My knee was busted. I was black and blue from the waist down, along both legs and my entire right side. And trust me, I don't bruise easily. There was a huge gash on my head, so they had to take me to the hospital in Gardnerville that night.

They booked me for resisting arrest. I spent the night in jail, pacing in my cell, ready to kill someone. Brian Peck got a call late that night from his friend, the district attorney. "Looks like we finally got your guy," he said. "Apparently, he's going back and forth like a caged panther."

The cops on duty taunted me. I probably deserved a lot of it. Here's this cop, just trying to do his job, and I kept shouting out, "Hey buddy! Hey buddy!" When he ignored me, I said, "Well, fuck you then, you piece of shit." Of course they're going to get on my ass for that. Of course they're going to ride me the rest of the night. They didn't know my story; I was just some angry guy in jail.

The next morning, the sergeant brought in a doctor to evaluate me. He asked about my medication and gave me two options: I could spend three days in jail or be put in a seventy-two-hour hold at a nearby psychiatric hospital, where I'd have access to doctors and medication. It seemed like an easy decision.

"I'll go to the hospital," I said.

Big mistake.

The next day, they drove me to Reno, at least an hour away. In the back seat of a cop car, there is no room—basically, I had to lie sideways. My knee and ribs were throbbing. My hands were cuffed and my legs were shackled. I felt like I was Hannibal Lecter. The cop in the front seat just blasted this heavy metal music the whole ride. It drove me crazy and I asked him to change it. The asshole just turned it up.

On the way, they stopped at an In-N-Out Burger and had a bite to eat while I lay there on my side with a gash across my head and a couple of banged up ribs. The driver was bald and into heavy metal. The other guy was okay. After his burger, he turned down the music, opened the partition and talked to me.

"What do you do?" he asked me.

"I'm a hockey coach with the Columbus Blue Jackets," I said. "I used to play in the NHL."

He was a cop in Nevada, so he wasn't a huge hockey fan. But when I told him about my jugular injury, he remembered it.

"Oh man, I know you!" he said.

From then on, I was suddenly this great guy. They both asked me a million questions.

We arrived at the mental hospital and they escorted me in, shuffling in the shackles. While Heavy Metal Cop checked me in, the other guy pulled me aside and gave me his card. "This will be a misdemeanor," he said. "It will all go away. Call me and we'll figure it out."

I took the card, but I saw right through him. Before he knew who I was, he'd assumed I was some cop hater—then, after finding out I was this old hockey pro, famous for a terrible injury, he turned into some goddamn jock sniffer. After everything I'd been through, I was grateful he was being nice, but it wasn't right.

On October 18, 2007, I was admitted to a full-out loony bin. The state mental hospital was full of batshit-crazy people. I knew I'd been drinking too much. I knew my obsessions were taking over my mind and that I was erratic and violent and a danger to myself and everyone around me. But holy shit—there were people running around naked in this place. There were people singing to themselves. One guy started throwing his food around. It was straight out of *One Flew Over the Cuckoo's Nest*. There's no better way to describe it. The head nurse was just like Nurse Ratched.

They made us line up single file for meals, like in prison. We had to line up at these locked doors, and they'd march us through several security doors. Most of these people suffered from some sort of schizophrenia. It was a state facility, so it was also filled with poor, homeless people who were just picked up off the street for being a nuisance. They were mentally ill, and they were just stuffed into this hospital without any real help. I sat down to eat, and one guy was trying to shove a hot dog into his forehead. He had mustard all over himself.

I knew I needed help, but I wasn't *crazy* crazy. I had to convince the doctors who interviewed me that I didn't belong in a loony bin. "I know I need help. I need proper medication or whatever. But you're not keeping me here—there's no goddamn way!" It was the worst three days of my life. It was just unbelievable hell in there.

Joanie came to visit me after my first night. When she saw me, she broke down and cried.

"I'm sorry," I said. "I'm not right. I know I need help. But I don't belong in here."

That place broke my heart. Nobody had anything. I asked Joanie to bring me a bunch of my clothes in a bag. The next day I asked for more, because I'd given them all away. Today, I swear there are homeless people walking around Reno in Florida Panthers and Columbus Blue Jackets sweats.

There was this old guy, Frank, just crying out from his bed. He was a giant of a man, probably six foot seven. "Help me! I need a nurse!" he kept yelling. "Help me! Please help me!" He was losing his mind. I ran over to the nurse's station and told miserable Ratched that this old guy needed to see someone.

"Oh, that's just Frank," she said. "He's just making a scene."

That isn't right, I thought. *This place is so screwed up. It's wrong.* I went in there and held his hand, and he was asleep in ten minutes. That was all the poor guy needed.

On my last day, I had to get a signature from a social worker to get clearance to leave. They had to be certain I wasn't going to hurt anybody on the outside. I sat there in the common area with my bag packed all afternoon, waiting to get the hell out. I kept asking the nurses when this social worker would be ready to see me, and they kept saying she was in a meeting. I didn't even know who this person was. Finally, a woman came out of an office and went into the nurses' station. I ran over—"Is that the social worker? I'm supposed to see her."

The nurse said they'd page her. I sat there for another twenty minutes, but she didn't get back to me. I went back up to the desk.

"Oh," the nurse said, "she might have left for the day."

You goddamn idiots!

"I'm here with my bags packed, waiting to talk to her!" I said. "I can't leave until she signs my clearance form."

"She must have slipped out," the nurse. "I'm sorry."

Joanie came to pick me up, but I still couldn't leave. I was close to freaking out again—starting to get paranoid that I'd never be able to get out of that wretched hellhole. I tried to stay calm, because I knew that if I snapped, they'd just think I was some kook, put me in a straitjacket and cart me away.

The nurse finally tracked down the social worker—she was on her way to her car—and called her back in. Then they couldn't find my paperwork. That took another half an hour. It felt like they were trying to trap me there. If I hadn't been competent, I'd have been lost in that mental hospital forever. I swear most of those patients didn't even know where they were.

After I escaped from the cuckoo's nest, I had to get a lawyer. I could have been up for assaulting a police officer. I didn't want to get nailed with anything worse than a misdemeanor. My job was in jeopardy because I wouldn't be able to travel out of the States to games in Canada. And the Blue Jackets certainly would have thought twice about employing a guy who fights with cops. I was already on the edge with them because of the bar brawl I'd been in in Nashville. Even though Pascal Leclaire and I had a great relationship, I knew the organization was worried about me.

My lawyer took care of everything. We went to court and I got off with a fine. They said I'd have to pay $250 to replace a flashlight on a cop's gun that I bit off during the struggle. The cop put a gun in my face and I had to pay for breaking it? Total horseshit. I mean, everything was under control at the bar until the cop on the motorcycle pulled up and got in my face. Then I got beat up in a parking lot, was taunted in jail and then got thrown in a mental hospital for three days, but still, the court said I was *almost* right.

Dudley went back to the Blackhawks after I was sent to the institution. He told Joanie to call him if I got out of control and to leave the house immediately. "You get on a plane if he gets angry," he told her. He was afraid I might hurt her. Duds always called things as he saw them. Joanie told him that, as violently as I was acting, she knew I'd never hurt her. I'd scream and yell, but nothing more. Still, Duds had never seen me so out of control. I looked like a madman, he said, like I was possessed with rage. It was unpredictable; one minute I'd be apologizing and trying to make everything seem okay, and the next I was spouting out *motherfuckers* and challenging every living thing to a fight.

When I got out of the state hospital, I agreed to meet with the doctor I had run away from at the start of the whole mess. He told me I had a chemical imbalance—which I'd heard many times before—and gave me prescriptions for a bunch of different pills. There were pills for anxiety, pills for sleeping, pills to calm me down. He prescribed me a cocktail of meds, at least six different kinds. It made me feel like I was being pulled in all these different directions. It seemed to make things worse.

I'm convinced a lot of my problems came from doctors. You watch these commercials for depression medication, and they warn you about side effects—"If you have signs of this and that and this and that . . ." One of them is always suicidal thoughts. If I'm depressed, why would I be taking medication that makes me suicidal? I think these doctors prescribe so much that the opposite effect happens. That's what happened to me.

The drinking just got worse through the spring and summer of 2008 as I kept trying to drown the suicidal thoughts, obsessions and rage. Nothing worked. It was like a high-pitched symphony of whistles, squealing louder and louder every day. My Jekyll-and-Hyde act was getting so wild and unpredictable that even my mother told Joanie that if she was worried for her safety, she needed to leave.

Joanie stayed with friends several times that summer. She couldn't sleep at night if she didn't. I'd be out in the barn, getting drunk all night, and then come in and start a fight. A few weekends, she flew back to her parents' place in San Antonio. They were always supportive of both of us—they could have told her to just leave me, but they knew I was sick and needed help. This wasn't me; it was a disease. "That's not the Clint you know," they said. I had friends tell her to leave me—"Jesus Christ, you can't stay there!" But Joanie's parents told her to do everything she could to get me into rehab. They knew it was the only way I'd survive.

One time, in early August, I threw all of her things on the lawn. Pictures, clothes, jewellery—the whole deal. I threw it all off the back porch. I dragged our bed outside. I broke a few of her porcelain dolls and piled them in pieces with the rest of it.

My God, the shit Joanie put up with. And she stuck by me. I had a complete nervous breakdown in the end. For lack of a better word, I was crazy. I'd wake up in the morning and be fine. I'd be good for about five or six hours a day. But as the day went on, I would become unbalanced and lose control of my ability to comprehend and rationalize. I had fits of madness.

That September, Joanie was back by my side, helping me work on some horses in Carson City. The NHL season hadn't opened yet. I wasn't full time with the Blue Jackets, so I was home for the week, doing some dentistry gigs and planning to head east to Columbus for the tail end of training camp.

The first weekend in October, we had a big party at our place. A bunch of friends came over, and I drank through the whole thing. It was messy. Predictably, later that night, I was irate. I picked another stupid fight with Joanie.

"You're only with me because I played hockey," I said, which was absurd—she'd never even seen me play. "You don't really love me."

The following Monday, October 6, 2008, Joanie left our house after we got in a huge fight. It was almost exactly a year since Dudley had come and saved my life and I wound up in the state loony bin. Neither of us can remember exactly what it was about. I was drunk again. Things were escalating, and I was out of control. Joanie was afraid. She thought that I'd calm down if she left, so she checked into the Carson Valley Inn. The next day at noon, Joanie went to a meeting of Al-Anon, the support group for family members of alcoholics. When it was over, she came home to check on me. I wasn't answering her phone calls.

It was two-thirty in the afternoon. The sky was overcast. She walked in the door and found my phones, which were switched off.

She went out the back sliding doors and called for me—I didn't answer. She walked up and around the side of the tack shed and saw me sitting there.

I wasn't right. I hadn't stopped drinking since she left. Hadn't slept. I was exhausted. My head was spinning. I was in blue jeans and shirtless. She wore a tie-dyed pink top and pants from her skating lessons.

I sat next to the tack shed, facing the mountains. She saw the gun lying on a wooden table beside me.

"Where were you?" she asked. "What are you doing out here?"

"I'm looking for rabbits," I said.

I was trembling. My face was red and sweating. The rage inside my head was full-strength. It was screaming. I couldn't shut it off.

"I can't stand being in my head," I said.

"What are we going to do about this?" she said.

I wasn't in control anymore. The monster inside me had taken over. I could feel my anger towards her, but I knew it was meant for me. *I have to make it stop.*

"Is this what you want?" I yelled.

"What?" She didn't understand.

"I can't do it anymore," I said. "I can't turn my head off. This is all I can think about. I can't live inside my head anymore."

I picked the gun up and pushed the barrel against my chin. It was like you see in the movies—on an angle to the back, towards my throat. She didn't have time to stop me. She didn't have time to scream.

I pulled the trigger. The bullet ripped through my chin and tore towards my brain.

27

I Did

THERE WERE NO FLASHBACKS. I DIDN'T RETURN TO THOSE COLD nights spent carving out dreams on the outdoor rink back of Elmwood Drive. There were no visions of Christmas mornings, no Saturday nights watching hockey around the television, no boxing matches in our old backyard. There were no smashed windows or broken vows. I didn't see my first NHL game or the one that sliced me open and drained my blood like sand in an hourglass, counting down to the end. There was just red darkness and the chaos I couldn't kill.

I opened my eyes and saw Joanie's screaming face. I put my hand on my chin and felt the blood between my fingers, falling faster and faster to the dirt. I stood there as the blood made red rivers down my chest. I bled like a stuck pig.

"See, Joanie?" I coughed. My mouth was numb. "Is that what you want?" Blood fell from my mouth and nose as I spoke. "Look what you made me do!"

My words slurred. I couldn't move the left side of my face.

Joanie was hysterical, fumbling with her phone as she tried to call for help. I started to walk away, waiting to die—pacing back and forth, trying to hold in the blood. Waiting to die, knowing it was coming. I went into the tack room and then walked out. Sat down and then got up. I went over to the barn, found a towel and pushed it under my chin, letting it absorb the blood. It was heavy and wet. I sat down, I got up, I stumbled back down. My eyes rolled back in my head.

Joanie was on the phone, yelling and screaming. "There's been an accident! My husband's been shot!"

"Where is the gun now?" the 911 operator asked Joanie. "You need to get it away from him."

She grabbed it and threw it as far as she could.

"I can fix this!" I yelled. "I can fix this. We don't need the cops." I found my shirt in the truck and put it on. The blood kept coming as I sat down and pushed the towel against my chin, trying to make it stop.

Joanie was yelling into the phone. "You guys need to get here! You need to be here!"

"Get off the phone—I can handle this!" I yelled. "I can fix this. I can stitch myself up." I didn't want the world to see me bleeding out again. It was a mistake, and I knew it then. It was just a mistake and I could fix it without the world knowing and seeing what I'd done. I think I was scared, like a wounded animal trying to escape a hunter. But I was also the triggerman.

The towel was soaked in blood. Everything felt light and I stumbled forward as I sat, but I caught myself. Joanie grabbed me. I could hear the sirens coming down the road.

The cops squealed into our yard and came out with their guns drawn, looking at Joanie as though she'd been the one who shot me. Five of them looked like they were ready to shoot. I was pacing around now, slumping occasionally—dizzy and fighting to stay conscious.

Joanie sat next to me as they yelled at her to move away. She refused. The cops kept yelling, "Ma'am, you need to move! Ma'am, you need to move!"

"No!" She put her arms around me, worried that the cops would try to finish the job.

"Fuck off," I coughed at them. "Mind your own business."

My dogs, Bob and Boon, sat next to me, leaning against my legs. The cops didn't know what to do. They kept yelling at Joanie to move, but she wouldn't. The dogs stayed put.

I stood up and starting walking to show the cops I could.

"Don't call an ambulance," I said. "I can fix this."

But the bleeding wouldn't stop. It came out of my mouth and the hole the bullet left in my chin. Part of my tongue and several of my teeth were gone. I could feel the hole in the roof of my mouth. The bullet was buried in my skull. I was certain I would die.

The ambulance roared in moments later. With the paramedics there, the cops backed away. I kept saying I was fine. "I can fix it. I don't need to get in the ambulance."

Joanie kept trying to help me. One of the cops was nice to her. "You need to listen to them," he said. He kept the other cops away. They seemed to think that Joanie had done it.

Her phone rang. A neighbour was listening to the police scanners. "Is everything okay, Joanie? Do you need me to come over?" she asked. Word rolled like a wave across Gardnerville. Joanie begged me to get into the ambulance. It was only going to get worse. *Damn it*—I let them take me.

The hospital was seven miles away. They rushed me in, all these goddamn people staring at me, getting involved in my business. I just wanted to run away and die. The doctors said they needed to airlift me to Reno. A helicopter landed on the pad out front. "Look, I'm fine. I don't need to go." I couldn't let them just carry me off. *You get up and keep moving*, I thought. They wheeled me out to the helicopter.

"I'm not getting in that thing. No way."

Joanie was still at the house, being questioned by the police. They wouldn't let her leave. I'd warned her not to tell them the truth—everything we had would be gone if she told them the truth. She told them it was a hunting accident. "He was cleaning his gun and it just went off." They didn't believe her.

It seemed like everyone else in town was at the hospital. You could almost feel that wave sweep across the town. "Clint's been shot . . . Clint's been shot . . . Clint's been shot . . ." There were at least thirty people there, staring at me with their faces of panicked horror. My third wife was there—she didn't live far from us, and we'd remained close after our divorce. Waco and Dave were there, too. Even Brian Peck was there—we'd hardly said a word to each other in months. I was on the stretcher, yelling at the nurses who were trying to sedate me, flailing like a shot cow in a slaughterhouse. *Might as well slice open my neck and get it over with.* Brian put his hand on my shoulder and pushed me down.

"Clint, you need to let them get you on this helicopter."

"Screw that," I said. "Just give me a Band-Aid."

Waco stood beside Brian, tears in both their eyes. "You've got to get on the chopper, man. You've got to."

Just give me a Band-Aid and let me finish this game.

Joanie arrived at the last minute. They strapped my arms and legs to the board. "Give him a lot of meds," Brian told one of the doctors. "Sedate him good. Because if he wakes up mid-flight, he'll take that helicopter down."

A numbness fell over me. I don't know how they managed to get that needle in, but it hit me fast and hard. I couldn't thrash, I couldn't fight, I couldn't yell. The rage stopped spinning. I closed my eyes and flew away.

2 8

The Damage Done

A FRIEND DROVE JOANIE TO RENO, ABOUT AN HOUR NORTH OF the house. She didn't know if I was dead or alive. All she knew was that, after the gun went off, the bullet went into my head and never came out. Anything could happen, and it probably wasn't good.

When she arrived, a doctor explained that there was little they could tell her, other than that I was still alive. And that she should go home and get some clothes, because it was going to be a while. The surgeons didn't know how much damage had occurred. They couldn't start surgery until X-rays revealed whether there was already swelling in my brain. If there was, surgery would have to wait. Joanie was told, very calmly, "We're not going to be able to get back to you for about another two to three hours."

The bullet had gone through the bottom of my chin, towards the back and left part of my mouth. It ricocheted off my left molars, went through part of my tongue and ripped through the right upper palate, through my sinus, close to my right eye. It stopped just millimeters from my brain. The X-rays showed little swelling, so the surgery went ahead. But removing the bullet was too risky. It remained lodged in my forehead.

I was out of surgery by the time Joanie got back from our ranch. They said I was doing fine. There wasn't any serious damage, other than the hole in the roof of my mouth. After surgery, a doctor told Joanie it looked as though I would survive. They needed to keep me unconscious for a while because they were still worried about possible swelling in my head, especially with the bullet still inside. My system needed to get rid of all the alcohol and the cocktail of prescription drugs I'd been taking. The doctor told Joanie the medication I was on shouldn't have been mixed together and that the dosages I'd been told to take by that pill-pushing doctor I'd seen after being in the state institution were crazy. What we thought would make me better had made things worse.

Before letting her into my part of the ICU, a nurse warned Joanie, "What you're going to see isn't good."

I wasn't in a private room; my bed was at the end of a large, open area, curtained off for privacy. It was kind of like a cul-de-sac, and I was in the first one on the right. The room was royal blue and white. The sheets were light blue on top with white stripes underneath. There were no windows.

I was unconscious, propped up with a brace around my neck. There was a breathing tube down my throat. Monitors beeped all around me. They let Joanie pull up some chairs, so she could make a bed to sleep on at night. It wasn't comfortable. It was awful for her. But they brought her blankets from the dryer. Joanie figured out where to get food and find a bathroom. Otherwise, she stayed by my side.

Later, everyone was gone. It was just me, unconscious, and the woman I'd blamed for putting me there. She was alone and scared. She tried to tell herself this wasn't her fault, but she couldn't stop believing that it was. Joanie had been trying to help, trying to save us, and now she sat there crying because she couldn't.

A police officer called Joanie and told her his report was done, and if she stood by her story that the shooting had been an accident, I would be able to leave at any time. As a suicide attempt, I wouldn't be let go. So she had the officers change their report to say that I had tried to kill myself. She knew I wouldn't get help if I could walk my own ass out of the hospital. If I was going to get the support I actually needed, it would have to be against my will.

With that decision, Joanie brought me back to life.

I was in and out of consciousness for a week. Joanie's sister came to be with her the day after the shooting. My mother arrived shortly after. I woke up once and the nurse asked me if I knew where I was.

"Buffalo," I said.

"No, Clint. You're in Reno," the nurse said. "You shot yourself."

I'd pass back out and wake up again a little while later. Every time they asked me where I was, it was the same hazy reply: *Buffalo . . . Buffalo . . . Buffalo . . .*

With all the sedatives, I was still confused about where I was and what had happened. But when the nurse asked me about Joanie, I kept saying the same thing: "I love my wife." A doctor told Joanie that that was my true personality. When people are put under sedation, he said, their true personality comes out. A lot of people that seem mean and ornery are really just mean and ornery. But I was just a nice cowboy, the doctor told her.

They kept trying to tell me that I had shot myself. The nurse told Joanie I needed to know right away why I was there so that I could properly process the trauma.

"Clint, do you understand that you shot yourself?" she kept asking. Eventually, I nodded that yes, I understood.

The nurse explained what all the machines attached to me were for.

"You have a hole in the roof of your mouth," she said. "We're going to give you something to drink, but we're going to thicken it up. It will have a weird texture." They had to thicken anything that could pass up through my mouth and into my nose. It was all very matter of fact. Joanie just stayed in the background.

When my mother came to see me, we both broke down. Here I was with a bullet in my head, still breathing. The woman who'd given me life and helped me fight through it—here she was, standing over me, in tears. And I knew it then.

I took her hand. "I'm here for a reason," I said. "I must be."

The news spread quickly, and reporters kept calling and trying to get into the hospital to find me. It got so bad that the hospital asked if they could officially discharge me but keep me at the hospital under the alias Roger Gordon. One woman called our home phone and Joanie's cell phone, claiming she was my aunt, had heard about the accident and wanted to know where I was being taken care of. Joanie told her she would call her back. She spoke to my mom, who confirmed I had no aunt by that name. It was another reporter. Next, the press somehow found out about Roger Gordon and started to hound the hospital again. We switched my name to Karl, because I loved the character Billy Bob Thornton played in the movie *Sling Blade*.

I was almost paralyzed on the right side of my face for the first little while. Between the hole in the roof of my mouth and the messed-up state of my tongue, I had a speech impediment. Everything I ate came up through my nose. I had a lot of macaroni and cheese—it was the only solid food I could eat. It was just terrible—terrible and painful.

The doctor said it was incredible that I was alive, that I could see and that I could function. "It just missed your eye. You have full vision," he said. "You didn't destroy your sinus cavity. It'll be hard to talk properly for quite some time, but eventually that will go away."

It was a goddamn miracle. There was a brief moment of joy. The blade, the pills, the bullet—nothing could take me down. *I'm the toughest motherfucker I know.* Then the reality hit—*I've really messed up this life of mine.* I'd be in the ICU for a week. But it was going to take a lot more time to fix a world I'd blown to pieces.

A man only has so many chances. I'd make the most of it this time. I spoke to my son, Jed, on the phone back in Calgary, and my daughter Kelli called me from Australia. Dallyn came in later that week. It broke my heart to have her see me like this, but her beautiful face was an inspiration.

Joanie called Rick Dudley. Days earlier, he had heard the news and thought he'd be making arrangements to attend a funeral.

My brother, Garth, called the NHL Players' Association to get help for me. They took care of everything. Andrew Galloway from the NHLPA told Joanie I had to go to rehab. The association would pay for it, but I had to do everything they said—for however long it took, whether it was thirty days, sixty, or more.

Joanie told me what was happening—that I was going straight to rehab, whether I wanted to or not. There was no choice. The NHLPA had made it clear. And Joanie said we were through if I didn't agree to take the help they were providing.

I wanted to go home. My mother and I tried to talk Joanie and the doctors into at least letting me go home before sending me to rehab.

"You're not coming home," Joanie said. "I'm sorry."

I wouldn't admit that it was a suicide attempt—but it didn't matter, because the police report said it was. Still, I was sure that if the Blue Jackets found out what I'd done, they'd fire me. So I stuck to my story—I was shooting rabbits; it was an accident.

My fears were unfounded. Scott Howson, the Blue Jackets' general manager, was very supportive. I don't think he really bought my story about the rabbits. I don't think anyone really did. He flew in from California to visit me the last day I was in the ICU.

"I'm going to be there for the opening game," I told him.

"Clint, you just need to take care of yourself. Do what the doctors say and your job will be waiting for you when you get back."

Okay, fine, I thought. *Thirty days and I'm out of here.*

They shipped me to rehab as soon as my face was surgically repaired and it was certain I was out of danger. It would take a while for my mouth to heal, but there was no permanent damage. The NHLPA sent a driver to pick me up at the Reno hospital and cart my sorry ass to a rehab facility just outside of San Francisco.

When we pulled out of the hospital, the driver said, "You probably don't remember me."

"What? No."

"I recognized you right away. I used to live in Saskatchewan. I was an alcoholic. You came to a meeting once in Regina."

There was too much going on—I had a hole in my chin and in the roof of my mouth, there was a bullet in my head and I was about to go away for being crazy. I couldn't process what he was saying.

"You were in Regina. At the AA meeting."

Holy shit.

He was a big guy, an ex-football player who played some games in the Canadian Football League. He told me he had been at that first Alcoholics Anonymous meeting I attended, and he remembered me because I'd played in the NHL. It was unbelievable. I can't remember his name anymore, but he drove me four hours from Reno to San Francisco. I was worried about so much at the time—my relationship with Joanie, my job with the Blue Jackets—but he helped put me at ease. I don't know if he worked for the rehab centre or the NHLPA, but his job was to drive people like me into the next stage of recovery. It was a long ride. I could have bailed at any time, but he just talked and listened and took me where I needed to go.

And he didn't just drive me there, he got me there—guided me there. A lot of things were coming together all of a sudden. I knew I was alive for a reason. I knew that I had gone to an AA meeting in Regina all those years ago for a reason. Faced with circumstances like these, it was hard to argue with divine intervention.

While I was on my way to San Francisco with my pseudo–guardian angel, Joanie went back to the ranch. It had been two weeks since she'd collected her clothes and moved into the ICU with me. She could still hear the chilling echoes of that violent afternoon. Her pink tie-dyed shirt was still stained with blood. She went out back to feed the horses, walking past the tack shed where I'd shot myself in front of her. Close to that terrible place, she stopped. There was no more blood. The rain or wind must have washed the rusty dust away. Joanie looked down by her feet, and a small white pebble caught her eye. She knelt down and looked closer.

My tooth.

The bullet had blown it right out of my mouth. It was completely intact. The sight of it didn't disturb her—she was just bewildered. *What are the chances?* she thought. Everything was blown to shit, but the pieces held together. A bullet ripped through my head, stopping mere millimeters from my brain. No permanent problems. Just pieces that needed to be put back together. *Maybe*, she thought. *Maybe everything can be whole again.*

Joanie picked up the tooth and turned it over in her fingers, brushing off the dirt. She walked back to the house, into our room, and opened a jewellery case she kept on our dresser. She hid it deep in the bottom and closed the lid.

2 9

Alcatraz

THE REHAB FACILITY WAS ON A HILL, SURROUNDED BY ART DECO homes with stunning views of San Francisco Bay. Along with the stunning sights came a pricey zip code—every driveway had a Porsche or two. This might have been somebody's paradise, but it was my hell. Trust me, rehab is always much nicer in the promo pictures.

From the window, I saw the dots of white sails drifting beneath the Golden Gate Bridge and along the shoreline. I watched them move slowly as the sun dropped over the city towards the sea. A large brown island pushed up in the middle of it all—this ugly piece of unwanted rock, stuck square in the middle of this picture of perfect happiness.

Alcatraz.

My "cell" was simple—a bed, a desk, some chairs. I marked off time served on a calendar on the wall. *Thirty days to freedom. Twenty-nine . . . Twenty-eight . . .*

The living quarters were in an old hotel. I had my own room, right across from the counsellors' and nurses' area. I had my own space when I arrived, which I thought was a privilege but turned out to be policy. I was a new arrival going through detox and on constant suicide watch. I was in that room for a month, which was supposed to be the length of a rehab "sentence." What a joke. I actually believed them. In reality, I was about to become the longest-serving patient the facility ever had.

There were no gates or guards or anything like that. I wasn't behind

196

bars. There was no law that kept me there. Technically, I was free to leave at any time, but they took away my cash and credit cards. I thought, *I might as well swim with the sharks across San Francisco Bay.* In my mind I was a man serving time, held against my will by a screwed-up system and a wife that wanted to put me away. *Joanie could get me out of there,* I thought. *She just needs to say the word and I'm gone. But she wants to see me bleed.*

I was a miserable prick. The first couple of weeks just drove me crazy. I wanted to get back to my job. Sure, I had shot myself, but I had obviously learned from my mistake. I messed up. Wasn't going to do that again. *Okay, I get it. Now let me get back and get rolling.* I didn't think I should be there. I didn't want to be there.

Everything irritated me. Everyone pissed me off. I was just a mean bastard. I scared everyone. I grew a beard that made me look kind of crazy. Just let it grow out, like I'd completely given up on shaving. You had to check out a razor every time you wanted to shave. It was just a pain in the ass.

It didn't take long for me to snap. A few days, tops. There was this one young guy who wouldn't stop talking. He always had something loud and obnoxious to say. He was like a goddamn mosquito buzzing around my ear. One afternoon, all the patients hung out in this common area, and this guy went off on one of his loud, annoying rants again. I absolutely lost it on him.

"You! Shut the hell up!" I shouted. "If you don't shut up, I'm going to throw you out that fucking window."

Everyone stopped and looked at me as if I'd shot the man. The room fell totally silent. The kid didn't say another word. Later, I found out he was on some kind of drug that was causing him to talk all the time. I felt bad about that. He ended up being a friend of mine.

I tried to escape after just a few days. I was mad at Joanie. I'd gotten really depressed and anxious. *I'm done with this shit,* I told myself. I packed my bags and marched out the door, but they managed to talk me out of it. They'd have to do that quite a few times before my time there was done.

That first week, I wasn't allowed to watch TV, and it was lights out by 10 P.M. There were no TVs in the rooms, so it was impossible to cheat the system. We weren't allowed cell phones—they search your bags and everything—but they didn't know I had two: a personal phone and another one issued by the Columbus Blue Jackets. I turned one in and hid the other. The scam didn't last long, though. I kept calling Joanie and leaving messages when she wouldn't answer. "You put me in a prison," I said. "I'm here because of you. I'm going to lose my job because of you." Joanie called the centre and ratted me out. They told her they had taken my cell phone already. She said, "No, you have *one* of his phones." She told them she'd call it until it rang enough for them to find it. She did, and they made me hand it over.

It was almost two weeks before they actually allowed me to make a sanctioned phone call. I wasn't even allowed to call my own mother. *Screw them and their rules.* I managed to get my hands on contraband cell phones that the other patients circulated (like the old inmates in Alcatraz, we had an underground economy). Through those first couple weeks, when it got dark, I'd climb these stairs next to the centre that led up to the road behind the buildings, and I'd sit on the steps and call my mom. If I couldn't get a cell phone, I'd go to a pay phone and call collect. She'd listen to me weep and tell me everything would be okay. She was the only person in the world that I believed was on my side. My entire life, she'd just loved and protected me. I needed her.

I told my mom it was all Joanie's fault. I told her Joanie was the only person who could get me out of there. "She's the devil shoving daggers into me," I said. "She won't help me." Part of the problem was that I still really loved Joanie, even though I thought she was being the cruellest person in the world. I needed to fix things by being home. If I was stuck in rehab, I reasoned, she'd probably just end up leaving me anyway. She didn't answer my calls because the rehab centre restricted our ability to contact loved ones during the early stages of our treatment.

Joanie came down to visit once a week. She didn't want me to be alone, even though she couldn't stay with me. She'd have to get permission to come and take me to dinner down on the swanky waterfront strip. Every time she did, I'd smile and play nice until we got down the hill and out of sight. I was just waiting. As soon as the building was out of earshot, I'd start barking. "You better get me the hell out of here," I'd say. "I'm going to lose my job because of you. You're the reason I'm here. You better quit saying stuff. They're going to keep me in here longer." It was always the same, and she always bit her lip and put up with it. She never backed down.

I told my mom to call Joanie and try to convince her to set me free. "He can hate me all he wants," Joanie told her. "If he hates me until the day I die, that's fine. He'll be alive."

My "warden" was Tina, a tough counsellor with attitude. She was younger—in her mid-thirties, maybe—all tatted up with long, black hair. Really pretty, but also really tough. She was responsible for assessing me—working with me one on one, evaluating my progress, stuff like that. At first, I was assigned to a guy I just didn't connect with. There was no way I was going to tell him shit about my life. I didn't like him at all, but after a couple weeks, he left rehab and I was reassigned to Tina. We met pretty much every day. At first, I hated her. I know she was doing her job, but Tina called me on my shit, and that was hard to face.

After a few weeks, Tina called Joanie and told her she thought I needed to be in there longer than a month. Joanie asked how long, and Tina recommended keeping me there for three to four months.

"You're kidding," Joanie said. "Have you told him?"

"No," Tina sighed. "We're going to."

"Well, be ready."

The next day, I met with Tina and she told me it looked like I'd have to stay through Christmas. It was early November. I lost my shit. "Screw you," I said. "I'm out of here." And I marched up to my room, packed everything up and went for the doors again. "Not a chance. Not a goddamn chance," I said. "I'm leaving now."

No one understood how panicked I was. There was a gun against my head and no one seemed to realize. *Thirty days and I'm out of here,* I thought. I could still save my job and my marriage. But if they made me stay longer than that, it was all over. I'd have nothing. So I packed my bags, put on my black cowboy hat and walked out the front door. I marched down the steep roads that wind down to the bay, dragging my wheeled suitcase behind me.

They sent one of their counsellors after me. He stayed about twenty feet behind me the whole time. I was yelling and screaming at him as I went along this busy street of shops by the water, packed with rich tourists. People looked at me like I was some crazy John Wayne or something. "Quit following me!" I yelled. "I'll break your neck!" I had no money, no phone. What was I going to do? I was walking around town with a suitcase and a cowboy hat and no money. I kept turning around and yelling at the guy. "Leave me alone! It's a free world. Go back to your hotel."

I thought about hitchhiking. It was a four-hour drive over the mountains to get home, and it was tough to find someone heading that way and willing to give a lift to a rehab fugitive. I'd have better luck with Joanie. I found a pay phone and called her collect. She answered. "You better get me a ticket," I said. "I'm heading to the airport." The centre had already called her. She said she wouldn't pay for a ticket and told me to go back to the facility. Then she hung up. *Shit*.

There was nothing else to do. I had to rethink my plan to get home. When I got back to the facility, they gave me a Breathalyzer test. I'd been walking for about an hour and a half, and they had a guy following me the whole time. They knew I hadn't had anything to drink. It was just another goddamn indignity.

I was convinced more than ever that Joanie was the only reason I couldn't get out of that place. I was so angry with her. I told the patients stories—only revealing tiny fractions of the truth—about how badly she had treated me before the gun accident. Tina started to think that Joanie might be part of the problem because of the way I framed everything. And I'd really convinced myself it was true. She wasn't taking my calls. She wouldn't listen to my mom. She wouldn't buy me a ticket home.

Experts working with the NHLPA and the NHL—Dr. David Lewis and Dr. Brian Shaw—counselled Joanie the whole time. I didn't know she was speaking with them. Like the rehab centre, they also told her not to answer my calls. It was a tough-love approach, and it was hard for her. She was worried sick about me.

I took Joanie's name off the official "call list" to get back at her for not taking my calls. It meant she was no longer approved to contact me or get updates on my progress from the counsellors. Joanie called Tina several times a day to check in on me, but now reception wouldn't take her calls. It also meant she couldn't come visit me at Thanksgiving. *That'll show her.*

But even though Joanie couldn't call in, I kept phoning her. I was still borrowing cell phones snuck in by other patients. When everyone went to sleep, I'd stay up all night, leaving long message after message on her voice mail. "You bitch. You better get me out of here. This is all your fault." Stuff like that, but often much worse.

Joanie didn't know what to do. She was hurt that I'd taken her off the call list and worried that she couldn't check on me. It was mean. I wasn't thinking about how much she cared about me and how agonizing it was not to be able to know how I was doing. She felt partly responsible for what I had done to myself. I blamed her outright, for starters. But beyond that bit of craziness, she worried that somehow she had driven me to pull the trigger; that life had been wonderful until she showed up and brought out the monster in me. That kind of guilt festers. And now I'd blocked her from calling in, as if she was some kind of crazy stalker I didn't want to talk to. Of all the things I did to hurt Joanie, this was one of the cruellest.

She didn't know what to do, so she called Andrew Galloway at the NHLPA, who had arranged for me to go to rehab. He helpfully suggested that the clinic might not be able to give *her* an update, but she was able to give *them* an update. It took her a while to figure out how to do it, but Joanie forwarded every message I had sent her to Tina's office phone one evening. She filled Tina's voice mailbox right up. When Tina came in the next morning, the light on her phone flashed with evidence.

She sat down and listened to every single one. The messages were terrible and abusive. It was embarrassing. Joanie also left a message with all the numbers I had called her from. She probably got five or six people in trouble. It was a disaster. I was busted.

30

Warriors

A LOT OF PEOPLE CAME THROUGH REHAB. SOME OF THEM WERE there for maybe a month, some a lot longer. Eventually, most would say, "Screw it, I'm leaving," and they'd just check themselves out.

After just a month, it seemed like I'd been there an eternity. I worried constantly that my career would be over. I asked the NHLPA's contact to tell me whether the Blue Jackets had filled my position, but he never got back to me. I searched the Internet for word that I'd been replaced but couldn't find anything. It felt like my career had been sabotaged. If I wanted to go back to work, I had to complete the program—and now Tina was making me stay even longer. I was stuck. It seemed like an infinite sentence.

When my first month was over, I was told to pack up and move into a room with another patient. Everyone had a roommate. A lot of people cycled through my life during that time. They'd move you all the time, switching up your roommates. It was always unsettling, but I liked most of my roommates. There were eight of them in the end.

The first didn't work out. He was this big, fat guy who was in there for drug addiction. I was really careful around him because someone had warned me that he was a snitch. We started off as friends, but it didn't take long for him to rat me out for using another patient's contraband cell phone to call Joanie. He got us both in trouble. What an asshole.

Unfortunately, he was just one of several miserable people I encountered in rehab. One supervisor made my life a nightmare. He was a drill sergeant. He'd always catch me with chew in my bottom lip and make me spit it out. Damn, I hated that. Talk about withdrawal. There was no chew, and caffeine and sugar were limited. Sure, the food was good and the scenery was nice—but all those shitty rules drove me crazy.

There was a small gym in one of the garages on site. It was always locked and you had to have permission to use it. Being active was one of the ways I dealt with my anxiety, and these assholes wouldn't even let me lift a weight. Eventually, I found an unlocked window and was able to sneak in and work out without them finding out. The window was up near the top of the garage, so I had to climb up and drop in. They didn't find out until I told another patient how to do it. He was this big guy who told me about all the steroids he did. He was in rehab for drug addiction. This donkey didn't cover his tracks—put the weights away, close the damn window, make it look like you weren't there. They busted us and locked the window. *Shit.*

Rehab was like jail, but it was also a lot like elementary school. As part of the program, we'd have mandatory group sessions every day. These were particularly annoying. We were assigned to specific groups with about five or six other patients. We'd sit there and bullshit about everything. "How are you feeling? What are you thinking about?" There was always some idiot who'd just babble on and on about themselves. Like anyone actually cared.

The groups were very general. We all had different problems. Most of the people in rehab had a dual diagnosis—some sort of anxiety or depression that had developed into alcoholism or drug addiction as a way to cope. But I convinced myself that the other inmates had nothing in common with me. Like the big gal who wouldn't stop eating; or the woman in her eighties who shopped so much her own goddamn kids put her away; or the heroin addict from L.A.; or the geriatric millionaire with a booze problem. *What the hell am I doing here with this cast of weirdo screw-ups and addicts?*

We'd gather morning, afternoon and night in various rooms that seemed pretty much exactly the same—the assembly room, the common room, the meeting area, etc. Always a circle of chairs and hour after hour of emotional show and tell.

The counsellors gave us assignments to complete during our free time. It was always weird shit. One counsellor wanted me to write a letter about why I love myself. Another wanted me to write a letter saying sorry to myself. I thought it was stupid and refused to do it at first. I'm not going to write some corny letter to myself. I knew where it was going and I wasn't going to fall for it.

The whole time, I kept a journal in a blue notebook. I'd asked Joanie to buy it for me while I was lying in that hospital bed in the ICU back in Reno. There was something about writing that I enjoyed. Getting it all out on paper was cathartic. But who wants to share that with a group of crazy strangers? *What's the point?* I wondered. *Are we all going to hug it out after?*

Eventually, though, I gave in and wrote a letter to myself. It was still corny—but okay, fine, it felt kind of good. After the exercise, we went around the room complimenting each other. Also corny. But again, it felt pretty damn good. I went back to my room and wrote down everything they had said about me in the blue notebook. They told me my "heart could heal the planet" and that I was "hilarious and a leader and a great speaker," and someone said that she saw "nothing but strength in me in every way." Another person complimented the beard I was growing, and one woman noted that I looked like the actor Hugh Jackman, while another said she liked my eyes and wished I wasn't married. I scribbled those things down, too.

"You make me feel safe," one person said.

"You're a warrior," said another.

I wrote it all down, because putting it on paper made it all seem real. I felt good about myself for the first time in a while, and even if that was something small, it was still something.

Sometimes, we had art class. My reaction: *Can it get any more like elementary school than this?* The counsellor would give us some theme to draw. It'd usually be some meaningful bullshit. And we'd always play these stupid games—trying to solve puzzles and problems—in our groups. Okay, that stuff was actually all right. I've always enjoyed trust falls. And some of the other team-building exercises were fun. But still, here we were, a bunch of grown-ass adults with grown-ass problems playing games like a bunch of teen counsellors from Camp Caribou! We even did a goddamn sweat lodge.

The kooks got on my nerves. I don't want to say that an eighty-something-year-old shopaholic doesn't have a legitimate problem, but how the hell am I supposed to relate to that? Her husband died and she just started shopping, buying up all these books and shit online. Her kids put her in rehab to make her stop. I guess I could appreciate the obsession that this old lady was dealing with. But at the time, I thought it was just crazy. At the other end of the spectrum, several patients suffered from addiction to hard drugs. A lot were hooked on heroin. I was surprised to find out how many. Oxycontin was another common addiction. I'd never touched an illicit drug in my life. Sure, I'd been down the dependence road before, but I really didn't think I was a true alcoholic. I drank too much, yes. But I managed to kick booze for eight years before. Well, okay . . . yeah, I developed a drinking problem . . . but it was strictly related to my OCD and depression . . . I mean, come on, I wasn't an *alcoholic* alcoholic—right? Just in case, my schedule included an AA meeting every night.

One of the guys who came through rehab was an Irish white supremacist. He had all these racist tattoos—swastikas, the iron cross, all that shit. He was big, too—probably six foot two or three—and thick. He had a marine haircut. It made him look intimidating. I felt his anger when I talked to him. When he got stressed, you just knew it was boiling over inside him. He was an alcoholic and would use the booze to channel his anger.

Worldviews aside, I related to this guy. He'd start out as this happy, funny, outgoing kind of guy and then snap into an angry beast. We were both pretty normal drinkers who would go out and have fun. But when the anger boiled out of him, he'd get really mean and resentful. In our AA meetings, he always talked about resentment. One day, our

AA counsellor asked us what the number one cause of a relapse is. I looked at the Irish white supremacist and *boom,* it came to me. I put my hand up. "Resentment," I said. I was right. I'm not Doctor-fucking-Phil here, but let's just call it an educated guess. I'd carried a lot of anger and resentment through life. It didn't matter that I'd been a pro hockey player. I could have been working my way up in business, in a factory or on the ice. Resentment exists in all those places.

I harboured a lot of resentment towards the people I cared about— particularly women. Women that I married and didn't know how to love. It was always a problem for me. Growing up, dating wasn't really a thing I did. Remember, I had one girlfriend before I started playing pro hockey. When I was young, my dad told me to stay away from women because they'd just screw me up. When I became a junior and pro prospect, people always told me women were only after one thing. When I did date, I figured they only liked me because I was a hockey player. It became a self-worth thing. *She doesn't like me; she likes what I do.* I assumed she was after what I might become and the financial benefits I might receive. Then, when I was in my first real adult relationship and thinking about breaking it off, she told me she was pregnant. I couldn't dismiss the thought that she'd gotten pregnant on purpose. Every relationship I have had was doomed by my unfair, preconceived ideas about women.

When I really tried to get to the root of my drinking problem, it always came back to this irrational resentment towards women. Not just the good-old-boy partying; I mean excessive self-medicating with alcohol to get rid of the pain. I was trying to protect myself, but all along I was sabotaging my ability to have a healthy relationship. I took it to an obsessive level.

31

Family Day

THE FIRST WEEK IN DECEMBER, WE HAD A SPECIAL WEEKEND FOR the families of the patients. Everyone had people come in to take part in addiction workshops and be part of all the constructive exercises and bullshit like that.

The events went on all day. In the first session, we had a big group meeting, and then we split off into smaller discussion groups. During the first meeting, I was laughing the whole time, making jokes. I felt my anxiety rising just having Joanie there beside me. I could see where this was heading: it was going to be her versus me again. I had learned a long time ago to use humour to ease tension and distract people from seeing the truth. *Take up all the time with jokes, and they won't have time to ask you something serious.* Walking to the next session, I prodded Joanie. "Everyone thinks I'm funny but you. Everyone likes me except you." She knew my behaviour, though—the jokes were a sign that I was getting anxious and nervous, and that I was trying to mask it.

When we got to the next session, there were about five patients grouped together with family members. We all sat in a big circle. There were about twenty people there. A guy from the Betty Ford Center, who was running the session, asked all the guests to share specific traits about their loved ones that they found particularly hard to deal with. Then the patient had a chance to respond and talk about all the things that frustrated them. It was kind of like: *When you do ____, I feel like ____.*

I knew right away this was going to piss me off. Everyone started spilling their guts, crying and hugging. When it was our turn, Joanie went first.

"When you blame me, it makes me—"

She didn't get to finish before I jumped out of my chair. "This is bullshit!" I shouted. "Do you see what I have to deal with?"

"Clint!" Tina yelled. "Clint! Sit down."

"Screw you," I said. "You let her talk, now let me talk."

It didn't matter what Joanie said. I had so much anger; I was just waiting to explode.

"Clint!" Tina said again.

I got up and tossed my chair against the wall. "You goddamn bunch of donkeys!" I shouted. "Why don't you all just go to hell? You too, Joanie."

She was crying now.

The doctor from the Betty Ford Center didn't know what to say. He just stared at me.

"Screw you and screw Betty Ford," I said. "You don't know shit."

And everyone just stared at me, frozen in fear, like I was an uncaged tiger at the zoo.

"Bunch of goddamn losers. What the hell are you looking at?"

"Get out," Tina said.

I went out to the lobby and paced back and forth, like I was holed up in a prison cell again. *Goddamn bitch. This is what she does—makes it my fault. Fuck her. To hell with this.* I sat down and tried to breathe. The monster was out of me. I needed to pull him back. This was the watch-what-you-fucking-say-because-I'll-rip-off-your-head-and-shit-down-your-neck version of me. In all the outbursts I'd had in rehab, they'd never experienced this from me, though they must have known it was inevitable. I mean, come on, I put a bullet in my own head. I had tried so hard to control the story, but here I was exposed again, bleeding out in front of everyone as they gasped at the horror.

Joanie was still inside the room, crying. I didn't give a shit about what anyone else in there was thinking. Tina came out into the lobby.

"You can't come back in, Clint," she said. "You're done for the day."

They let Joanie stay in the group, and she did. I just sat in the lobby all morning until I returned from Pluto.

The staff told Joanie she didn't have to talk to me, but she came and sat with me at lunch. She and Tina had spoken about my outburst. Tina told her not to take it personally—she hadn't done anything wrong—and that it was perfectly understandable if she just wanted to leave.

"Don't worry about Clint," Tina said. "He's an adult. He can handle his feelings. He'll be fine. Don't worry about offending him."

Joanie said she could take care of me. She was calm when she sat down.

"I'm sorry," I said. "I just get so mad at you sometimes."

"I'm really sorry you feel that way," she said, "but I'll see you next weekend."

"Are you sure you're coming back?" I said. "Goddamn it, I'm sorry. I just hate you sometimes. Please come back."

Joanie went out into the parking lot and started to drive away. I ran after her.

"Are you coming back? Will you come back?" I was panicking. I couldn't lose her and I thought she'd be gone forever.

"Yes," Joanie said again. "I'll be back again next weekend. Clint—I love you." And she left.

When I went into my session with Tina on Monday, she ripped me a new asshole. She went on for half an hour about all the things I needed to deal with. I told her I thought she had let me down. I'm sure she realized I wasn't ready to be in a setting like that with Joanie, but she had rushed me because of this stupid goddamn family weekend. I was convinced she had done it because the NHLPA wanted to know she was getting results.

"I trusted you, Tina," I said, "and now I think we have a problem."

We didn't speak for a few days after that, but then we started working together again because I knew she was the only person in that place who could really help me.

Two weeks later, Joanie went to the Betty Ford Center in Palm Springs to take part in a special program for families of people suffering from addiction. When the counsellors at the rehab centre recommended the clinic to her, Joanie was upset. She thought I'd convinced everyone that this was all her fault. Her parents urged her to go—she had nothing to lose, they said, and she could use the time away. It turned out to be the most important thing Joanie did through this whole painful ordeal. Whatever she learned there really helped. When she came back, things started to change. She was angry before—and I couldn't blame her. At the time, I was also filled with rage. But my anger was about me; I didn't stop to think about what I had done to her. When I saw her after that Betty Ford trip, she just seemed softer. More patient, more understanding—like everything didn't have to be a fight. She had learned a lot about mental illness and addiction, and how to deal with people who suffer from both. She learned not to take things personally. After a while, people in her position start to really believe that it's their fault—*I am doing this to him. I'm ruining his life. I'm making him miserable.* And the counterbalance to that is instinctively to respond with anger and hurt, so she'd lash out at me.

There were about thirty-odd people with loved ones suffering from addiction or some kind of mental illness at the Betty Ford course. Joanie listened to them all share the hurtful things that their loved ones had said. It was identical to what I had been saying. She realized that my circumstances weren't so special—I was acting like so many other people do. They explained that it was like a kid who isn't allowed to go out because he hasn't cleaned his room. There's a lack of understanding and perspective.

They taught her that, by taking me on in our battles, she was actually enabling my behaviour. As bad as she felt, they told her to let it go; it wasn't her fault. And so she stopped taking things personally. "I have nothing to do with this," she finally told herself. "I'm fine."

The few friends that I made in rehab through those first couple of months had pretty much the same attitude as me. You know, misery loves company. We sat around and complained together. We'd bitch about the shitty rules and swap our woe-is-me tales of life on the outside. Everyone had their own version of the victim story. I mostly complained about Joanie. I let everyone know that she was the real reason I was stuck there. She was the one who messed with my mind so much that I tried to put a bullet through it.

I got along well with a couple of young guys from Philadelphia who were both, I'd guess, in their mid-twenties. They had gone to high school together but hadn't seen each other since then. Rehab was their reunion. Both were big hockey fans, so we had that in common. The Flyers had been my favorite team growing up, and I had also played in the NHL. They were pretty impressed with that. They knew all about my injury—they remembered seeing it on TV and on the Internet.

One of the other guys there was a mixed martial arts fighter. He said he was actually part of the UFC and was on his way up the chain. His whole body was covered in tattoos, and he was jacked. Another rehab centre had sent him to this facility because he kept getting in fights there. If a patient got violent with another patient, they always got sent away.

We tried to get the MMA guy to fight with the juice monkey who had screwed up my gym scam. The fighter was so insecure. I kept telling him, "Man, that guy is way bigger than you. He could probably kick your ass." And the MMA guy would get all upset. At first, I thought he was joking. He was huge—there was no way our little comments should have bothered him. "You're a little pussy compared to that guy," I'd say, and he'd just start going crazy. "Fuck you!" he'd yell. "I'll whip his ass!" Steroids. I'm telling you—never do them.

Some really messed-up stuff went on in that place. It kept me entertained, at least. Like the meeting where two female patients got into a huge fistfight. And then there was the guy who must have had a sex addiction or something, because he and another patient were sleeping together—which was strictly against the rules, of course. And then he banged one of the housekeepers who came regularly to clean the place.

One of the other patients was there for eating too much. She was a big girl. We got along well and became close friends. You could tell she was a genuine person, honest and kind. She used to have an important office job, but she wasn't able to control her eating and it became a serious problem. Everything fell apart for her, and she ended up sitting next to me in rehab. This one time, she got extremely mad at me. There was this old, wrinkly guy who always walked around in loose shorts. He'd fall asleep during meetings and never wore underwear. In a meeting, we were going around the room, talking about whatever feelings we were dealing with that day, and this old guy's nuts were hanging out while he snoozed away. It was so disgusting and yet so hilarious. I couldn't stop laughing. My friend thought that was so mean and was furious with me after that. She didn't talk to me for a week. Otherwise, though, we got along well. A lot of the patients would come and go, so we never really got a chance to connect. But she became like family on the inside. It was a *Shawshank Redemption* kind of scenario.

After she got out, we kept in touch for a while. I was still doing my time—had been for a couple months and would be there for a while longer. It was encouraging to hear about her new life out there in the real world. Ever since she was young, she had always dreamed of being some sort of actress. She had a perfect voice for radio or TV—I always told her that. A while after she left, I got an email from her about the commercial she'd landed as a voice actress. She thanked me for encouraging her. She wasn't young, but she finally got a chance to follow her dream.

Many of the stories from rehab, though, don't have happy endings. The success rate for full recovery if you stuck with the program was something like 4 per cent, we were told. That's a grim reality.

One guy came in for a single afternoon before he was shipped out to hospital because his liver was messed up from too much cocaine over too many years. They did a standard blood test when he arrived and realized he probably shouldn't even have been alive at that point.

Boozing was probably the most common addiction at the clinic. Some of the people who suffered from alcoholism really shocked me. One of my roommates was a rich old guy with grey hair who was there for a month. He owned an oil company—I mean, this guy was an incredibly successful alcoholic. I liked him a lot and I admired that he was able to check himself into rehab when he knew he needed it, when he felt himself slipping even if he hadn't had a drink. That took a lot of strength and wisdom.

One of my best friends was a woman from New Jersey. She was also an alcoholic. She had really short hair and a thick Jersey accent. We used to talk about all the problems she was having with her husband. We really connected. Her husband ended up leaving her while she was in rehab. That was a common occurrence. I remember another patient having her husband come visit her, only to have him tell her he was through. He just couldn't take it anymore, so he broke her heart and left. So I was lucky—it was amazing that Joanie still spoke to me at all.

I stayed in touch with my friend from New Jersey for a while after she got out. But it wasn't long—maybe a few weeks—before the emails stopped abruptly. A short time later, we were told that she had passed away. She took a few steps back into the real world and drank herself to death.

You wouldn't believe some of these stories. They thought *I* was special because I had a bullet in my head, but some of their tales were just crazy. The heroin stories were always the worst. There was one nice guy I met who had tattoos all over his body. He was really interesting, really down to earth. He'd just been remarried. We talked a lot about our relationships. One day, he showed me his track marks. He told me all kinds of stories about his dark desperation. He used to shoot up at work.

The drug stories always shocked me. The crazy places these people would get stoned, all the time they wasted, and so much money just snorted up their nose or shot into their veins. So much money—more than most people could make in a year. It was so sad.

After my family day outburst and her session at Betty Ford, Joanie started coming down to visit me every weekend. It was like she'd doubled down on me. Eventually, she starting coming down on Thursdays and leaving on Sundays. She was gentler, kinder, even though I still blamed her for everything. But that was just my insecurity and confusion. I was crazy. I'd look around and try to find a reason for feeling the way I did. Joanie was closest to me, so she became my emotional punching bag. I don't know that I can fully understand how badly I hurt her. She carries the memory of that terrible day with her. I imagine that she always will. She never left my side, even when I tried to drive her away—even when I blamed her for my behaviour. Even when I put a gun to my chin, pulled the trigger and blamed her.

While at the Betty Ford Center, Joanie wrote about that day in her journal. When I see it through her eyes, the enormity of what I did breaks my heart. It makes the reality that she stayed with me that much more of a miracle.

Joanie's Journal
October 7, 2008, around 2:30 p.m., I sat not more than two arms' lengths away. What only took a second to happen seems to last forever as it plays through my head over and over again. What could I have done to stop this? I came home to my husband sitting behind a shed with a gun lying in front of him. In an instant he grabbed the gun, stood up and faced me, looked at me and said, "This is what I have been thinking about"—at that moment he placed the gun under his chin. While he stared at me you could hear a dull pop sound. His mouth and nose filled with blood. His chin swelled up with blood. He stood looking at me and said, "Look what you made me do." I thought he was gone.

As I dialed 911 he walked into the tack shed, grabbed a paper towel that he placed under his chin, walked over to the back of his truck and put his shirt on—continuing to walk around he went into the barn and grabbed a towel. He came out of the barn and sat down and started to pass out. I was losing him. The lady on the phone kept saying "Hang on someone will be there soon"—soon wasn't coming soon enough.

Then he got up and walked back to the tack shed and sat

down in front of it. As he sat with his chin resting in his hand, I started to lose him again. He was slouching over, his eyes starting to roll back. Then he stood up and went to where everything started—behind the tack shed, and he sat down.

The police showed up. There were so many—they seemed scared. No ambulance yet. None of the policemen seemed to help. Finally the paramedics showed up. I don't remember seeing the ambulance arrive, can't remember Clint being put into the ambulance. Waco showed up. Louise showed up. The police kept asking what happened over and over again. I was afraid they were going to show up and be mean, aggressive and forceful so I told the lady on the phone it was an accident and he was shooting rabbits. I told the same story to the police.

Louise drove me to the hospital in Gardnerville. When I walked in there were so many people. Blood everywhere. I heard them talking about putting a trach in his throat. There was so much noise. They wouldn't let me stay in the ER room. Everything seemed to get loud and anxious and they led me out of the room. Told me to go to the hospital in Reno and that Clint would be flown there by helicopter. Louise drove me to the hospital. When I got there a few minutes later a lady doctor came out to see me, told me they were having a plastic surgeon doctor come and look at Clint and they might do surgery that night. I was asked about a donor card. I was told they might put a trach in his throat again. Plastic surgeon came out to talk to me and said he was taking Clint into surgery that night. He sounded very positive—first sound that everything will be all right. The doctor said I should go home if I needed to because the surgery would be a few more hours and I could see him after. Mary took me home to get my car. I grabbed a few things and went back to the hospital.

During one of Joanie's visits shortly after she went to the Betty Ford Center, I was ranting and raving at her in the lunchroom. She walked away from me. A counsellor went over to see if she was okay. "You know, you don't have to take that from him," he said.

"I'm fine," Joanie said. "I'm going to go say goodbye."

She walked back over to me. I was still furious with her, seething.

"I'm sorry you feel this way," she said.

"Screw you," I growled. "Get the hell out."

Joanie didn't flinch. "I hope you have a nice weekend," she said. "I'm sorry you feel the way you do. But I still love you."

"Fuck you."

And she left—just walked out the door. I caught up to her and apologized before she got in the car.

If Joanie was willing to do whatever it took to help me survive this—to help *us* survive this—I was going to do whatever it took, too. I fully bought into the program then. Even if I hated every minute of it, I owed it to the people who stood by me to see this through.

32

Post-Traumatic

I FIRST LEARNED ABOUT POST-TRAUMATIC STRESS DISORDER IN January 2009. Tina kept bringing it up, suggesting that there might have been more to my jugular injury than the scar across my neck.

I thought it was complete bullshit. I was a professional hockey player, not a Vietnam vet.

"Clint, you're messed up," she said. "And do you know why you're messed up? It's because of that accident in Buffalo."

I blew her off. "Whatever, I was back playing in ten days," I said. "I would have come back sooner, but they said I couldn't until the stitches came out. I was brought up tough. You get on the horse, you get bucked off, you get up and get back on the horse. When that's your mental makeup for forty-eight years, you stand by it. Don't give me this crock of shit."

"Well, what was your life like after the accident?" she asked.

"Severe obsessive-compulsive disorder, my depression got really bad, constant nightmares and eventually insomnia," I said. "And then I started self-medicating." *Shit.*

Tina said she thought one of the reasons the NHL Players' Association was trying to help me with this rehab stuff was that I hadn't received any help back then. That was her theory, anyway. Who knows? She focused on the skate-blade accident as the catalyst for my psychological issues, but also tied in the things that had happened to me earlier in life. I had nightmares for years after my dad smashed in those windows in the middle of winter. The cop-car sirens haunted me and the cold consumed me. I thought we were going to freeze to death. Then he left one day and didn't come back. There's trauma in that.

After the accident, the effects of that trauma sent me into even more of a spiral. I swallowed a handful of sleeping pills and chased it with a bottle of whiskey. My heart stopped. My NHL career ended. There's trauma in that, too.

The rage has always been there. That switch goes on and I'm a monster. I was channelling things I couldn't even begin to comprehend. Suddenly, I was drinking my face off, taking on cops, and walking into gyms and picking on the biggest goons I could find. Normal people don't do that shit. The roof of my mouth was barely healed, and there was a bullet lodged millimeters from my brain.

Yeah, I knew something about trauma—but I had no clue how to deal with it. I kept fighting Tina on this. Post-traumatic stress? Was she crazy? My entire career was defined by that injury and my ability to come back from it quickly. That wasn't my problem. It was proof that I could take on anything.

It took me a good month to buy into her reasoning.

"No," I said. "This is all bullshit."

"Did you think you were going to die?" she replied.

"Well, yeah, I thought I was going to die. But we've been through this. I handled all that."

"Don't you think it was traumatic?"

"I got over it in a few days. I was fine."

During one of our sessions, Tina handed me this book called *Waking the Tiger* by Peter Levine, a renowned expert in trauma. The first chapter is about a young impala getting attacked by a cheetah. As soon as the cheetah lunges for the impala, it falls down like it's dead. The impala isn't pretending to be dead; its instincts have pushed it into an altered state of consciousness that all mammals experience when death is imminent. We often talk about "fight or flight" as the two main responses to danger, but the third response is to freeze. That impulse can do two things for the impala. If the cheetah thinks the impala is dead, it might drag the motionless prey to its lair to feed to its cubs. When it has a moment to escape, the impala will wake up and make a break for it. It shakes its body, literally ridding itself of the traumatic stress. On the other hand, if the impala doesn't have a chance to escape, its altered consciousness means it won't suffer when the cheetah rips it apart.

I really like animals, and this story had lots of action, so I bought in. Tina explained the concept to me. As humans, we're taught to not do what the impala does. We're taught to be tough, especially men. We're taught to fight. And we're taught to contain the natural instincts that help shake out the trauma that cripples us. Don't seek help. Don't cry, especially not in public. "Unlike wild animals," Dr. Levine writes, "when threatened, we humans have never found it easy to resolve the dilemma of whether to fight or flee." This stuff was a bit much for me to take in at the time, but the more I read and discussed it with Tina, the more it started to make sense. The lasting effects of trauma are the result of that negative moment being trapped inside of us, frozen and without resolution. It destroys us from the inside.

"The long-term, alarming, debilitating, and often bizarre symptoms of PTSD develop when we cannot complete the process of moving in, through and out of the 'immobility' or 'freezing' state," Levine said. That impala collapsed when it saw a cheetah chasing it down at seventy miles per hour. On the outside, the impala looked dead and gone. But on the inside, its nervous system was still spinning at seventy miles per hour. It's like slamming on the gas and the brake pedals in your car at the same time, Levine says. All that energy has to go somewhere. As a human, we aren't very efficient at getting rid of it. It comes out in the form of anxiety, depression and dysfunctional behaviour. When we can't get rid of these problems, we become fixated on them—returning, again and again, like a moth to a flame. The result, Levine says, is that many become so riddled with fear and anxiety, we're never capable of being comfortable inside ourselves.

That was chapter one.

Fuck. Me. It was all I needed to read. Two decades of hell, distilled into a few pages.

A couple days after my crash course in trauma, I got a panicked call from Joanie. She had been on her way from Gardnerville to visit me in rehab. The roads were icy through the mountains, and on one of the hills, another car slammed into her.

She wasn't hurt, but it was a big enough wreck that a number of cops came, an ambulance roared up, and it was a tense, terrible scene. The last time she'd seen anything like it, I was gushing blood with a bullet in my head.

"Clint, I was so proud," she said over the phone. "I held it together. I didn't even tear up until I got back in the car. And then I just started to shake and couldn't stop crying."

"Christ, Joanie," I said. "That's exactly what you're supposed to do! That's exactly it."

After that, Tina started doing these exercises with me, like word association and listening to the noises you'd hear in a quiet room—stuff like that. It was amazing how this shit just poured out of me. I cried for three days, uncontrollably. She didn't know it was going to be a three-day deal. It takes most people three *hours.* Every time she saw me, I broke out in tears.

"I don't know—you did some voodoo shit to me," I said. "Now I'm a frickin' blubbering baby."

I cried more than I'd ever cried in my life. Two decades of unaddressed trauma poured out of me in three days. I think it scared Tina to see how deeply messed up I really was.

We are a toxic bunch, aren't we? We want everything to stay inside, where it doesn't belong. If it stays inside, it's toxic. Our society stays toxic because of it. If I'm going to cry, I'm going to cry, because that's the way I'm made. If I'm depressed, I'm just going to say I'm depressed. What else am I going to do? I can't deny it. It's nature, and we need to do what nature intends us to do.

I started to realize that my anxiety always got worse as soon as the sun started to go down. Maybe it was because that's when my dad would come home—I don't know. He'd come home and be drunk and there would be a fight. I really started to wonder whether all this childhood trauma was a major factor in my anxiety. Who really knows? Still, talking about it with Tina helped me get a lot of this shit to the surface.

During one of our sessions, Tina had me draw a picture of myself on a plain black piece of paper. Not just a self-portrait, but a picture showing the pieces inside me. I drew a white outline of a man with yellow bolts of electricity charging through him. There were these large blue cylinders, rolling up and down him. In his head, there was a man walking back and forth on a tightrope. The bolts showed the chaotic energy constantly bouncing around inside my mind. The steamrollers were the part of me constantly trying to contain it all—pushing down on my chest, trying to smooth it all out. The man was angry. He never stopped moving, never stopped yelling—just went back and forth, back and forth, yelling and screaming. He was the part of me that I always heard talking. He represented my obsessions and doubts and insecurity. He was my rage. The source of everything, guarding my mind on a tightrope.

Most of these exercises weren't even associated with the skate accident. It was weird: at the end of each one, I'd have tears streaming down my face. I think that made Tina a little bit worried, to be honest. There was no cognitive beginning or end to it. It just happened.

She did the same thing with the gun incident. It was caused by trauma and was causing new trauma, a vicious cycle. I had no idea about all this emotional therapy shit. *Why do we drink? Why are we the way we are? Why do we think about suicide? Why?* I'd never given it a second thought.

I fought that place so hard. I hated it. I had thought, *Thirty days and I'm gone.* I wanted to get back to my job, back to my marriage, back to my life. I just wanted to get out of there. I'd been to enough therapists and psychiatrists to know that I was a little bit off. It was always the same: OCD—check. Depression—check. I've got some issues. Give me some pills and let me get on with life until it all falls apart again. So in rehab, I was just the same. *Yeah, I had too much to drink. Yeah, I have a drinking problem. Yeah, it was just an accident. And now I've done my thirty days and I'm better now.*

I didn't even have a clue until early February. Tina is the reason I got there. I owe everything to her, because she is the one who convinced me I was still in so much denial after the jugular vein accident. Shit was flying because I never dealt with the reality of trauma. Now I look back and realize how my life spiralled downward after that accident. The whole time, I was like, *Tina, fuck off.* But, like Joanie and Dudley, that woman helped save my life.

I got out in April. When it was time to finally leave, six months after it all began, I knew I was a different man. There was no doubt it had helped. I was no longer a jaded asshole who hated everyone. When I first arrived, everyone was scared of me. At the same time that people liked me and saw that I was a nice guy, they also saw that I was a monster. Everything had changed. I now understood myself better than I ever had before. I had bought in. I was even mentoring other patients and had become friends with some of these guys who came into the program after me.

A couple of weeks before I left, they let me go home for a weekend. By that point, I had done my time. This was a test, like being on parole. It had been half a year since I had sat in that shed and pulled the trigger. I was pretty emotional. I knew I'd have to turn around and head back to the rehab clinic in a day. But seeing the ranch, my horses, my dogs, felt like a beautiful return, like a roaring ovation in an arena when you're weak from almost dying but rushing with life. It wasn't difficult to be back at the spot where the shooting happened. That was the past. This was now. And this was home.

• • •

When you leave rehab, they put on this big graduation ceremony for you. Everyone shows up like it's high school. Most people are in rehab for a short period of time, but because I'd been there for half a year, all the counsellors and doctors and staff members showed up. That had never happened before. I was the longest-standing resident they had ever had.

All of the characters I met there helped me in some special way. As much as I wanted to push them all away, we became a sort of team. It didn't matter if we were in there because of heroin, alcohol, overspending, overeating or attempting suicide. We understood each other because we could see that we all had broken pieces. We just needed a little help to find our way to wholeness. I hope I gave them back a fraction of what they gave me.

I stood at the front of the room and talked about everything I had gone through and about how painful the last six months had been. It hurt like hell, but I knew I was a better man for it.

Most patients there dealt with addiction, but I had a bullet in my head. I was crying. I can't remember everything I said. When I was done, everyone got up—the doctors, the counsellors, the patients—everyone I had dragged through this hell with me. They all stood and clapped and cheered while I cried.

33

On the Outside

BACK ON THE RANCH, BACK IN THE WORLD, MY DAYS NEEDED A routine. I signed up for a regular AA meeting and found a church to go to. Our neighbour was a pastor, so we joined his congregation. I needed to surround myself with good feelings and good friends.

I needed to repair my relationship with Joanie. I'd shattered it to pieces, and it was my responsibility to put it back together again. It will be difficult for people to believe this, but I loved her so much. Even when I hated her, even when I blamed her for putting me into rehab and convinced myself that she was keeping me there—even when I spouted off terrible things that I could never pull back, I loved Joanie so damn much. Still, I'd tried to push her away. Looking back, I guess that's something I've done in a lot of my relationships. But with Joanie, it was gigantic. I was emotionally abusive to her. I was an animal—I mean, off the charts. But that wasn't me. Or, at least, it wasn't the real me.

The bearded man who threatened to throw people out of windows in rehab, that angry son of a bitch buried deep inside of me, was gone. I had no intention of letting him return. Now I had to make up for the damage he had caused. Even as we tried to move forward, Joanie blamed herself for a long time. I was always thinking, "Poor me, poor me." I didn't even think about how this shit affected her.

Logic told her it wasn't her fault, but poisonous thoughts haunted her—*What could I have done? What did I do?* I tried to pull her out of that. Despite everything, Joanie stayed. I owed her my life.

We did our best to get back to living. We redid the tack shed, painted it up and changed some things to make it look more like an old-time saloon. We did a lot of work around the ranch, planting trees and redoing the gardens. I got back on the horses. We had lots of friends over to ride with us and enjoy the ranch. My old happy ways returned.

Joanie and I have the same sense of humour. We were able to look back on a lot of the shit we'd been through and laugh—getting into a fight with those goons at the gym, giving away my clothes in a psych ward, stuff like that. Laughter is a good way to deal with a dark past.

Slowly, life felt good again. We were falling back in love.

Returning to the real world wasn't easy. Getting back into a daily routine, adjusting to social settings, trying to deal with the pressures of finding work—it was overwhelming.

My biggest worry in rehab wasn't that I wouldn't be able to quit drinking or get control of my disease. It was that I'd never get my job back. There was a very real possibility that I might never work in the NHL again. It was the main anxiety I faced while cooped up in rehab. The NHLPA said the deal was that I had to stay in rehab if I wanted to keep my job. If I left before I was ready, I was done. But I knew it would all go to shit anyway.

The Blue Jackets had told me there was a job waiting for me when I got back. But in my mind, I'd been thinking, *You think this is my first time in the NHL? I know how this works.*

When I got out of rehab, I got in touch with Scott Howson, the general manager in Columbus, and said, "Look, I'm out. You know, I'd really like to get back in the saddle." He said exactly what I thought he'd say. "We're just going to keep it status quo for the time being. We're going to the playoffs. We don't want to make another change."

I wasn't surprised at how it turned out. And I really wasn't angry about it. The Blue Jackets had been very good to me. Scott was incredibly supportive, and I owe him a lot. I'm sure he really meant what he said at the time, but I knew my job was gone.

Scott said, "At the end of the season, we're definitely interested, but we're just going to wait and see. We'll talk in a couple weeks." A couple weeks went by, and he hadn't called. I'd heard the rumblings that they'd let Steve Mason have his old goalie coach come and work with him. So I called him back. When we finally connected, Scott let me down easy. It wasn't a knock on me or my skills, he said. "Mase really likes you, but you haven't worked with him that much . . ."

My history spoke for itself. I'd worked with Luongo and Leclaire and had all kinds of success with them, but nothing is guaranteed when you coach in the NHL, especially when you're a goalie coach. I hadn't worked with Mason all year. Understandably, I was a tough sell. "Listen, we're going to talk to Mason's goalie coach at the combine in Toronto," Scott said. "We're going to offer him the job, but if he doesn't take it, we're coming right back to you."

"Yeah, I figured that," I said. "I knew that."

Scott was kind of shocked. "How did you know that?"

"Listen, Scott," I said. "I don't want to go into detail, but I knew I didn't have a chance to work with Mason much and build a rapport. Didn't get a chance to put my stamp on him like I did with Leclaire and Luongo."

I think that kind of made him feel better. Columbus was great through everything. I'll never say a bad thing about the organization. Gary Agnew, one of the coaches, was particularly supportive through everything, and I owe him and the rest of that Blue Jackets staff a lot of gratitude.

That fall was difficult. I'd only been out of rehab a few months, and the anniversary of the shooting was coming up quickly in October. Any opportunities in the hockey world were fading fast at that point. I sat there on my ranch, staring at the mountains, thinking I'd still be sitting there when there was snow on them. *Boy, did I screw my life up*, I thought.

Usually in September, I was off at training camp. I'd be going back and forth between the ranch and Columbus, Florida or whichever team needed my help. But here I was, an NHL goalie coach with a great track record, and I couldn't even get an interview.

Money was a problem. Thankfully, the NHLPA had taken care of most of our bills while I was in rehab, but now I was closing in on a year without a steady paycheque. The horse dentistry brought in some money, but nowhere near what we'd need to get by.

And I could tell I was drifting back into depression—I was much more aware of where my mind was heading now than I was before rehab.

Depression was so common in my life at this point that it felt like the return of an old friend you've been trying to ditch because he's a bum, but he keeps coming back again. Look, we've all been sad, we've all been blue, lost a job—whatever. But to get to that clinically depressed state is something that's hard to describe. If you've felt it, you've felt it.

I carried depression throughout my life. It affected my ability to play hockey, it affected my marriages and it affected friendships. It took a long time to realize that it was a disease related to a chemical imbalance in my brain. Even when I was told that, it was hard to really comprehend. You feel weak—like a failure. The world outside your mind doesn't understand what's going on inside you. You don't understand it, either, so you're screwed.

Physical pain doesn't destroy me. I can take a broken leg—my pain tolerance is extremely high in that sense. When I was in the worst of the worst of my depression and anxiety, I'd pray to God, *Bust my leg—a compound fracture. I can take that. I can't take this.* When I had back surgery, I practically crawled into the hospital—it was the most excruciating pain. I'd take that any day over the torment and anguish of depression.

What kept me going as a kid was being able to put all my energy into hockey. Hockey, hockey, hockey—all day, every day, into the night. You can't be sad on the ice. You just play the game and make that your life. When I look back on my career, I can't help but think about how much better I could have been if I had had control of my depression and OCD.

Maybe I don't give myself enough credit for what I accomplished in the NHL. But in my heart of hearts, I really believe that my mental condition ended my career. I was a good goalie. I could have been great.

This all swirled through my mind as I sat back at my ranch, staring at the mountains, waiting for the season to change.

I was healthy. I wasn't chasing demons anymore. It was under control now. I understood my medication, which I was taking in properly regulated doses. And I understood my mind better than I ever had before. I could control my moods and sense when things were starting to go awry. Still, it was hard to convince people that my ship could still sail after everyone had watched it sink.

I didn't know if I'd ever be invited back into the NHL fraternity. Maybe I'd gone too far to come home again. There was still such a stigma around mental illness. On the surface, I'd received a lot of support. I knew my close friends, like Rick Dudley, would never turn their backs on me. But there was an asterisk beside my name now; the footnote read "crazy." My reputation brought to mind words like unpredictable, uncontrollable, uncooperative, unhinged—unemployable. Who the hell hires crazy?

The bills piled up. It would take a while to rebuild my equine dentistry clientele. And even if Joanie and I could get that back off the ground, it likely wouldn't pay enough to get us out of the hole. And my heart was in hockey. It was the only place I ever belonged, but now it had no place for me.

The first anniversary of the shooting was difficult. I tried to make October 7 blend into the rest of the month by keeping myself busy. It wasn't a significant day—just a terrible one that I wanted to forget. But for a week and a half, Joanie kept saying that we'd have to do something on Wednesday. It was like she'd marked the date in her head. A lot of the details remained hazy for me. But not for Joanie—she's the one who saw everything. I just did it and was unconscious. She saw the shit go down. Joanie will never be able to wipe away that stain.

I understood that, but she also marked it in the calendar. I didn't think it was a good thing to do. Maybe it was still the "get knocked off, you get back on" mentality, but I really didn't want to dwell on it. I don't think the body and mind are connected through a date. I needed to guard and monitor myself against revisiting that dark time. I was aware that it could hit me anytime—maybe that day, maybe in three weeks. It was impossible to know, especially with me.

We decided to just get out of the house that day—maybe go to a movie. I'd seen the trailer for that zombie movie with Woody Harrelson. It looked good. Or maybe, I suggested, we'd just go out for a hamburger.

Figuratively, I wanted to get back on the horse and move on, and stop letting the past seep back into our lives. What better way than to literally get in the saddle—like the time, soon after, when I rode naked around the ranch, getting my pasty-white ass cheeks burned in the desert sun. I sent pictures to my buddies—I'm sure I sent one to Chris Reichart and Dean Kennedy, my old friends from the Sabres days. I know for sure that Duds has seen my full-moon riding. I posted one to Coleman, too. Naked ranching is the kind of activity that tells the world you're back and riding free. The cowboy goalie had returned—even if that bucking bronco was about to knock my naked ass back to the dirt.

34

Relapse

A YEAR WENT BY WITHOUT HOCKEY. NO JOBS, NO CONSULTING gigs, nothing. I'd watch games and see what all these guys were doing wrong—it was infuriating. I needed another chance to prove myself. Still, all season, nobody in the hockey world so much as looked my way. So I went heavy into horses, trying to scrape out my living with the dentistry thing.

An opportunity came up that took me to upstate New York to work with the horses of a few high-profile people, like Martha Stewart and Calvin Klein. It had been arranged as a kind of test gig by this vet from Florida I'd been connected with. I flew all the way to New York from Nevada. The vet from Florida liked the work I did, so she invited me to come down to Florida to work with her. She said they'd provide an apartment and everything. So I made the trip in my silver pickup truck from Nevada.

When I got to Florida, some of the Ottawa Senators staff happened to be on a southern scouting trip, and I connected with them. Pascal Leclaire, my goalie in Columbus, was now playing for the Senators, and we'd kept in touch. Bryan Murray, my old coach in Washington, was Ottawa's general manger. The team was looking for a new goalie coach. It was the perfect situation.

We set up a meeting between me, Murray and the entire coaching staff at the hotel the Senators staff were staying at. It went very well. They seemed eager to hire me.

Meanwhile, the dentistry job fell apart. When I got to the vet's place, she showed me the apartment I was supposed to stay in. It was this little room above the barn. It was absolutely disgusting—piss on the sheets and bed, mouse shit everywhere. It took me five days of driving across the States to get to this hole? Screw that. I got in my truck and drove home, hoping that my phone would ring and the Senators would offer me the job.

A few days went by. Nothing. A couple more. Nothing. A week. Nothing. Another week. Still nothing. I started to get stressed out. I followed up with the Senators but still didn't hear back from Bryan. The anxiety of being so close to this job started to build. My head started to race again, and I needed to keep things in check. One night, I went to my regular AA meeting. I'd go to several a week; I'd been really good about attending since I got out of rehab.

But that day, when the meeting was over, my anxiety was still there. I couldn't shake it. On the drive home, I called Joanie and told her I was going to grab a coffee with a couple of the guys from AA. Then I pulled into a bar called French. I had a few beers. And then a few more. I was alone.

Joanie phoned several times, but I just let it go to voice mail. "Where are you?" she asked. "It's been two hours."

What made me drink? Well, what didn't? There was the guilt that I felt over screwing up and losing my job in the first place. Or my NHL exile. Or my disappearing bank balance—I used to be an NHL hockey player, and here I was, flat broke. Or the shooting itself, and how the world viewed me now: as just another breathing disaster waiting to implode.

So yeah, I downed my drink and had the bartender pour me another.

I left the bar in my Dodge pickup with the Canuck Ranch logo on it. A few minutes on the road, and red lights filled my rearview mirror. *Shit!*

The cop said I was weaving across the road. He gave me a Breathalyzer test. I blew high—really high. Double the legal limit. The cop put me in the back of his cruiser and took me to the local jail.

The officer who booked me at the local did horseshoeing on the side, so we knew each other. "Clint, I wish I could do something," he said. But there was nothing he could do—nothing he *should* do. I was busted. I had messed up. After spending six months getting my life back together, I threw it all away in one night. I had all the tools, but I still couldn't stop myself.

They kept me in the cell overnight. I cried all night in that damn jail. I'd ruined everything. The local paper caught wind of the story, and the Associated Press picked it up. By morning, news of the DUI was everywhere.

Bryan Murray called me. He had read about it in the Ottawa papers and asked if it was true. The Senators were going to hire me, but now there was no way they could. It was too much of a shitstorm.

"I understand, Bryan," I said. "I'm sorry."

I was so pissed off at myself. I was so close, and then I screwed it all up with my stupid binge. It wasn't just the Senators job; now everyone would assume I was a loose cannon. I felt like hope was completely gone. I think it's important for people to know that recovery is a battle. Sometimes you lose, but you have to keep fighting.

Once again, thank God for Rick Dudley. After Joanie and her wonderful parents, Duds had been the first friend to visit me in rehab. And just as he had done many times before, he came through when I needed him most. He called me during the summer of 2010. Duds always said there wasn't a situation a player could face that I couldn't relate to. As shitty as everything I had gone through had been, it had made me a good coach. Rick knew that.

By this time, he was the associate general manager of the Atlanta Thrashers, back with Don Waddell. The guys who had given me a chance in San Diego almost two decades earlier, when I lost my goaltending spot in the NHL, gave me another chance to return. The circle seemed complete.

"Are you ready?" he asked. "Can you do it?"

"Yes," I said. "I'm ready."

Atlanta was an important opportunity for me. The Thrashers gave me a fresh start in the NHL. It was a contract under which I was supposed to be with the team for two weeks at a time, but I'd often stay for the whole month. I loved being around the team. Our staff was great. The team's strength coach, Barry Brennan, let me stay at his condo. He and I had worked together with the Columbus Blue Jackets. It was nice to actually stay with a friend instead of living out of a hotel. Craig Ramsay was the Thrashers' head coach—he was a great guy to work with. My goalies were veteran Chris Mason, whom I'd had in Florida, and young Ondrej Pavelec, who reminded me a lot of Pascal Leclaire. He was such a nice kid.

I found out the Thrashers were leaving Atlanta in 2011 the way pretty much everyone else did: through the press. It took me by surprise. I waited for a long time to see whether I'd be making the move to Winnipeg with the team. It was an anxious time, and a decision was taking way too long. Finally, I asked for permission to talk to other teams—I couldn't afford to go jobless. Duane Sutter told me his brother Brent was looking for a new goalie coach in Calgary, but they had just wrapped up interviews. I called up the Flames' GM, Jay Feaster, and sent my application in right away. He called me in for an interview, and I was in Calgary the next day.

Shortly after, the Flames offered me the job. I was heading home to Alberta.

Lucky One

CALGARY HAS ALWAYS FELT LIKE HOME TO ME, SO THERE WAS comfort in returning to the city. The Flames were a great organization. I got to work with one of the best goalies of his generation in Miikka Kiprusoff and helped develop the young goaltenders in their system. Kipper was a good guy to work with, but there's only so much you can do for a superstar like that. And near the end of his career, you could tell that he just wanted out. He didn't even want to play his final year.

I enjoyed being part of the team mostly because of the relationships I managed to build with players. As a coach, I go out of my way to connect with them. I enjoy shooting the shit with struggling forwards next to the pool at the Anaheim Hilton, or cheering up a journeyman goalie after a bad game in St. Louis.

The hockey world is tough, especially as a goalie coach. It's better than it used to be. At least now, on most teams, the goalie coach has a full-time gig. But they don't pay you like the other coaches. They say goaltending is the most important position, but goaltending instructors don't get paid like it is. You're living contract to contract—that's stressful. A new GM comes, a new head coach comes, and you're done. That's why it's cool being self-employed: it's your job, it's your show. You don't have to worry about someone not liking you and giving you the boot. Being self-employed with my horse business is fun, though it's not without its challenges. When the economy dips, you hurt.

I love being part of the game because it lets me connect with people beyond it. In Calgary, I started to share my story at high schools. I'd stand in front of the entire school at an assembly and talk about the demons I faced and how close they came to killing me. Every time, students would line up afterwards to talk to me. Some of them opened up about their own struggles with depression and other forms of mental illness. I recognized the fear and confusion in their faces. I understood the hopelessness they faced. I did my best to encourage them to get the help they need. The first step is to let go and seek it. Nobody can conquer mental illness on their own—believe me, I've tried. I've been through enough to know now that sometimes you need help getting up. That's why I really enjoy the opportunity to help people through my public speaking. I like that my story might have an impact on people.

This book wasn't easy to write. It took me back to a lot of places I never wanted to see again. I heard stories from people that I love about the things I did—the things I couldn't fully see—and realized how painful and terrible it was for them. Every damn page of this book hurt. Deep down, I really wanted to finish this, but I didn't realize that revisiting this turmoil was going to affect me the way it did. In the process of writing this book, my anxiety started to build again. As the words came together and I saw them on the page, the anxiety continued to grow—stronger and stronger until it consumed me like it had so many terrible times before. Over the course of three months, starting in October, as the contents of the book were reported and drafts were passed around, I started to lose control of my ability to deal with the anxiety, and the depression started to resurface.

During one of the Flames' west coast road trips, Joanie and my daughter Dallyn came to stay with me in San Jose. Dallyn is a teenager now. She's a very pretty girl. A brunette. She's super-outgoing and she loves to ride. She's a natural, just like kids who put on skates and are zooming around the ice right away. Being on the road all the time (and being divorced three times) makes it hard for me to see my kids as regularly as I'd like to. We used to get together at Christmas all the time when they were younger. When we get to visit, it's hard, because you enjoy the moment, but then you start realizing that you only have a day or two before you have to say goodbye.

I was thinking about that as we sat in the hotel room in San Jose. Joanie was on her iPad, Dallyn was doing homework, and I was just sitting there in a chair. I started tearing up, trying not to cry. It had been a hard week. I still struggle with depression—the disease doesn't go away, you just learn to manage it with medication and experience. But I'd been recalling a lot of painful memories putting this book together. I had re-read my journal from the rehab centre and was planning to visit with Tina for the first time since I left, because she lived in the area.

"Dallyn, come here," I said. She came over and sat on the armrest and put her arm around me.

"You know I get depressed, right?" My eyes were wet. "I can walk around, go in the bathroom and cry. But then I'm hiding from you and I'm hiding from Joanie. You know I get depressed and I cry."

"Yeah, Dad," she said.

"And I'm crying now. Are you okay with that?"

"Yeah." She rubbed my back.

I told her that the shooting had nothing to do with her. I suffered from an illness—that was all. I needed her to understand that none of this was her fault. Depression is a terrible disease that takes too many lives and leaves too many people thinking they played a part in the tragic end of the person they loved and lost.

"Do you ever get depressed?" I asked Dallyn. I know it can be a hereditary condition. I'd be devastated to learn that she felt the same way I had.

I never found out whether my father suffered like I did. Alcohol consumed him and was a battle for me—an attempt to deal with problems I couldn't grasp. I've always wondered if my father might have understood my obsessions and compulsions. I wonder if he understood depression. Was he haunted too? I wonder if that might have changed things between us. Had he gotten help, could it have saved my family a lot of pain and anger? I'll never know.

"No, Dad," Dallyn said.

"Thank God. Do you understand it, though?"

I explained the disease to her. I told her about OCD and depression and post-traumatic stress. I told her about chemical imbalances and the shame and the guilt and the feeling of helplessness. I told her because I don't believe in hiding anymore. Too many people do that. The truth is ugly; it might be difficult to share with the people you love. But you owe it to them and to yourself to do so. Held inside, the truth is destructive.

I hugged my daughter and felt so lucky to be alive. My life was far from perfect, but I still had it. And I had a beautiful wife who had loved me through the darkest times. I had three incredible children who meant everything to me. I had a strong, wonderful mother and a loyal brother and sister whom I love very much. I had friends who would drop anything to be by my side when I needed them. I was the luckiest man in the world, but once again, I could feel it falling apart.

During a game against the Vancouver Canucks in January, my old friend John Tortorella tried to get into our dressing room between periods to fight our coach, Bob Hartley, after a brawl-filled first period. Torts thought Hartley was to blame. The ordeal was caught on camera—excited little John Tortorella trying to push through a wall of Flames players, including enforcer Brian McGrattan, who could pretty much flick him aside. I was inside the locker room, and when I heard that John was trying to get into our room, something snapped inside of me. It was like I was back on the ice, taking on the world. I charged out and shoved my way through our players until McGrattan caught a hold of me. Torts was gone by then—and he was lucky. The camera caught the vicious snarl across my face. Someone was challenging my team, and I didn't care who it was. You stand up for your boys. I've fought my own brother, so an old hockey pal? Wouldn't think twice about flattening his nose. Don't get me wrong: we would have made up afterwards. A fistfight is a fistfight—no hard feelings.

But that incident really had nothing to do with what was going on with my emotional and mental state at the time. It was just instinct. Writing and editing the book was stressing me out, and eventually it started to show. In February, I started to self-medicate again, turning to alcohol to crank down my anxiety. Joanie was back home at our ranch in Nevada, while I was in Calgary with the team or away on road trips. When I wasn't distracted by my job as the Flames' goalie coach, I was alone with my thoughts—my words, my story, my book. They haunted me. I entered a depressive state, compounding my anxiety. It was the same thing all over again, and I could feel it rising inside of me. It affected my work. I didn't realize that others could tell, but they knew. My anxiety began showing up in my personality at the rink. I used to be so good at hiding it.

On March 26, 2014, I was called into an office at the Saddledome. Brian Burke, the team president, was there along with Bob Hartley, the head coach. There was another familiar face too: Dan Cronin. Dan is a part of the NHLPA's substance abuse program, and he helped me get to rehab after the shooting incident. Now he was set to help me again.

Brian said my behaviour with the team had seemed depressive and erratic. He asked if I had been drinking. I was in shock. *How could they tell?* But I should have known by now: you can't hide these things. Not truly. They asked me if I wanted to go to a treatment centre to get help. They offered to send me. "Yes," I managed to say. "And I need help with my mental state as well."

I was gone that day.

The players' association sent me to a rehab facility in Los Angeles. I cried through the first two and a half days—I was so low. I was so sad. *Here we go again.* It was shameful. I felt like I had let everyone down. But I was in a different place, experience-wise, than I was the first time. I knew what lay ahead. There was no denial this time. I had to deal with mental issues, anger issues and alcohol issues. There were no wasted days.

We worked a lot, specifically on my anger during my sessions with therapists at the clinic. They helped me find ways to deal with the anger and anxiety that overcame me at times. We talked about what to do when I'm feeling the rage build up—I know where it comes from, but I needed tools to control it.

The words "Thy will be done" have always echoed in the back of my mind, lingering from my various experiences with faith. Those words came back to me when I was in rehab for a second time. I'd say them over and over as I walked around the grounds of that facility in Los Angeles, a city where a few months earlier I had sat down by the pool of a hotel during a Flames road trip and laid out my thoughts for this book. Here I was again, in the middle of a new chapter that seemed to take me back to the beginning. "Thy will be done," I said—because every time I've fallen, there has been something there, waiting to catch me. A blade was millimeters away from ending my life. A handful of pills stopped my heart. A bullet is lodged in my forehead next to my brain. A narrow margin exists between life and death. I have clung to the finest of threads and returned—eyes blinking, heart beating—only by the grace of something much larger than me.

Call it God, call it fate or call it blind luck. Any way I look at it, it breaks down to one simple, essential thing. I call it purpose.

But "purpose" isn't easy, and mine was going to be a daily battle. I tried to change my habits and make sure I was focused on staying in the right emotional, mental and spiritual state. It was like an essential mental tune-up. But again, these issues don't just go away. I expect that they will return, but each time they do I know I'll be stronger than I was before.

Once again, the NHLPA and NHL were a great help. Dan Cronin and Andrew Galloway from the players' association had been there when I first went into rehab, and they were a big support in getting me help a second time. They do a fantastic job of taking care of players and employees who need help. When I suffered the jugular injury back in '89, no one mentioned anything about mental health to me. We've come a long way in the last twenty-five years. More and more teams are becoming conscious of these issues. The Calgary Flames have their own team psychologist, and many other NHL teams do too.

I think a lot of the attention on mental health is the result of all the information coming out about the links between post-concussion syndromes, like CTE (chronic traumatic encephalopathy), and depression. Sometimes I wonder if head trauma affected me. For years, we'd see players get hit in the head by a check or in a fight, and it'd be diagnosed as "getting your bell rung." The players would shake it off and get back out there. No one considered the permanent implications of brain injuries. Now, with everything I've been through, it just makes me wonder. I'm sure a lot of other former players think about it too.

Mental illness is still too often considered a private issue because its effects go unseen. At every NHL training camp, experts come to speak to players about the dangers of substance abuse, gambling, and so on. They did these annual sessions back when I played, too. But now, they also take time to talk about mental health. That wasn't even a phrase hockey players would have known the meaning of back in my day. Mental illness was a reality then, but not one that we knew how to face. Today, that's changing. But a group session does little to actually encourage someone who is struggling to get real, meaningful help. I'd like to see a system set up where a player can seek confidential support and know that his coaches, the general manager and ownership won't be informed about it. It has to be confidential. There is so much denial amongst players because they think they are going to ruin their careers—their lives—if they actually seek help. A twenty-four-hour help line with assured confidentiality, or something like that, is the next step forward for the NHL.

In August 2011, Rick Rypien, a young man who played in the Vancouver Canucks' system, killed himself after a long, painful battle with depression. I had always respected the way Rick played the game—his competitiveness, his attitude, the way he fought guys much bigger than him. I had heard that he was struggling and I wanted to reach out to him. By then, most people in the hockey world knew part of my story. They all knew about the skate-blade accident, and most had deduced that the shooting incident wasn't really an accident that happened while I was shooting rabbits on the ranch. But I hadn't discussed the reality of my struggle in depth. When the terrible news about Rick came out, I broke down. I don't think that I could have saved him, but I know I could have helped. I know that I could have, at the very least, looked him in the eye and told him I knew what he was going through.

You have to understand one thing: I was very sick. People who are going through this kind of thing don't know what the hell they're doing. When I pulled the trigger, I had no idea where my head was. The last thing I was thinking about was checking out permanently. It was a random thing. It wasn't about leaving my loved ones or anything. Looking back, I wonder why I wasn't thinking about them. But you're not thinking about anything. It's hard to explain. Trying to describe depression to someone who has never really had it is hard. If you were to break your back, the pain would be excruciating. You can try to describe that, but someone listening is going to say, "I can imagine it was." Unless you experience it, you can't know. If you break your leg—your femur—right in half and it's sticking out of your skin, it looks gross, but no one else can really feel it. I felt it and I'm trying to describe it. I was in so much pain.

Eventually, I hope, we will get to a point where the stigma that surrounds mental illness will diminish so that no one feels they need to fight it alone. We need to be at a place where people seek help for mental illness just like they would for any physical ailment. We have come a long way in this regard as a society. And in sports, we are getting closer. We are getting better at realizing that being "tough" has nothing to do with suffering in silence.

On April 26, 2014, I got out of rehab and flew back to Calgary. It was a Saturday. Joanie flew in the next day. Before I had gone into rehab, she told me, "Remember, we are a team." I called her every day while I was in the facility. Joanie and her family—along with my strong, wonderful mother—have been my team all along. They never let me down. They never stopped fighting for me.

Back in Calgary, Joanie and I started packing up the things we planned to take back to the ranch in Nevada for the summer. The rebuilding Flames hadn't made the playoffs and the season was done. I didn't go back to the Saddledome at all. Brian Burke called me that Tuesday. He asked if the doctors had prepared me for the possibility that I wouldn't be returning to the team. "You know we can't have you back," he said. I thanked him for helping me through the season and for getting me the treatment I needed. I have a great deal of respect for Brian. He said the team would look to help me out in any way possible as I moved on to the next chapter of my life.

And with that, it was done. I was no longer a member of the Calgary Flames' coaching staff. I was officially unemployed, facing a great, terrifying unknown—with my life about to be splayed out across the pages of this book.

We rented a U-Haul trailer and packed up everything in our condo, hitched it to the back of my silver pickup and started out on the twenty-two-hour trip back to Nevada. It was hard to drive out of Calgary and leave everything behind. Joanie and I didn't say much as we drove down the highway and the city disappeared behind us. Nothing needed to be said. The last bump was behind me now; I had no idea how many were ahead. But right then, we were moving forward, moving on. We stopped for the night in Great Falls, Montana, and I found an AA meeting to attend. I had committed to going to one every day, and I planned to see that through.

I nearly bled out in front of thousands. This book is about sharing the rest of me, because I know there's a reason why I'm still breathing. I have post-traumatic stress disorder, obsessive-compulsive disorder, depression and alcoholism. I still have meds to take and wounds to heal. I still have a long, rough ride, but I'm tightening my grip and holding on—because this life is a crazy game and I'm determined to win it.

The next morning, Joanie and I started out on the last leg of our trip home. As the truck rolled south towards the desert, through the mountains of Idaho, I thought about all the places I had been and dreamed of all the places I might still go. It was a beautiful, perfect day and the road was wide open. It stretched out in front of us, fading in the distance, reaching for an end I couldn't see.

Afterword

by Joanie Malarchuk

THE QUESTIONS I GET ASKED THE MOST ARE, "WHY DID YOU STAY?" and "How did you do it?"

Looking back now, when I ask myself those questions, I honestly don't know. I was seeing my best friend struggling within himself, watching every day as his mind turned on him and he couldn't shut it off. I knew little about mental illness, depression or obsessive-compulsive disorder (OCD) and nothing about self-medicating. I soon learned that what I thought I knew about those things didn't even come close to what was true.

My first meeting with Clint was a surprise. I saw him through a window, saying to me, "Wow, you are beautiful!" That made my day. I thought, *Now there's a handsome Marlboro Man*. I was right. Clint is a cowboy: tough on the outside and kind, caring and soft on the inside. He has that cowboy country politeness (he opens doors for you; it's always ladies first), but he can also skate. I'm a figure skater, so we had skating in common. I knew nothing about hockey, though. I had never heard about him or his accident. In the past, I had coached a few hockey players on their skating skills, but I had no knowledge of the game. The only hockey game I had ever watched was the Miracle on Ice game at the 1980 Olympics.

Most of the people who knew me back when I met Clint weren't sure if he would be a good fit for me. They would say, "You know, he only ever wears jeans and cowboy boots." That was perfect. My mom's side of the family is from Bandera, Texas, the Cowboy Capital of the World. He fit right in. My dad really liked Clint too. They had the same taste in music—old, classic country. Clint would put on his favourite songs, and I think I knew almost every one he played. I grew up listening to those songs.

Clint had told me when I met him that he had OCD. He would also have a few beers once in a while, and I thought nothing of it. He was handsome, confident and social, a well-liked guy, no red flags. We even had a few discussions about my being a figure skating coach and look-ing for that certain undefinable trait in a young athlete, not knowing that in his case, that trait was a touch of OCD.

My first experience with how OCD can affect a person was when Clint's luggage was lost during a trip to Canada. His OCD medication was in his checked bag. He assured me that he would be fine, and after two days with no luggage or medication, he sounded a bit anxious on the phone, but nothing seemed unusual. Then five days later, still with no luggage or medication, he missed his flight home. He couldn't get himself to leave his hotel room. So I helped the only way I knew how: I changed his flight, and then I talked him through the whole day.

Over the phone I told him to just go downstairs to the lobby. Then I called the lobby and had a desk clerk look for Clint and call him a taxi. Then I called Clint, asked if he was in the lobby and told him to get into the taxi and ask to go to the airport. I estimated how long it would take to get to the airport, and then I called him again and told him to go to the ticket counter. This went on all day. Three connecting flights and many hours later, he came walking off the plane with a smile on his face, as if nothing had happened. At that moment I learned how great an actor he can be around people.

We saw a doctor after this incident and thought Clint was on his way to getting better. Until one day when I came home to find that he had split his chin open and stitched it up himself with a needle and thread. Some of the medication he was on made him drowsy, and he had slipped in the bathroom and suffered a nasty cut. He had cleaned everything up, so the bathroom was spotless. I never would have known anything had happened if it hadn't been for the stitches.

I couldn't tell you exactly when those few beers once in a while started to become more. Looking back now, I can see that there was a gradual increase in his drinking and that he was drinking more often by himself. This probably sounds naive, but I thought that if he was drinking (self-medicating) too much I would notice, because he would be stumbling around, slurring his words or passing out. That isn't what I saw. I didn't know what self-medicating looked like or what OCD looked like when it was out of control.

Months went by before Clint started acting noticeably different. My first thought was that he was just taking everything too personally. He started picking apart and analyzing everything I said, down to the tone I said it in. His entire personality would change, like Dr. Jekyll and Mr. Hyde.

Looking back, I feel like I should have known that his OCD was getting worse and that his medication probably wasn't having an effect anymore. But I didn't know. It slowly got to the point where there were about two hours in the morning when everything seemed fine. That was when I would try to talk about things, day-to-day things. I would try to talk about what was going on with him and getting him some help. He would always say that he had everything under control and he could take care of it.

Throughout the day I could see him getting wound up tighter and tighter. His mind would start going a mile a minute. I knew when his head was racing because he would play Johnny Cash over the speakers in the barn, loud. He would isolate himself. He stayed outside and in the barn, just keeping himself busy, watering trees, cleaning horse stalls, finding things to fix, working out and drinking. I couldn't get him to eat. He was too busy and always said, "I'll eat later."

Later was usually when people would show up. He would stop what he was doing and laugh, joke around and become the life of the party.

But as soon as everyone had gone and he came inside for the night, his thoughts would turn on him. It seemed like he just couldn't trust anything; his mind was questioning everything, so he asked questions for reassurance. Again and again and again the same questions, for hours. If you answered "white" he wanted "black," and vice versa. It didn't matter what we were arguing about. After hours of this, he would fall asleep from exhaustion.

I didn't sleep much. I started to think that if I could see a rough spell coming on, I might be able to help stop it from consuming him that day. He said that drinking helped stop his head from racing, but it would only help for a short bit. Then the more he drank, the more his head would race and the harder he would crash.

He talked about not wanting to be in his head anymore, not wanting to live this way. Then the next day, for those few morning hours, he was Clint: kind, caring, reassuring, loving, helpful and hopeful. I was able to breathe in those moments and feel hope that things would get better.

I tried for so long to get help. I became consumed with just getting through the day, sometimes minute by minute. I had Clint's friends helping me. I was calling doctors every day, all day, over and over again. The answers I got were, "We are not taking any new patients," or, "Yes, we can see him in a month," or, "Sorry, the doctor is out, but here is a brochure. Have a nice day." I tried to get Clint some sort of emergency care or help. I was told that unless he had harmed himself or someone else, there was nothing anyone could do.

That's when I started feeling helpless. My thoughts and fears were that Clint was never going to get the help he needed, that he was not just going to hurt himself but that he was going to end his life, then the help would be too late. My best friend, my husband, the love of my life needed help, and I couldn't find it for him. Leaving was never an option. I knew in my heart who Clint was and that what was happening to him was not his choice or his fault.

My family provided a huge amount of support to me. My mom and dad, my sisters and Clint's mom were always there to talk to me and support me in helping Clint, reminding me that Clint was sick and he just needed help.

Tuesday October 7, 2008, 2:30 P.M. The worst day of my life also turned out to be a blessing in disguise. I hadn't stayed at our house the night before. That day at noon I had gone to my first Al-Anon meeting. Driving home after the meeting, I called Clint's phone but there was no answer. I remember feeling anxious and getting increasingly worried because he always had a couple of phones with him and always answered.

When I got home, the house seemed unusually quiet. I saw Clint's phones lying by the back door. There was a weird, uneasy stillness in the air as I walked outside looking for him. I found him sitting alone. I remember having a fear of saying the wrong thing or nothing at all, or saying too much or not enough.

I sat on a stool in front of him, and almost instantly he became tense, hyper and mad. He told me he didn't want to be in his head anymore. He became more and more frustrated. I kept telling myself to stay calm, stay calm. I don't remember feeling anything when I saw and heard the gun go off.

Maybe it was because of shock or panic, but without thinking, I called 911. Clint was bleeding but walking around. I panicked when he sat down and it looked like I was losing him. I shook him to keep him awake until the paramedics and police arrived. They finally showed up, but after all their questioning I wondered if they thought that I had pulled the trigger.

I believe in my heart that if that day had not happened, Clint would not have gotten the help he needed, and there is a good chance that he would not be here today.

I wasn't sure about being a part of this book and opening up to the public. I knew people would relate to what Clint had gone through. But I was also worried that people might say I should have seen the breaking point coming and ask why I didn't do more to help. Even though Clint struggled to write this book, he gradually became more at ease with himself and talking about his demons. There was never a lot of talk like this before—it was the elephant in the room. Well, now the elephant had a name: mental illness. That's when I knew it didn't matter what people thought. This was what happened. We have both learned that you are only as sick as your secrets, so we said, "Let's give them the whole story."

Seven years and a book later, as devastating as some of those events were, Clint and I can look back on them all and even laugh at some of the stuff we experienced. We went through a lot, and we learned a lot. I think I look at people differently now. I'm not so quick to judge people these days.

I once lived with the feeling that the bottom was going to fall out at any moment. But not anymore.

Today, I have the Clint I know and fell in love with, all day, every day. We made it.

—Gardnerville, Nevada, August 2015

Acknowledgements

IT TOOK A GREAT DEAL OF LOVE AND SUPPORT FROM A LOT OF people for this book to get done. First, I'd like to thank my mother, Jean Ilene Jones, for being a constant support in my life through the good and bad. You are the strongest woman I know. I'd like to thank my three wonderful kids—Kelli, Jed and Dallyn—for bringing me so much joy, making me so proud, and giving me a reason to wake up every morning. To my siblings, Terry and Garth, thank you for being a support throughout my life. I'll always look up to you. To my in-laws, John and Elenora Goodley—you have welcomed me into your family and stood by me through the hardest times. I'm eternally grateful for everything you've done for me.

This memoir wouldn't have gotten off the ground if it weren't for the efforts of my good friend Randy Sieminski, who spent hours recording our conversations when we first dreamed up the idea for a book. Those recordings were an essential backbone for this memoir. I can't thank you enough. We finally got there.

Likewise, dozens of friends and teammates agreed to be interviewed, pulling the details of these stories together. I can't thank all of you in this space, but I appreciate the time and care you put into making these stories as complete as possible. For their ongoing support in my life, I'd like to thank Chris Reichart, Mitch Korn, Gary Agnew, Barry Brennan, Steve Ludzik, Jordan Fenton, Dr. Brian Peck, Bob Strumm,

Dean Kennedy and Coleman Robinson. I don't think I would be alive if it weren't for Rick Dudley. Rick, thank you for always answering the call.

As I continue to learn about my struggle with OCD, depression and PTSD, I need to thank Bill and Tina for helping me make sense of the debilitating diseases I've dealt with all my life. You were a light after years of darkness.

I'd like to thank HarperCollins Canada and Jim Gifford for believing in this book and guiding it to completion. It was always about so much more than hockey, and I thank you for recognizing that this was an important story to tell. Likewise, to my agent Rick Broadhead for his enthusiasm and support throughout this process. To my friend Dan Robson for all his support, patience and understanding when he knew this wasn't easy for me. When I relapsed in the process of writing this book, Jim, Rick and Dan told me to just focus on getting the help I needed and not to worry about the manuscript. Just get better, they said. Thank you for that support.

Finally, to my beautiful wife, Joanie, who stood by me through it all. No man deserves the patience, love and grace you have shown me. There are no words strong enough to thank you for that. I love you, always.

I sat in my barn on a July afternoon going over the final edits of this book. I've done a lot of drinking in my barn, but this time it never crossed my mind. I went in the house and found Joanie in the kitchen. I started to cry. She asked, "What part?" I said, "All of it." She gave me a hug. And that was it. I didn't take a drink. Didn't want to. And that's something—that's everything. Thank you for reading this book. And if you're struggling, like they say in AA, "Do the next right thing." And keep going.

—CM
www.malarchuk.com
canuckranch@yahoo.com

Acknowledgements

I'd like to echo Clint's gratitude to HarperCollins Canada for taking on this project with passion and enthusiasm from the start. My thanks to Jim Gifford for his encouragement and guidance as an editor and to Lloyd Davis for his thorough edits and helpful suggestions. Thanks to Noelle Zitzer for her edits and support, and to Patricia MacDonald for carefully proofing these pages.

I also thank Rick Broadhead for believing in this story and taking a chance on me.

My colleagues at *Sportsnet* magazine have been enormously supportive and patient throughout this process. My editors saw the value in this story when I first pitched it for our pages, and without them I would have never had a chance to be part of a project like this.

Thank you to Clint's friends, former teammates and players who took the time to add their perspective to the story of this remarkable life. Your contributions were essential. And to my own friends and family for their endless support and for providing feedback throughout the process. To Jayme, as always—for keeping me going despite so many sleepless nights filled with bourbon and clementines.

Finally, to Clint and Joanie—for trusting me with the fragile details of your lives and for the honour of putting your story on these pages. Joanie, your strength and grace astound me. Clint, your heart is the toughest part of you. It's the reason I know you'll win this fight and inspire others along the way.

—DR

Index

AA. *See* Alcoholics Anonymous
Ace (horse), 132
Adirondack Red Wings, 58
Agnew, Gary, 159, 227
AHL. *See* American Hockey League
Al-Anon, 183
Alberta Junior Hockey League, 29
Alcoholics Anonymous (AA), 122, 194,
    206, 207, 225, 232, 243
American Hockey League (AHL), 47,
    49, 58, 61, 109, 114, 150
Anaheim Ducks, 120
Anderson, Glenn, 65
Andreychuk, Dave, 83, 98
Arniel, Scott, 114
Associated Press, 233
Atlanta Thrashers, 233, 234
    C.M. as goalie coach of, 233–34
Audette, Donald, 94

Bank of America Center, 136
Barrasso, Tom, 94
Bauer, Jodi, 43, 49
Beaupre, Don, 81
Benning, Jim, 29
Bergeron, Michel, 47, 65

Betty Ford Center, 209, 211
Binghamton Rangers, 110
Black Rain, 93
Blount, Rachel, 118
Bonk, Radek, 124
Bossy, Mike, 48
Boston Bruins, 59, 60, 82, 91, 98, 111,
    126
Bouchard, Dan, 46
Bourque, Ray, 60
Brennan, Barry, 234
Brodeur, Martin, 145
Brown, Keith, 29
Bruce, Winston, 75
Bryzgalov, Ilya, 2
Buffalo, NY, 91, 95
Buffalo Sabres, 3, 47–48, 66, 114
    C.M. traded to, 81–82
    1988–89 season, 81, 82–83, 84–91
    1989–90 season, 94, 96, 97, 98
    1990–91 season, 100–01
    1991–92 season, 108, 109, 110–12
    1992–93 season, 115
    training camp, 93–94, 102, 112
Bulat, Jeff, 34
Bure, Pavel, 94
Burke, Brian, 239, 242–43

Burke, Sean, 71
Buskas, Rod, 134
Butsch, Dr. John, 88, 105, 106, 107

Calgary, AB, 67, 73–74, 92, 121, 235
Calgary Centennials, 26
Calgary Flames, 234, 235, 240, 242–43
  C.M. as goalie coach of, 234, 238,
    239, 243
Calgary Stampede, 75
Canadian Athletic Club, 26
Canadian Olympic team, 112, 113, 120
Canuck Ranch, xi, xii, 127–28
Carpenter, Bobby, 43
Carson City Hospital, 169–70
Chabot, Fred, 112
Chelios, Chris, 44
Cheveldae, Tim, 134
Chicago Blackhawks, 63–64, 149
Christian, Dave, 71
Cloutier, Jacques, 87, 90, 93
CNN, 119
Cohen, Alan, 147
Columbus Blue Jackets, 158, 193, 227
  C.M. as goalie coach of, 157, 158,
    159, 161, 162, 173, 181, 183,
    226–27
Columbus Dispatch, 157
Cronin, Dan, 239, 240
Crosby, Sidney, 65

Daneyko, Ken, 29
Dave (friend), 165, 188
DeGray, Dale, 114
Demers, Jacques, 49–50
Demitra, Pavol, 134
Detroit Red Wings, 63
Dionne, Marcel, 83
Donnelly, Gord, 60
Draper, Tom, 112

Druce, John, 79–80
Dryden, Dave, 32
Duchesne, Gaetan, 67
Dudley, Rick "Duds," 147, 148
  as C.M.'s friend, 152, 173–75,
    176–77, 181–82, 183, 193, 229,
    230, 233
  as coach, 94, 100–01, 111, 112–13,
    116, 120, 147
  as general manager, 140, 147,
    148–49, 158
  as hockey player, 51, 124, 148
Dupont, Andre "Moose," 45, 46

Edmonton, AB, 5, 8, 9, 10, 19, 26
Edmonton Oilers, 32, 48, 66, 80
Edmonton Oil Kings, 28–29
Erie County Medical Center, 106

Feaster, Jay, 234
Fedorov, Sergei, 94
Filion, Maurice, 43
Finch, Bill, 5, 6, 7
Flook, Dr., 22
Florida Panthers, 140, 143, 146, 147, 157
  C.M. as goalie coach of, 140, 141,
    142–43, 150, 158
Foligno, Mike, 98
Fort Saskatchewan, AB, 29
Fort Saskatchewan Traders, 29–30, 34, 36
Francis, Ron, 44
Fredericton, NB, 47, 50
Fredericton Capitals, 49, 50
Fredericton Express, 47, 48, 49, 50, 58, 59
Fuhr, Grant, 44, 48, 65

Gaetz, Link, 124
Galley, Garry, 70
Galloway, Andrew, 193, 201, 240

Gamble, Troy, 124, 125
Gardnerville ranch, 156, 161, 166, 223, 226, 227, 230
Gillies, Clark, 48
Gillis, Paul, 60, 91
Good Friday Massacre, 58
Goodley, Joanie (later Joanie Malarchuk), 150–53, 154, 155–56
Goring, Butch, 124
Gosselin, Mario, 59, 60, 66, 91
Goulet, Michel, 60, 62, 65
Granato, Tony, 83
Grande Prairie, AB, 5, 6, 11
Grant, Danny, 49
Gregson, Terry, 85
Gretzky, Wayne, 65, 66, 106
Grimson, Stu, 124

Haldol, 110, 114, 117
Hall, Glenn, 2, 33
Hamel, Jean, 58
Hartford Whalers, 66
Hartley, Bob, 239
Hasek, Dominik, 112, 115
Hawerchuk, Dale, 43, 65
Haworth, Alan, 67
Hay, Denny, 128
Hay, Rod, 128
Hextall, Ron, 65, 71
Hitchcock, Ken, 26, 158, 159
Hockey News, 127
Hodge, Ken, 36, 39
Houda, Doug, 93
Housley, Phil, 83, 98
Houston Aeros, 124
Howe, Mark, 65
Howson, Scott, 193, 226–27
Hrudey, Kelly, 16–17, 21
Hunter, Dale, 46, 51, 60–61, 62–63, 67, 69–70, 71, 78, 111

Idaho, 135
Idaho Steelheads, 135, 136
    C.M. as coach of, 135
International Hockey League (IHL), 27, 112, 114, 120, 133

Jasper Place Composite High School, 30–31
Johansson, Calle, 81
Jokinen, Olli, 157
Joseph, Curtis, 133-34

Keenan, Mike, 71, 140, 141, 142–43, 158
Kelley, Jim, 99
Kennedy, Dean, 95, 98, 230
Kiprusoff, Miikka, 145, 235
Knickle, Rick, 114
Krupp, Uwe, 85
Kurri, Jari, 65–66

Lafleur, Guy, 83
LaFontaine, Pat, 83, 106
LaForest, Mark, 63, 110, 112
Las Vegas, NV, 121, 123, 134
Las Vegas Thunder, 120, 123–24, 135
    C.M. as assistant coach and GM of, 132, 133
    C.M. as head coach of, 133, 134, 135, 137–38
    C.M.'s salary, 127, 135
    1993–94 season, 123, 125
    1994–95 season, 128
    1995–96 season, 132, 134
    1996–97 season, 134
    1997–98 season, 133
    training camp, 121, 122
Leclaire, Pascal, 158, 159, 181, 227, 231, 234

Ledyard, Grant, 81, 82, 87, 98

Leetch, Brian, 83

Legace, Manny, 134

Lemieux, Mario, 65

Levine, Dr. Peter, 219–20

Lewis, Dr. David, 201

Lindbergh, Pelle, 33

Lisk, Dick, 37

Lisk, Mary Lou, 37

Loewen, Darcy, 94

Los Angeles Kings, 69

Los Angeles rehab facility, 239–40

Los Angeles Times, 118–19

Loughran, Matt, 136, 154

Lowney's Save and Score contest, 27–28

Ludzik, Steve, 147, 155, 173

Luongo, Roberto, 140, 142, 143–44, 158, 227

MacArthur, Clarke, 157

MacInnis, Al, 44

MacLean, Doug, 158–59

MacLean, John, 72

Madison Square Garden, 83

Malarchuk, Clint
  adolescence, 28–32, 34, 35–3
  and baseball, 52, 54, 67
  and boxing, 9, 52, 58, 93
  childhood, 4, 5–16, 17–23, 24–28, 100, 102, 153, 163, 222, 228
  on coaching, 133, 134, 137–38, 140–41, 144, 145, 146, 235
  children of, 55, 68, 71, 108, 113, 120–21, 134, 150, 152, 155, 192, 236–38
  community work of, 95, 107, 125, 135, 236
  and depression and anxiety, 21–22, 29, 36, 37, 56, 68–69, 79–80, 93, 95–97, 103–04, 107, 108, 114–16, 139, 153, 154, 228, 236, 237
  and drinking, xi, xii, 73, 102, 105, 107–09, 121–22, 138–39, 154, 156, 161–62, 165, 166, 167, 182, 183, 206–07, 232–33, 239
  and drugs, illicit, 107, 206
  and drugs, prescribed, xii, 104, 105–06, 108, 109, 110, 117–18, 123, 152, 153, 166, 167, 182, 190, 229
  and fans, 64–65, 90–91, 107, 124, 125, 126, 136
  and fighting, 29, 55, 57–59, 63, 110, 124–25, 148, 162, 167–69, 174, 238
  on goalie partners, 97–98
  on goaltending, 1–2, 28, 32–34, 48, 57, 64, 65, 72, 83, 95, 144–46
  and homesickness, 28, 30, 37, 42
  as horse dentist, 138, 140, 158, 183, 228, 229, 231, 232, 235
  injuries, 3, 18, 34–35, 47, 54–55, 100–01, 240–41. *See also* jugular injury
  and insomnia, 92, 95–96, 97, 103, 104, 106, 115, 153, 154, 155, 182
  jokes and pranks, love of, 50, 61–62, 69–70, 74–75, 77–78, 134, 147, 208
  jugular injury, 85–91, 92, 93, 102, 179, 218, 219, 222, 223, 240
  junior hockey career, 28–30, 34–40, 42
  on loyalty, importance of, 136, 159
  and media, 88, 89, 94, 99, 106, 107, 118, 119, 141, 157, 192
  mental breakdown, 168–83
  on mental illness in pro sports, 2–3, 119, 240–41, 242
  minor hockey career, 47, 48–51, 55, 58, 59
  on NHL career, 119, 228–29
  and nightmares, 92, 97, 159, 219

and OCD (obsessive-compulsive disorder), 25, 48–49, 95, 96, 102, 103, 104, 106, 107, 109, 118, 123, 139, 153–54, 162–64, 182, 229

and physical pain, 18, 34, 100, 104, 116, 155, 177, 228

pre-game routine, 61, 84–85, 96–97, 144–45

Pro Set hockey card, 91

and PTSD (post-traumatic stress disorder), 218–21, 223

and ranching, 4, 5–7, 28, 79, 92, 121, 127, 135, 156

and rehab, 165, 183, 193. *See also* Los Angeles rehab facility; San Francisco rehab facility

relapses, 231–33, 238–39, 240

relationships with women, 152–53, 163–64, 207

religious beliefs, 43, 239–40

retirement from playing, 132

and rodeo riding, 6, 73, 75–76

skate blade accident. *See* jugular injury

and suicidal thoughts, 105–06, 108, 115, 116, 165, 173, 174, 182

suicide attempt (2008), xi, xii, 183–88, 189–95, 223, 229–30, 242

on trades, 80–82

trouble with law, 41–42, 70, 167, 176–79, 181, 219, 232–33

wives of, xi, 52–56, 68, 71, 98, 103, 105, 115, 116, 117, 120, 127, 128, 134–35, 150. *See also* Joanie Malarchuk

workout regime, 28, 35, 36, 38, 42, 49, 51, 64, 73, 92–93

and writing book, 236, 237, 238, 239, 240

Malarchuk, Dallyn (daughter), 134, 150, 152, 155, 192, 236–38

Malarchuk, Garth (brother), 8, 9, 10, 17, 18–20, 25, 34, 42, 52, 53–54, 67, 88, 129, 193

as C.M.'s father figure, 27, 92

hockey career of, 11, 26–27

Malarchuk, Jean (mother), 15–16, 18, 19, 22, 23, 41, 42, 54, 67, 155–56, 242

and C.M.'s hockey career, 29, 34, 59, 60, 86, 88, 97, 100, 129, 132

and C.M.'s suicide attempt, 191

marriage of, 12–13, 16, 24–25, 131

as single mother, 25, 31, 37

Malarchuk, Jed (son), 120, 121, 152, 192

Malarchuk, Joanie (wife; earlier Joanie Goodley)

car accident, 221

and C.M.'s suicide attempt, xi, xii, 184–88, 189–91, 192, 193, 194–95, 211, 215–16, 229–30

marriage to C.M., 161, 162, 165, 166, 167–68, 169–72, 173, 174–77, 180, 181–83, 225–26

parents of, 152, 182–83, 211, 242

supports C.M. in rehab, 197, 198–99, 200–02, 208–10, 242

Malarchuk, Kelli (daughter), 55, 68, 71, 108, 113, 120–21, 152, 192

Malarchuk, Mike (father), 8–9, 10, 11, 22, 26, 27, 37, 42, 52, 92, 129–31, 132

alcoholism of, 11, 12–13, 21, 24–25, 130, 131,139, 222, 237

death of, 136–37

Malarchuk, Terry (sister), 10, 11, 12–13, 19, 22, 25, 88, 89, 129, 132, 137

Malkin, Evgeni, 65

Martin, Grant, 57

Martin, Jacques, 158

Mason, Chris, 234

Mason, Steve, 227
May, Darrell, 40
McGill, Waco, 165, 169, 170, 171, 172, 188
McGrattan, Brian, 238
McSorley, Chris, 133
Meagher, Rick, 85
Meehan, Gerry, 81
Messier, Mark, 29, 65
Mogilny, Alexander, 83, 94–95, 98–99
Momesso, Sergio, 99
Montreal Canadiens, 58, 63, 66
Moorer, Michael, 146–47
Morrow, Ken, 48
Muckler, John, 112
Mullen, Brian, 83
Muller, Kirk, 73
Murray, Bryan, 71, 72, 80, 81, 141, 231, 232, 233
Murray, Terry, 144–45

National Finals Rodeo (NFR), 128
National Hockey League (NHL), 45, 47, 48, 201
    All-Stars, 64–65
    C.M.'s first career shutout in, 59
    C.M.'s first game in, 47–48
    C.M.'s last game in, 111
    1981 draft, 43–44
    1992 expansion draft, 112
    2004 lockout, 150
Nevada Foundation for Child Cancer, 125–26
Neverett, Tim, 134
New Jersey Devils, 71, 72
New York Islanders, 48, 66, 71
New York Rangers, 82–83
NHL. See National Hockey League
NHL Players' Association (NHLPA), 193, 201, 210, 218, 226, 228, 239, 240
Nolan, Owen, 111

OCD (obsessive-compulsive disorder), 25, 48–49, 95, 96, 102, 103, 104, 106, 107, 109, 118, 123, 139, 153–54, 162–64, 182, 229
On Goaltending (Plante), 2, 28
Orap, 114, 117
Orr, Bobby, 27
Ottawa Senators, 112, 128, 231–32, 233
Ovechkin, Alex, 65

Papke, Cecil, 11
Papke, Murray, 11
Parent, Bernie, 33
Park, Brad, 63
Pavelec, Ondrej, 234
Peale, Norman Vincent, 43
Peck, Brian, 166–67, 169, 170–72, 178, 188
Peeters, Pete, 71, 72, 73, 81, 144
Philadelphia Flyers, 33, 71, 212
Pittsburgh Penguins, 80
Pizzutelli, Jim, 86–88, 89, 90, 97, 111
Plante, Jacques, 2, 28
Plasse, Michel, 46–47
Poile, David, 67, 70, 75–76
Portland, OR, 36
Portland Winterhawks, 28, 29, 30, 36–39, 42
post-traumatic stress disorder (PTSD), 218–20, 223
Potvin, Denis, 48
Prime Ticket, 119
Prince George Cougars, 138
Prozac, 109, 114, 117
PTSD. See post-traumatic stress disorder
Puppa, Daren, 81, 94, 97, 98, 100, 101, 108, 112, 115

Quebec City, QC, 61
Quebec Nordiques, 61–62, 90, 111
    C.M. drafted by, 43, 44
    1981–82 season, 47–48
    1983–84 season, 55, 58, 59
    1984–85 season, 59
    1985–86 season, 59, 63, 66
    1986–87 season, 60, 66, 67
    Rendez-Vous 87, 64–65
    training camp, 45, 46
Quinney, Ken, 133

Raglan, Herb, 111
Ramsay, Craig, 234
Ramsey, Mike, 98
Ray, Rob, 94, 111
Reagan, President Ronald, 78–79
Regina, SK, 122
Reichart, Chris, 115, 116, 230
Rheaume, Manon, 128
Richard, Jacques, 47
Ridley, Mike, 80–81
Robinson, Coleman, 73–74, 132
Rochefort, Normand, 65
Rochester Americans, 109–10, 114
Roy, Patrick, 2, 33, 63, 145
Ruff, Lindy, 114
Runnin' Rebels, 123
Rypien, Rick, 241

Sakic, Joe, 67, 111
Salei, Ruslan, 134
San Antonio Rampage, 150, 158
San Antonio Rodeo, 151
San Diego, CA, 117, 118
San Diego Gulls, 114
    C.M. sent to, 112, 113, 114
    C.M.'s leave of absence from,
        116–18
    1992–93 season, 115, 116, 119, 120

San Francisco rehab facility, 196
    C.M.'s first week at, 196–98
    C.M.'s release from, 223–24
    counsellors at, 199, 200–04, 205,
        207, 209–10, 217, 218–19, 221,
        223, 224, 237
    patients at, 197, 198, 203–04,
        206–07, 211–14, 224
    program, 204–06, 208, 213, 217, 221,
        222, 223
    visits from Joanie, 198–99, 208–10,
        211, 214–15, 216–17
Sator, Ted, 94
Sauve, Daniel, 126
Sauvé, J.F., 63
Sawchuk, Terry, 2
Schneider, Cory, 144
Sevigny, Richard, 58
Shaw, Dr. Brian, 201
Sidorkiewicz, Peter, 112
Simonick, Rip, 82, 86, 87, 91
Slap Shot, 45
Sleigher, Louis, 58
Smith, Billy, 48, 66
St. Albert Saints, 29
St. Louis Blues, 3, 84, 99
Stahl, Dr. Stephen, 116–18, 121, 152
Stamkos, Steven, 65
Stanley Cup, 48
Stanwyck, Barbara, 79
Stastny, Peter, 58, 59, 60
Stickney, Hank, 123
Stickney, Ken, 123
Strumm, Bob, 120, 123, 124, 126, 127,
        133, 134, 135
Sundin, Mats, 111
Sutter, Brent, 234
Sutter, Duane, 158, 234

Tampa Bay Lightning, 112,
        149

Tarkanian, Jerry, 123
Teen Ranch prospect camp, 158
Thomas and Mack Center, 123, 128
Tina (rehab counsellor), 199, 200,
    201–02, 203, 209–10, 218–19,
    221, 222, 223, 237
Tonelli, John, 48
Toporowski, Kerry, 124, 125
Toronto, ON, 153
Toronto Maple Leafs, 28
Toronto Star, 106
Toronto Toros, 26–27
Tortorella, John, 238
Tremblay, Mario, 58
Tretiak, Vladislav, 33, 84
Trottier, Bryan, 48
Turgeon, Pierre, 83, 98
Tuttle, Steve, 85, 99

United Cycle, 26

Vanbiesbrouck, John, 43, 83
Van Boxmeer, John, 134
Vancouver Canucks, 40, 90, 144, 238
Van Halen, 62
Verbeek, Pat, 73

Waddell, Don, 116, 233
Waking the Tiger (Levine), 219–20
Washington, DC, 78
Washington Capitals, 26, 33
    C.M. traded to, 67–68
    1987–88 season, 68, 71–73
    1988–89 season, 77, 82
Washington Post, 76
Watters, Bill, 28
West Coast Hockey League, 135
Western Hockey League, 28, 138
Westgate Chevy midget team, 24
Wey, Mr., 31
What About Bob?, 153
Williams, Tiger, 58–59, 62, 63
Wilson, Doug, 65

Yashin, Alexei, 128
Young, Wendell, 112

Zednik, Richard, 157
Zoloft, 117, 118, 152, 153, 156